South Asia State, Society and Development

South Asia State, Society and Development

Edited

Gull Mohammad Wani

GYAN

First Published, 2018

Published by

Gyan Publishing House
5, Ansari Road
Daryaganj, New Delhi-110002
Phone: 9811692060
E-mail: books@gyanbooks.com

Printed at: G. Print Process, Delhi.

Cataloging in Publication Data—DK
Courtesy: D.K. Agencies (P) Ltd. <docinfo@dkagencies.com>

South Asia state, society and development / edited by Gull Wani.
pages cm
ISBN 9788121214148

1. Regional planning—South Asia. 2. Marginality, Social—South Asia. 3. Marginality, Social—India—Jammu and Kashmir. 4. Women—Political activity—South Asia. 5. Women—Political activity—India—Jammu and Kashmir. 6. South Asia—Politics and government. 7. Jammu and Kashmir (India)—Politics and government. I. Wani, Gull Mohd., 1961- editor.

LCC DS341.S68 2017 | DDC 954 23

Contents

POLITICS AND GOVERNANCE IN JAMMU AND KASHMIR

Preface

The book is an intellectual labour born out of passion and deep commitment for regional harmony in the region. The compendium emanated out of teaching a group of students drawn from the South Asia to Kashmir University. I had the privilege of directing a Master's Programme in "Kashmir and South Asia Studies" at Kashmir University during 2013-2016. It is in one sense a follow-up of the digest being published at the Institute of Kashmir Studies at the university. The book is the by-product of a unique experience of teaching the Kashmir and South Asia course to a select group of students from different countries of the South Asia. The three years experience of teaching such a mix of local and South Asia youth together in the challenging academic and political environment of Kashmir valley gives me the confidence about the huge 'soft power' available to us which of course can be employed towards building bridges of unity and solidarity across people and states. In order to make the course innovative and invigorating leading experts on South Asia were invited for special lectures which added content and quality to the teaching programme. In fact, some of the contributors to this volume happen to be the same experts who visited the institute for special lectures. The other contributions are from the local teaching faculty and students. It was in this academic setting that the idea of a book of an interdisciplinary nature came to my mind. My request to different scholars to contribute for this volume was readily honoured.

It is always fascinating for editors to constantly encourage and sometimes needle the authors particularly the young ones to accomplish their work within the stipulated time. It has taken great deal of time and patience to bring this work to fruition. I respect and admire all the contributors who worked with patience and in line with the requirements of this volume.

Gull Mohammad Wani

Introduction

The book focuses on issues of regional understanding, gender, identity and resources in Kashmir and the larger region of South Asia. It reflects our optimism about potential of peace and growth of 'enlightened regionalism' in South Asia which can be promoted and enhanced not through ivory tower initiatives or high profile conferences being conducted in the national capitals but through the use of 'soft power' and cultural exchanges involving youth and common people. As already mentioned, we realised the power and significance of involving educational institutions and students in the process of regional understanding only when students from SAARC countries were admitted by us to a two years post graduation programme at Kashmir University. We were also able to attract good number of scholars from the region for extension lectures so that we understand the internal complexity of the South Asian region. It was at that time that the significance of an enlightened regionalism attracted our attention. At a time in regional and global history when nation-state is again making a forceful come back we cannot afford to sidetrack the project of enlightened regionalism in South Asia. The region is central to the life, livelihood and future of the people living in this part of the world. Each one of us, people in general and youth in particular, have to earn direct social and economic benefits if regional friction and tension is removed and colonial borders are made irrelevant.

The book attempts a different if not unique conceptualisation of South Asia as a region. The conceptualisation captured our attention when we started looking at the larger region from a place like Kashmir which has remained a cause for inter-state irritation between India and Pakistan and has also affected the working of SAARC as a regional organisation. Our understanding is based on the faith that nation-state cannot be the only template for promoting regionalism in South Asia and academics and peaceniks need to debate the issue of *muffasilisation* of the region so that regions/provinces in each country can also be involved in the integration process. This approach is useful in differentiating SAARC from South Asia so that focus remains upon people and their day-to-day livelihood matters. Many of the conflict resolution mechanisms advanced in relation to Kashmir dispute were also in recognition of the fact that Jammu and Kashmir should act as a bridge for connecting rather than disrupting the relations and lives of the people. However, the contemporary regional and global political context is increasingly turning negative and the regional organisations including SAARC are bracing up to a new challenge. It is imperative to examine these negative trends which could hinder a better understanding in South Asia.

First, there is a virtual revolt against globalisation in developed world and the global south is not free from it. The idea that economic globalisation and liberalisation are the only routes to progress is being contested. The election of Donald Trumph as President of USA has dented the so called 'Washington Consensus'. The President-elect has promised to break the free trade agreements. Donald Trump is not the only leader capitalising on the current negativity in west. The withdrawal of Britain from European Union in 2016 is an indicator of distrust against globalisation and supranational economic arrangements. Media reports are now focused on what is called as 'Frexit' as France hold elections in next couple of months and may follow the British path. The fact is that EU was seen till 2008 as a very successful regional project and many countries in Central and Eastern Europe wanted to be part of the grouping to reap social and economic benefits. The EU also inspired many leaders outside Europe who also aspired for similar arrangements to reap benefits from regional integration but there are definite irritants in the integration process. Indian Political Scientist Pratap Bhanu Mehta opined that "there is politics of fear rather than hope and all guiding values of the post-Berlin world have fallen by the wayside. The idea that increasing globalisation, mobility of labour and capital is a sustainable political project has temporarily bitten the dust. The romantic idea that forms of economic interdependence would reduce the risk of armed conflict in different parts of world has come under strain".

Second, while South Asian Association for Regional Cooperation (SAARC) is yet to make an international impact, countries within have started drifting from its grand vision. The BJP-led NDA government of Narendra Modi in India decided not to participate in the 19th SAARC summit which was to be held in Pakistan. This according to Nepal-based journalist Kanak Mani Dixit "represented the triumph of ultra-patriotism which is the flag of populist demagogues and which equates allegiance to the state with loyalty to the government of the day". The fact of the matter is that India cannot escape from South Asia. It has to grow from within the region. A country which cannot integrate with its own region cannot integrate with other regions of the world. India according to some people has become "hyper-arbitrary state". State is empowered in an unprecedented manner to regulate the life of the people. An Indian policy-maker according to former national security advisor Shiv Shanker Menon must deal with several Pakistan's: with civil society, the Pakistani business, the army and the ISI and the religious right (which extends from political parties to Jehadi Tanzeems). One man who prophetically hated nationalism in South Asia was Rabindranath Tagore who won Nobel when Europe was seeped in nationalism and fighting wars that killed millions of its people.

Third, current regional/global politico-economic changes indicate revival of the nation state. In fact, the idea of death of nation-state model of development was premature. Across South Asia we are witnessing the emergence of what French scholar Christophe Jaffrelot describes as "national-populism and to some extent authoritarianism". In fact, nationalism is back with vengeance not as a harbinger of a new civic commitment but as a new collective narcissism. Donald Trumph too wants to restore American military advantage and make "America great again". In South Asia political/power elite with help from security establishment wants to keep the flag of the nation-state flying. Nation-states were sought to be superseded through the EU, ASEAN, and SAARC partly because they tended to designate external enemies and go to war with these in order to attain internal consolidation. These states also indulge in politics of exclusion and marginalisation. In South

Asia many ethnic groups have tough time at the hands of nation-state which by its very nature is resistant to demands of identity and autonomy of different groups. Kashmir and Tamil issues respectively in India and Sri Lanka are the cases in point. Today when exclusionary forces are making a comeback one is reminded of the farewell address of George Washington in September 17, 1796. He said "the nation which indulges towards another habitual hatred or a habitual fondness is in some degree a slave. It is a slave to its animosity or to its affection either of which is sufficient to lead it astray from its duty and its interests". Moreover, liberal intellectuals in many parts of South Asia realise the need for developing a new narrative of the region that can be owned by all and help in promoting commonalities within the region and across countries. This realisation has dawned in the disturbing context of evidence in many countries that history writing is being manipulated by the governing elite to suit their party/community agendas. This will have serious implications on pluralism and secular nation-building in each country of the region. In his book: "Identity and Violence: Illusion of Destiny" (2006) Amratya Sen writes that "state cannot survive through an enforced identity. A perfect citizen is one who has multiple identities rather than a single one".

Fourth, regional integration and connectivity has also suffered in recent times due to a noticeable trend towards de-democratisation leading to weakening of institutions and processes. In many parts of the world experts are worried about today's mix of nationalism, corporatism and popular discontent. A new crop of leaders is emerging who relate directly to the people situating themselves above parties and institutions. There is widespread support for illiberalism. Indian historian Ramachandra Guha refers to "India as the republic of un-freedom". The freedom of expression is incrementally contained in the name of national interest and national security. The academic institutions with liberal reputation are being squeezed. The NGO sector especially those working on governance accountability are being targeted. Under the Foreign Contribution (Regulation) Act the government can now target trade unions, student unions, youth forums as organisations of political nature and inhibit their role in the process of democratisation of polity and society. Media, judiciary and academic institutions are feeling the heat of an oppressive state in South Asia.

Impunity is becoming biggest threat to media freedom. The committee to protect journalists (CPJ) recently claimed that Afghanistan, Pakistan, Bangladesh and India are among the 13 most dangerous countries for journalists. The South Asian countries can neither attain the goal of sustainable development nor that of good governance without accountability and all that is not possible unless we learn to tolerate dissent. More than 100 journalists have been killed in Pakistan since 2005 and 95 have lost life in India since 1990. Most countries in South Asia have become "elections-only democracy" and India as a leading democracy is experiencing many troubles. Kishore Mehbubani, faculty at the Singapore National University, wrote about "closing of the Indian mind". Pratap Bhanu Mehta states that "China has an open mind but a closed society. India has an open society but a closing mind". The RSS/BJP today adopt fascistic methods of appropriation of popular symbols, create a false consciousness of deprivation amongst the majority community and appeal to extreme jingoism as their methods to advance.

It is in the above backdrop that this volume attains significance. The contributors have within their own areas of specialisation suggested how problems within the region of South Asia can be addressed so that inter-state tension can be removed. There are of course certain areas where we need to work hard and press upon institutions and governments in the region for necessary policy intervention. There is utmost need for strengthening secular/democratic people's struggles in South Asia. A common ground must be found to integrate popular social movements so that we are able to create scope for a South Asian citizen. South Asians tend to instinctively recognise and connect with each other as South Asians, but the idea of South Asia does not come naturally to people of the region. The ownership of the idea of South Asia cannot be only left for governments in the respective countries, non-governmental actors and agencies have to play a more important role. Some of the tasks at hand are:

First, the countries within the region of South Asia need to focus on reviving inclusive economic growth to catch-up with aspirations of different sections of society particularly the youth. The political/ bureaucratic elite are exploiting the resentment of the voters who are left behind by a model of development giving rise to inequalities. We are face to face with a political order marked by frustrations due to growing joblessness. India and other countries in the region need to do genuine thinking on post-reform economic strategy. The so called "fourth industrial revolution" further necessitates it. Economic growth rates may be good but may not yield job creation because of mechnisation. Technologies like artificial intelligence, robotics and big data can prove more disruptive than earlier economic/technical transformations. There is a virtual consensus among political/policy-making circles that more connectivity and economic and infrastructural linkages among countries in South Asia will help in fighting poverty, exclusion and exploitation of youth and other sections of the region. Most of the wars being fought in the region are internal to the countries and hence cannot be fought by the nation-state alone. Kanak Mani Dixit rightly proposes South Asian regionalism as a "social justice project". The network of cross-border connectivity projects like highways, transmission lines can be alternative to high military budgets of countries of the region.

Second, the regionalism in South Asia yesterday, today and tomorrow will always have collision with the nature of nationalism of states born after colonial withdrawal. It is a nationalism anchored by the nation-state of the European variety. This nationalism in South Asia has generated dual categories of 'minorities' and 'majoritarianism' thus plunging old societies in South Asia in new turmoil. After construction of nation-state in France the advocacy of federalism became a capital offence. The project of nation-state involves privileging one socio-cultural identity over others. The identity group is always the community having numerical majority. The nation-state according to Dipankar Gupta should have the concept of "territoriality" which got firmly established by the partition of India in 1947. The nation-state policies have been historically pursued by following variety of routes from soft to downright brutal, by encouraging voluntary assimilation and resorting to coercion that might in the extreme involve ethnic cleansing. In South Asia, many ethnic minorities have been victims of this nation-state power projection. For promotion of the value of enlightened regionalism in South Asia the model of 'state-nation' provides better way than the one under 'nation-state'. A notable book "Crafting State-Nations" by Alfred Stepan, Juan Linz and Yogindra

Yadav provides remarkable insight in this matter. The authors propose a new concept of 'State-Nation' to capture the essence of the relationship between states and nationhood. This model is relevant for South Asia where countries have strong territorially based diversity. State-nation policies work on two levels: creation of a sense of belonging with respect to the larger political community, while simultaneously institutionally safeguarding politically salient diversities such as language, religion and culturally sacred norms. Federalism is normally a necessary condition for the protection of territorially specific diversities. Having two or more political identities is not subversive to the nation. In retrospect, the separation of Bangladesh from Pakistan in 1971 could have been averted had the latter accepted to recognise the dual identity of the people of East Pakistan. Further, the pain in the body-politic of Jammu and Kashmir, Baluchistan, and North-East of Sri Lanka may not go easily unless we recognise the fact that pluralism is the destiny of these states.

Third, it is significant to recognise that SAARC as a regional association and South Asia as a regional conglomeration of people deserve separate academic attention. The South Asian Association for Regional Cooperation is a state to state or government to government forum for interaction and for taking regional cooperation forward while as South Asia is and continues to be a dynamic area where people and cultures interact. The SAARC can fail or the countries within may find new and alternative regional groupings keeping in view their interests but people and divided families in South Asia cannot move away from the region. Hence what is required is to look beyond nation-state but certainly not ignoring it as far as regional understanding is concerned. This involves the use of soft power in its varied forms to connect the people and cultures in the larger region of South Asia. Sports linkages, business and music will keep the idea of South Asia alive and kicking. Religious tourism has great scope in connecting communities in a region like South Asia where too many religious places are located in one country but the devotees in a different country. This should prompt the countries within to think of a SAARC airline to connect all the national capitals in the region. Further we need to appreciate the power of culture to humanise relations while parochial politics is bent upon demonising the same. Junoon was the first and only Pakistani rock band to perform in Srinagar in May 2008. It performed at the edge of the Dal Lake for thousands of Kashmir students and South Asian leaders who had come to attend the inauguration of the institute of Kashmir Studies. Cricket lovers in India and Pakistan have over the decades become a peace constituency unto themselves. Cricket diplomacy created its own impact in bilateral relations between India and Pakistan on many difficult occasions. The exclusion of Pakistani actors from performing in Bollywood amounts to killing the soft power of India and snapping cricketing ties has also disillusioned millions in both countries. For three years at Institute of Kashmir Studies we learnt the significance of soft power by admitting students from across the South Asia. South Asia can be made a regional education market to further boost the soft power.

Finally, after 1991 new type of collective interaction between sub-national states and international bodies, MNCs and foreign governments has become a norm. State/provincial governments have become crucial in economic diplomacy. In India peripheral and border states have demonstrated eagerness to integrate and interact with their ethnic counterparts across the border. This urge for more commerce and people to people contact may help in not only regional harmony but also in defusing certain tensions as well. There is a strong body of scholarly opinion advocating the need for inclusion of new stakeholders into the India-Pakistan peace process especially the Chief Ministers of the border states. The Chief Ministers of the two Punjab's have recently shown strong desire for cross-border cooperation in trade and sports activities. New Delhi should also encourage the Chief Minister of Rajasthan to reach out to her counterpart across the border in the Sind province of Pakistan. At Attari-Wagah border in April 2012, the Chief Minister of Punjab Shri Prakash Singh Badal underlined Punjab's interest in reconciliation with Pakistan. In September 2012, an 18-member delegation led by Union Commerce Secretary S.R. Rao had visited Pakistan with Punjab Chief Secretary Rakesh Singh. It was decided to dismantle negative trade list by the end of October and 600 items will be traded through Attari-Wagah border. The Punjab chief secretary told media people that with more items allowed to be traded through land route, the economy of the state will benefit a lot as much more business will come to the state. It was also decided to open Hussainwala and Abohar routes between India and Pakistan and the relics of

Maharaja Ranjit Singh which are in Pakistan's Punjab be brought to Punjab in India for a six month exhibition at the Gobindgarh Fort. It was also decided that joint sporting events will be held between both Punjabs. During the 2014 Indian parliamentary elections, Mr. Arun Jaitley contested elections from Amritsar and had a difficult time to convince the Punjab based traders about the commitment of BJP led government to Punjab-Punjab cooperation. He eventually lost from Amritsar. The seat was won by Amrinder Singh of Congress party who is an ardent advocate of cooperation across regions in Punjab. The likely inauguration of twelve new check posts will improve connectivity with neighbouring countries including Nepal, Myanmar and Bangladesh. One way to make Cross LoC trade less contentious is to make it less exceptional. This can be done by forcing India and Pakistan to reframe their frontier policies and mobilise stakeholders in border regions. From the Indian side Punjab, Bengal and Kutch can be engaged as connectors of trade across the divides. India needs to have a strategic vision rooted in creating a large and vibrant Asian regional market. This market will constitute a significant and growing part of global demand for products due to the demographic shift. This vision would mean strengthening Pakistan to be an effective regional hub that connects the Asia-wide market. There is equally a feeling in Pakistan that due to ethnic mix economic growth has to be regionally balanced and any such strategy has to be rooted in history and geography. Ijaz Nabi, Professor of Economics at the Lahore University of Management Sciences (LUMS) thus outlines the strategic vision of trade between India and Pakistan. "The three principal regions of modern day Pakistan, Peshawar, Lahore and Upper Sind were connectors of the lands to their West and North-Iran, Central Asia and China and those to the East-India and as such became centres of trade, commerce and culture. This flourishing activity made them growth nodes that brought prosperity to their surrounding regions." The new bonhomie found in Indian Punjab recently should make us understand how in Malwa region near about hundred trucks carrying dry fruits and other items from Afghanistan and Pakistan used to pass through Hussainwala before the 1971 war. The cross-LoC trade in erstwhile Jammu and Kashmir state, at theoretical level in particular, needs to be framed in the discourse of theory of soft borders. The soft border concept moves beyond state sovereignty, territory and borders seeking a movement through people, economy and trade. Addressing a rally at the launch of Amritsar-Nankana Sahib bus service on 24th March 2006 former Indian Prime Minister Dr Manmohan Singh said: "borders cannot be redrawn but we can work towards making them just a line on the map. People on both sides of the LoC should be able to move freely and trade with one another. I also envisage the two parts of Kashmir can with active encouragement of the governments of India and Pakistan work out a cooperative and consultative mechanism in solving problems of social and economic development of the region". Since 2005 the LoC was opened for movement of divided families and in 2008 for trade. This process needs to be addressed within the larger framework of regional/ humane governance. There is also case for federalising the foreign policy-making in South Asian countries. In fact, in its 2014 election manifesto, the Bharatiya Janata Party mentioned the significance of creating a new spirit of cooperation and collaboration between New Delhi and the states arguing: "Team India shall not be limited to the Prime Minister led team sitting in New Delhi, but will also include Chief Ministers and other functionaries as equal partners". All other countries in South Asia need to involve their regional governments in foreign policy making. It would provide an additional impetus for regional harmony. It is encouraging that regional governments in Pakistan have also started participating in such ventures. The Chief Minister of Sind Murad Ali Shah recently returned from China with bouquet of projects for his province relating to the China-Pakistan Economic Corridor. Earlier Pakistan's Punjab Chief Minister also visited China many times to invite more and more Chinese investment for his province.

The contributors to this volume have delved into the issues that have potential to further promote equitable development and harmony in South Asia. Javid Ahmad while "theorising a Theory of Global Justice" holds that the spheres of injustice have increased manifold. The suffering caused by global poverty in the post-Cold War era are far huge than miseries brought by the wars including great wars of the entire 20th century. The scholars and academics are yet to adequately respond to the hugely unjust conditions and suggest a practical guide to remedy injustice/s. Though the philosophers have turned their attention towards global justice, but it is largely confined to the western countries. It suffers, what author calls, inadequate theorisation. Significant in this connection is how Amartya Sen is turning to non-western traditions. This brings a shift in *form* and *content* of the theory of justice to build up a case for inclusive global justice theory. We need to look at problems in South Asia from inclusive justice theory. In his paper on "Decoding the Meanings of Development and Welfare in Indian Politics" Prof. KC Suri while examining the capitalist model of economic development and socialist model as choices of post-colonial Indian state analyses its transition to economic reforms in 1991 making development synonymous with economic growth. This led to a sort of unbridled capitalism giving rise to corruption and crony capitalism. The developing countries in South Asia like India face a tension between development, understood as allowing primacy to free market and emphasis on economic growth, and welfare, understood as state providing succor and support to the needy people. The tension between development and welfare does not go away by attempts at tight-rope walking between the two, but by integrating them in a way that simultaneously ensures economic growth as well as welfare, which together would lead to governance. Sangeeta Thapliyal in her paper focuses on the changing notions of security from the traditional state centric to human security. The international politics at large has been influenced by the realist paradigm of territorial security, which believes that a state is secure if its territories are secured. The concept of security in its widened form brings in political, societal, economic and environmental threats to a state. Related to the people centric notion of security is the concept of human security which gives primacy to an individual as a referent of security rather than a state. The author holds that India has a huge task of dealing with both the territorial security challenges faced from outside and the internal security challenges of mitigating poverty, hunger and disease. This holds relevance for the entire South Asian region. The paper on "Neighbourhood First: A Reality Check" by Prof. S. D. Muni focuses on Modi's neighbourhood initiatives since he took over as Prime Minister. The author believes that the real challenge of India's neighbourhood policy has always been in dealing with China and Pakistan. But the relations with other smaller neighbours have not improved substantially. India stands alienated in

Nepal. India's sympathies in Maldives oscillate between the ousted President Nasheed and the new regime led by President Abdulla Yameen. Relationships with Bhutan, Afghanistan, Bangladesh, and Sri Lanka are generally friction free but without any new significant development under Modi, except for the change of regime in Sri Lanka and ratification of 'Land Boundary Agreement' with Bangladesh. SAARC remains a slow and uninspiring instrument of regional integration. Efforts to activate sub-regional mechanisms to enhance connectivity are being made, but results look far and few. But PM Modi did try to build a good neighbourly relations; he visited almost all the countries in the neighbourhood. But the initiatives lacked adequate preparation and a credible road map. There is also a "delivery deficit" on promises made and agreements concluded. The author highlights some external factors impacting India's neighbourhood policy.

The paper titled "Liberalisation, Peace Process and India-Pakistan Trade" by Dr. Sajad Padder and Prof. Gull Wani focuses on the India-Pakistan trade relations from 1947 onwards. In 1996, India and Pakistan became signatories to the South Asia Preferential Trade Agreement requiring member states to reform tariffs and increase intra-regional trade. In the same year, India granted to Pakistan the 'Most Favoured Nation Status' and Pakistan decided to expand its positive list (imports from India) to include 596 items. The positive list went on expanding till 2012 when it was finally replaced by a negative list of 1209 items. The present volume of official bilateral trade hovers around US$ 2.3 billion. But the bilateral trade balance is heavily in favor of India. The authors argue that the greater India-Pakistan trade will increase the prospects of peace in South Asia. The paper on "Gender, Equality and Governance in South Asia" by Seema Kazi portrays the dismal picture on women's empowerment in South Asia. The author holds that the women's movements in South Asia are part of wider civil society mobilisations that emerged in response to popular disillusionment with the state and its inability to administer democratic governance and ensure distributive justice. South Asia's feminist movements against state violence, authoritarianism, religious chauvinism and equitable development sought to advance the goals of gender equality and women's democratic rights. The author believes that the class dimensions of this struggle cannot be underestimated: a large majority of South Asian women are poor, illiterate, undernourished and unemployed.

The contributors to this work while looking at South Asia are not in any case underestimating the concept of regions within the region. The state of Jammu and Kashmir looms large in several of these contributions. The beauty of this conceptualisation lies in the importance of a shared identity critical to regional peace and harmony in the greater region of South Asia. Prof. Rekha Chowdhary focuses on the conflict situation and multiple identity politics in Jammu and Kashmir. The author believes that the only way the conflict situation in the context of multiple identities and divergent political positions can be resolved is through the process of consensus building. In a diverse society like Jammu and Kashmir where each identity marker is internally differentiated and overlaps with other identity markers, the identity politics assumes a complex character. This complexity is provided by the fact that there is no clear cut context of 'majority' or 'minority'. Each of the identities while asserting its collective numerical strength also simultaneously voices its victimisation as a minority. Thus, the Kashmiri identity politics while asserting the numerical dominance within the state, bemoans the marginalisation of 'Kashmiris' and 'Muslims' in the larger context of Indian state. Those asserting the regional identity of Jammu claim that this region is larger in territorial terms in comparison to Kashmir but complain about its political marginalisation vis-à-vis Kashmir region. Gujjars claim to be the third largest demographic grouping after 'Muslims' and 'Hindus' but again lament their backwardness vis-à-vis other people of the state. The complexity that has been generated by the multiple identity politics of the state has made the conflict-resolution a challenging task. Prof. Rekha Saxena in her paper "Jammu and Kashmir: A Test case in India's Asymmetrical Federal Governance" attempts to decode the problem and panacea of the Kashmir tangle in Indian federal system. The paper is divided into four main sections. The first section provides an account of the theoretical debate on asymmetrical federalism and the second looks into the historical roots of the Kashmir problem. Section third examines the political history of Kashmir and the fourth debates Article

370 as an epitome of the constitutional asymmetry in Indian constitution. The author recommends a federal solution for Kashmir tangle. Dr. Nyla Ali Khan in her essay "Story of Kashmiri Women in Indian-Administered Kashmir: Dialectic of Resistance and Accommodation" holds that inadequate attention has been paid to the gender dimension of the armed conflict in the Kashmir, which stymies even further the emergence of peace, political liberty, socio-economic reconstruction, and egalitarian democratisation. Women in Kashmir have been greatly affected by the armed insurgency and counter-insurgency in the region, they are largely absent in decision-making bodies at the local, regional, and national levels. New efforts and new forums are required not just in Indian-administered Kashmir but in other parts of the South Asia for the germination of new ideas, broad based coalition politics that transcends organisational divides, and gives women the space and leeway to make important political decision.

At the risk of sounding repetitive I once again stress the fact that the book tries to capture the multiple realities in South Asia. My endeavour has been to highlight nuanced opinions of scholars and academics who teach, research and are busy in peace-building process in the region. I earnestly hope that the readers will take this opportunity to engage with the opinions of contributors in the book.

List of Contributors

Professor Gull Mohammad Wani

Professor Gull Wani served as the director of the Institute of Kashmir Studies at the University of Kashmir, Srinagar from 2013-16. Presently, he is teaching at the Department of Political Science in the same University. His most recent book is 'Kashmir: Identity, Autonomy and Self-Rule' which was published in 2011. Professor Wani is a part of several peace initiatives and has participated in several track II meetings between India and Pakistan.

Professor S.D. Muni

Professor S.D. Muni was India's Special Envoy to Southeast Asian countries on UN Security Council Reforms (2005-06) and served as India's Ambassador to Lao PDR (1997-1999). In 2005, the Sri Lankan President bestowed on him 'Sri Lanka Ratna', the highest Sri Lankan civilian honour for a non-national. He superannuated from Jawaharlal Nehru University, New Delhi, India in 2006 after 33 years of service.

Professor K.C. Suri

K.C. Suri is a Professor of Political Science at the Central University of Hyderabad. Professor Suri's areas of research interest are Indian democracy and political process, politics of public policies, political parties, elections and voting, and state politics in India. His publications include Political Parties in South Asia: The Challenge of Change, International IDEA, Stockholm, 2007; Electoral Politics in Indian States (Co-editor), Oxford University Press, New Delhi, 2009; and (Editor): ICSSR Research Surveys and Explorations: Political Science: Indian Democracy, Volume 2, Oxford University Press, New Delhi, 2013. As the recipient of Endeavour Executive Award, Government of Australia, he was a visiting scholar at School of International and Political Studies, Deakin University, Melbourne, Australia during July-October 2010.

Professor Rekha Chowdhary

Rekha Chowdhary is presently ICSSR National Fellow and is affiliated with University of Jammu. Earlier she served as Professor of Political Science in University of Jammu. She wrote a number of books and research papers. Her most recent book is 'Jammu and Kashmir: Politics of Identity and Separatism' published by Routledge (2015). Besides the present ICSSR Award, she has availed various other Awards and fellowships which include: Fulbright Fellowship that she availed in SAIS, Johns Hopkins University; Washington DC, Commonwealth Fellowship which she availed in QEH, Oxford University; Ford Foundation funded South Asia Visiting Scholars Programme Fellowship.

Professor Sangeeta Thapliyal

Professor **Sangeeta Thnapliyal** is the Chairperson at the Centre for Inner Asian Studies, Jawaharlal Nehru University, New Delhi. She works on strategic issues concerning the South Asia region. Her areas of research include Water Security in South Asia and Regional Cooperation. Her previous work experience includes Director, Department of Strategic and Regional Studies, University of Jammu, Observer Research Foundation, Delhi Policy Group and the Institute of Defence and Strategic Studies.

Professor Nyla Ali Khan

Professor Nyla Ali Khan is a faculty member at the University of Oklahoma in the US and member of Scholars Strategy Network. She is author of 'The Fiction of Nationality in an Era of Transnationalism', 'Islam, Women, and Violence in Kashmir: Between Indian and Pakistan', 'The Parchment of Kashmir: History, Society, and Polity', and 'The Life of a Kashmiri Woman: Dialectic of Resistance and Accommodation'.

Professor Rekha Saxena

Professor Rekha Saxena is a faculty member in the Department of Political Science at the University of Delhi. She was a Doctoral and Faculty Research Fellow of the Shastri Indo-Canadian Institute at the Department of Political Studies and Institute of Intergovernmental Relations at Queen's University in Canada in 1999-2000 and 2003 respectively. Apart from a number of publications to her credit, she has worked on various projects with research institutes and governmental, nongovernmental organisations in India like the

Centre for the Study of Developing Societies, University Grants Commission, Inter-State Council Secretariat, and Union Ministry of Home Affairs.

Humra Quraishi

Humra Quraishi is a Delhi-based writer-columnist-journalist. She wrote a book on Kashmir titled, *Kashmir: The Untold Story* and has co-authored two books with Khushwant Singh—*The Good, The Bad and The Ridiculous* and *Absolute Khushwant*.

Dr. Seema Kazi

Seema Kazi is a Senior Fellow at the Centre for Women's Development Studies (CWDS), New Delhi. She has obtained her PhD from London School of Economics.

Dr. Sanjeda Warsi

Dr. Sanjeda Warsi is a Sr. Assistant Professor at the Department of Political Science, University of Kashmir, Srinagar.

Javid Ahmad Dar

Javid Ahmad Dar is an Assistant Professor at the Department of Political Science, University of Kashmir, Srinagar. He is pursuing his PhD in the Department of Political Science, University of Delhi.

Dr. Sajad Padder

A recipient of Doctoral Fellowship awarded by the Indian Council of Social Science Research, Sajad Padder did his PhD in the Department of Political Science, University of Kashmir, Srinagar.

Farah Qayoom

Farah Qayoom is an Assistant Professor at the Department of Sociology, University of Kashmir, Srinagar.

Sehar Iqbal

Sehar Iqbal is a Kashmir based women's rights activist and a PhD fellow at the UNESCO-Madanjeet Singh Institute of Kashmir Studies, University of Kashmir, Srinagar.

Dr. Khan Touseef Osman

Dr. Khan Touseef Osman is an Assistant Professor at the Department of English, Daffodil International University, Bangladesh. He did his PhD from the *UNESCO-Madanjeet Singh Institute of Kashmir Studies, University of Kashmir, Srinagar.*

Pawan Bali

Pawan Bali is a journalist and conflict resolution consultant based in Washington DC. She has completed her Masters' in Peace and Conflict Resolution from American University, Washington DC and works on South Asia Policy.

Wajahat Qazi

Wajahat Qazi did his Masters in International Relations from the University of Aberdeen.

Subarna Dhar

Subarna Dhar is a Bangladesh based human rights activist. She did her Master's from the *UNESCO-Madanjeet Singh Institute of Kashmir Studies, University of Kashmir, Srinagar.*

Shafinur Nahar

Shafinur Nahar is a Bangladesh based writer and columnist. She did her Master's from the *UNESCO-Madanjeet Singh Institute of Kashmir Studies, University of Kashmir, Srinagar.*

Kabita Kharka

Kabita Kharka, a Bhutan based young entrepreneur did her Master's from the *UNESCO-Madanjeet Singh Institute of Kashmir Studies, University of Kashmir, Srinagar.*

Bishnu Pokharel

Bishnu Pokharel is a Nepal based journalist who did his Master's from the *UNESCO-Madanjeet Singh Institute of Kashmir Studies, University of Kashmir, Srinagar.*

Mohammad Zakaria

Mohammad Zakaria is a Bangladesh based young journalist who did his Master's from the *UNESCO-Madanjeet Singh Institute of Kashmir Studies, University of Kashmir, Srinagar.*

Conceptual Framework

1

Theorising a Theory of Global Justice: A case for Inclusive Perspectives

— Javid Ahmad Dar

I. Introduction

There is a broader agreement that global justice is the *most* urgent academic agenda of the world *for* the prevalence of global injustice is an indisputable fact. One of the least controversial claims even any thinking mind, not to speak of a theorist or philosopher, can make is, what Thomas Nagel states, 'we do not live in a just world.'[1] And add to this Martin Luther King's far-reaching concern that he made in a letter from Birmingham Jail in 1963: 'Injustice anywhere is a threat to justice everywhere.' It is hard to discover disagreements over such indispensable concerns which, in my opinion, no sensible individual can reasonably reject. The realisation of global justice is far more a difficult terrain than is inversely true of the prompt diagnosis of the problem. The reason is that the *theorisation* of global justice is a very 'daunting (academic) task' whether done through 'contextualisation'[2] or de-contextualisation.[3] 'Theorising theory', here used in the title, comes from a well-crafted and widely referred paper of Prof. Bhikhu Parekh that he wrote in the context of *discipline* of Contemporary Political Theory.[4] It appositely captures the attempt of broadening the base/foundation of contemporary debate of global justice that suffers a particular 'parochial' problem. It is precisely this *problem* in contemporary debate that we must address to make a theory of global justice a truly globally-informed theory. The presentation, hence, is titled as: 'Theorising a Theory of Global Justice: A case for Inclusive Perspectives'.

II. 'Contemporary' Debates of Global Justice: the beginning

The debate of global justice has received a great deal of academic attention since 1970's and many philosophers are engaged over the proper understanding the issues of global justice. It is becoming increasingly difficult for academic departments like Political Science and Philosophy to ignore this topic in their academic courses. This theme is becoming overwhelmingly popular to such an extent that in a short span of almost last two and half decades 'a veritable publishing industry' developed around the theme.[5]

The contemporary debate of global justice was well inaugurated in early 1970's by a path-breaking paper of Peter Singer, 'Famine, Affluence and Morality' published in *Philosophy and Public Affairs.*[6] Singer was inspired by the famines of Bangladesh and made a (moral) demand to affluent persons of developed nations to donate some part of their income to charitable causes *beyond* their borders. Singer underlines a 'moral obligation' for the affluent persons that 'if it is in our power to prevent something bad from happening…we ought, morally, to do it.'[7] His latest work *The Life You can Save* (2009) reiterates the moral 'duty' of the rich to 'end world poverty'.[8] There are two important aspects of Singer's call for assisting the global poor. First, he termed such help as 'obligation' rather a mere charity. He thought that such a moral obligation must be done from some sort of a 'sense of duty'. Second, he made 'persons' as prime actors/agents of such an obligation rather a state. His call on person/s has had important influence on the theory of global justice. There are theoretical problems with Singer's line of argument (I shall be discussing them in a while).

The early years of the decade of 1970's saw, at least, two very important academic developments in the general theory of justice. The first is *the* classic treatise on social distributive justice written by John Rawls, his *magnum opus*, *A Theory of Justice* (1971); a work that undisputedly shifted the paradigm of the discipline of political philosophy, and finally emerged as a most influential work of the Twentieth Century on the subject. Second, an influential essay by Peter Singer titled 'Famine, Affluence and Morality' (1972) that attempts to address a broader domain of justice. The two are *not* comparable in terms of their theoretical density, methodological accuracy and reach of arguments, but the two *overlap* in a concern to 'benefit' the 'left-out' disadvantaged people. Interestingly, Peter Singer's essay does not mention Rawls's *Theory,* meaning thereby that the paper was neither influenced by Rawls's *theoretical formulation* nor by his *ethical consideration* of significance of pursuit of justice. While John Rawls made domestic social justice the subject-matter of his *Theory* and tried to *extend* his thesis to international level only in 1999, Peter Singer was only occupied with justice beyond borders.

This shall not lead us to confusion that the domains of domestic and global justice are strictly 'bordered'. It is important to keep in mind that the domains of local and global justice are *not* distinct and separate. In many a cases, a seemingly specific domestic injustice can be a problem of global justice. Sometimes a particular pattern of injustice related with ethnicity, religion, race, or caste in a particular country can become an agenda for global justice. Apartheid, for example, is a clear illustration of it. With this point in view, I, thus, deem the domains of global and domestic/local justice as 'overlapping'. Keeping these two points, birth and 'overlapping' domain, let us try to understand issues, or more precisely the handicaps, that beset the contemporary notions of global justice. There are two sets of problems: the nature of theory, and problems in very *theorisation.* The latter is more a serious issue for the academicians belonging to non-Western world, therefore, a major concern for this presentation also.

III. Nature of Global Justice: the Problems

The concepts and theories of global are not adequately developed *for* the entire discourse is yet in the embryonic stage. There is a definite lack of multiple theories which could identify the central questions, discuss various theoretical frameworks, explore consistent theory from local to world scale, and seek the possible answers for the pursuit of global justice. I shall briefly highly some ambiguities which bear the 'disputed' nature of global justice out.

(a) Positive duties beyond borders

As discussed above, Peter Singer's well-initiated debate of global justice has two important features: firstly, he goes beyond the line of 'charity' to 'obligation' done from, using a Kantian phrase, a 'sense of duty', and secondly, he appeals the 'affluent persons' rather the developed nations to help the global poor. It is a moral duty of the affluent West to help the world poor.

There are two major problems with Singer's line of positive duty or *moral obligation* argument. First, moral obligation may not 'inevitably' be the form and content of justice. Justice, instead, is a matter of right legitimately claimed by the individuals/societies which are justifiable by the mutual agreements reached by them and, finally, enforceable by a centralised power. It primarily involves the question of sovereignty (I discuss this issue below). And second, humanitarian assistance is warranted in peculiar times, say for example, like famines and extreme chronic poverty. In this sense, justice becomes *particularly situational* (that has a utility in particular situation) rather a *general problem* of socio-economic distribution. Thomas Nagel (2005) has another point to make here. He argues that there is *no* clarity what obligations are we supposed to follow individually and collectively as 'basic duties of humanity'. This approach, Nagel argues, reduces the problem of global justice to mere global poverty and the principle of humanitarian assistance has a limited application in 'absolute' need only. It is deemed to fail in the problems of 'relative' need. Justice cannot be reduced to *mere* humanitarian assistance rather justice 'is concerned with the relations between the conditions of different classes of people, and the causes of inequality between them.'[9]

(b) Negative duties towards global poor

There is a thinking line that deems positive duties towards global poor as 'less' stringent. They are 'less' stringent in so far as they ask a person 'to do' something for others rather than restricting the personal conduct from 'harming' others. 'Not to harm others' is a negative duty of persons. It is comparatively more stringent than a positive duty of assisting others. A well-developed notion of global justice based on negative duties framework is theorised by Thomas Pogge.

The contemporary world poverty presents a catastrophic picture. Pogge argues that in the first fifteen years of post-Cold War period, 270 million people died 'prematurely' from 'poverty related causes' and this figure (270 million) is 'considerably larger than the 200-million death toll from all the wars, civil wars, genocides and other government repression of the entire 20th century combined.'[10] Additionally, billions of people have suffered from: hunger, malnutrition, child labour, trafficking, and lack of access to basic healthcare and safe drinking water, lack of shelter, basic sanitation, electricity, and elementary education in the same period.[11] Who is responsible? The answer is simple: the citizens of the developed countries. Pogge confessedly writes: 'we (the citizens of the affluent countries) are *harming* the global poor— ...we are active participants in the largest, though not the gravest, crime against humanity ever committed.'[12] There is a 'radical inequality' between global rich and poor and it is principally the leaders of the developed states who shape and enforce conditions that cause global poverty. The post-Cold War scenario offered 'exceptionally favourable' conditions for eradication of global poverty, but the affluent states have surprisingly done 'very little' in this regard. Without any serious implication on them, the developed states 'had both the power and the funds to make major effort toward poverty eradication.'[13] Conversely, they *actively* produced poverty and affected, thus, billions of lives. In fact, they added to world poverty *manifold* which has had disastrous implications on the global poor. It is in this context, Pogge argues that the citizens of the affluent countries have 'violated the *negative* duties' (duties not to harm others) by perpetuating poverty and miseries in the developing world. He lays focus on two kinds of negative duties: (a) duties not to harm; and (b) duties 'to avert harms that one's own past conduct may cause in the future.'[14] The duties of the latter kind are of both natures —positive as well as negative— and, are, therefore, termed as intermediate duties.

If we follow this view, there are obviously certain requirements for the establishment of global justice. A legitimate institutional framework that 'prevents' the people from doing harm to others is all but a must. It will require regulating (or limiting) the private holdings of the individuals; and fairness would ultimately demand a *redistribution* of the resources *to remedy the past injustices.* This also necessitates, as

Nagel points out, for the establishment of a 'common system of institutions' for the world 'as a whole' to realise a universal standard of opportunities available to the people of the world.[15] If it is correct, then *the* most fundamental condition for the pursuit of justice at the world scale is existence of global sovereignty which is almost impossible to achieve in the present nation-state world order. In other words, the absence of global sovereignty and the presence of national sovereignty pose problems for this 'remedial' notion of global justice. This brings us to a very crucial point, that is, the relationship between the attainment of justice and existence of sovereignty. It is here one can make a quick comparison between domestic and global theories of justice. With the state sovereignty in the background, domestic theories of justice saw a tremendous theory building and optimism of applicability within the national jurisdiction of the states. With non-existent global sovereignty, is reverse true of global justicc?

(c) Justice and Sovereignty: is global justice possible?

One of the most profound foundational works that spoke of relationship between justice and sovereignty is Thomas Hobbes's *The Leviathan* (1651). For Hobbes, 'moral motive' cannot be the *condition* for actualising justice; though it may influence in discovering the principles of justice. Justice as the collective interest of *all* is actualised when *all* the members of society *conform* to the mutual agreement reached to safeguard the interests of *all.* For justice (as well as injustice), a centralised power with a coercive capacity is all but a must. In one word, there is no justice (or even injustice) in the absence of sovereignty. He wrote with clarity:

> ...before the names of just, and unjust can have place, there must be some coercive power, to compel men equally to the performance of their covenants, by the terror of some punishment, greater than the benefit they expect by the breach of their covenant...So that the nature of justice consists in keeping of valid covenants, but the validity of covenants begins not but with the constitution of a civil power sufficient to compel men to keep them: and then it is also that propriety begins.[16]

Picking this Hobbesian line, Nagel (2005) wrote a well-meaning essay, 'The Problem of Global Justice', that addresses the problem through Hobbes's *condition* of sovereignty and Rawls's *concern* for equality. Both the accounts (Hobbes's and Rawls's) tend to agree for the existence of a global *institutional* mechanism to ensure global justice. Such an institutional approach *fundamentally* requires global sovereignty which is *no-where* existent. Thomas Nagel himself argues: 'if Hobbes is right, the idea of global justice without a world government is a chimera.'[17]

Following 'Hobbesian spirit', Nagel holds that the *primary* condition for global justice 'is the concentration of power' or 'a centralised power at world scale' and only then the issues of legitimacy and justice are *gradually* considered.[18] These global structures of power, however, might be 'illegitimate' in the beginning and would ultimately gain legitimacy through expanded democracy. For the moment, there are *no such* global institutions *or* globally centralised power. One of the most vibrant impediments in establishing global sovereignty is the existence of national sovereignty. The nation-states are *the* major actors in the global arena. It is for this reason that there is a huge pessimism about the possibility of global justice. We have identified some problems in the *nature* of contemporary theories of global justice; there are definite problems in the *very* theorisation too.

IV. Parochialism and Contemporary Theory of Global Justice

The incontrovertibility of global justice is perhaps proportionate to the lack of global character of the debates of global justice. Despite having global significance, the debate is confined to the scholars of the West on the one hand, and is deeply influenced by the Western intellectual traditions on the other. As a consequence, the very 'base' of the theory remains quite 'thin'. I shall be briefly highlighting some of the problems in the very theorisation of these contemporary debates which in turn would emerge as a subject matter for an (urgent) academic agenda for us (people in the developing world).

(a) Inadequate Theorisation

The available literature on the subject fairly makes us realise the problem of global justice. But, we *fail* to receive a fine comprehensive introduction that would introduce the debates through varied angles and through the varied voices from the different regions of the world. This results in, what can be loosely called, *inadequate* theorisation: the inadequacy becomes evident with a mere survey of literature. Some call it a 'thin' theory. For an adequate theorisation of this subject, it remains necessary, as Sebatiano Maffetone and Akash Singh Rathore (2012) hold, to recognise and accommodate 'more (global) voices into this (global) debate of global reach and significance.'[19] This requires not only serious thinking about the plural worldviews and wide inclusion of voices of globally marginalised people, it also asks for new epistemological and ontological foundation of International Relations of persons, states and institutions. Additionally, the broad base of theory also necessitates how we define, describe, debate the contours of a just world society and global agency. However, the problem is that very few people are active in this important subject. This is one of the major causes of *inadequate theorisation* and must be addressed to broaden the theoretical foreground of such vital theory as global justice.

(b) Parochialism of contemporary dominant approach: Sen's Alternative

There is a well-developed western philosophic tradition that holds that justice emanates from the 'perfect' institutions conceived through an impartial mechanism. This impartiality is featured by 'pure rationality' conditioned by, using Rawls's terminology, 'most favourable conditions' *uninfluenced* by the social and natural contingencies. This is famously called the Social Contract tradition and was followed by philosophers like Thomas Hobbes, John Locke, Jean Jacques Rousseau, Immanuel Kant and John Rawls. The existence of global institutions is a necessary *precondition* for the pursuit of global justice and the problems with this line of thinking are evident as we discussed them above. This approach is centrally focused on the establishment of the 'perfect' institutions and structures for the pursuit of justice. These 'institutions' can be conceived through deductive-logic with a scope of universal application. There are objections to this 'perfect' institutional framework. Amartya Sen is a major critique of this transcendentalist approach to global justice. Sen is of the view that this transcendental institutionalism is 'parochial' in character precisely for the reason that it ignores and underestimates the vast practices and the rich intellectual traditions of non-western world. This underlines, what he calls, the 'parochial' foundation of theory of justice.

The institution-focussed notions of justice, as transcendentalists propagate, do not concentrate on the consequential aspects of functioning of institutions and structures and cannot explore the influence of societal factors such as social behaviour, social norms and practical, cultural past and intellectual traditions on the actual life of individuals and institutions governing them. This approach 'closes' itself for examining the influence of internal and external social contingencies and historico-philosophic character of the society. Drawing from Indian classical Sanskrit vocabulary for two ways of understanding justice, *niti* and *nyaya*, Sen differentiates between *organisation-focused* notion of justice (*niti*) and *realisation-focused* practice of justice that emphasises on the *actual* lives rather *ideal* institutions (*nayaya*). Fundamental to his thinking that *ideals* are *irrelevant* when the matter is of choosing from two *actual* situations. In the actual practice, individuals and societies *compare* the situations and choose a *lesser* unjust practices. The justice is related *not* only with the institutions and structures but justice is *fundamentally* a matter of *judging the societies themselves.* The institutions are, thus, secondary to comprehensive realisation of justice.[20] Sen's *comparative* approach has an advantage that it can duly regard the cultural milieu and intellectual traditions of a particular society, it opens it up for a broader *open impartiality*: the world societies. This 'Impartial Spectator', as Adam Smith would call it, would critically scrutinize the societies and the world, resultantly, turns into a wide reasoning sphere at large where cultures find space and recognition. Such an engagement 'turns' a society 'on' to an 'open question' coming from somewhere else and through this, what I can call, *deliberative*[21] comparative approach the remediable injustices can be identified and finally eliminated. As a matter of fact, the realisation of justice lies in the removal of injustices from the actual societies rather dreaming a *perfectly* just society. Amartya Sen here follows the approaches of Aristotle, Adam Smith, John Stuart Mill and Karl Marx. The very basic approach they all had was that there must be a constant evaluation and critical examination of different situations, institutions, behaviours, norms and practices.

It has huge merits and is immensely helpful in re-shaping the contemporary debates to make them *truly* global.

(c) Challenging the Western dominance: a need for de-parochialisation

Amartya Sen's rejection of the dominant western tradition results in two-fold *de-parochialism*: One, in the *form* and second, in the *content* of global justice theory. He pushes for the inclusion of non-western ideas and traditions in the very theorisation on the one hand, and speaks about the grammar of injustices on the other. This has opened up a possibility for the non-western scholars to break the ice. Following Sen's de-parochial approach, few non-western theorists wrote provocative essays to take a departure from dominant western line of thinking apart from asserting the 'agency' prominence of global poor in the whole debate of global justice.

The global justice debate suffers *monologue*: it is located in western academia and dominated by the western scholars. The non-western world seems at the receiving end *for* the very foundational features of the theory *exclude* the developing world from active role in realisation of justice. Neera Chandoke (2012) argues that the scholars from the 'global poor' 'are excluded from the debate by definitional fiat.'[22] By the very definition, it tries to demand and justify the moral account of assisting the global poor. While the western rich are morally obliged to help the poor of world who live beyond their borders, the global poor are defined 'as if they are mere recipients both of processes as well as obligations that emanate from elsewhere.'[23] These theories reduce the global poor to a passive receptor who on the one hand faces the great military and technological *might* of the developed countries and, on the other hand, depends on their *aid* and *assistance* to come of the wretched conditions of poverty and ill-health. Both ways, he is a receptor. Raising a very serious question, Chandoke writes: 'are we who live in the developing world, fated to remain consumers of acts, whether these are those of harm, or of duty, performed by the West?.'[24] In short, 'the western theories of global justice are not based on active cooperation of world peoples' who share rights and duties to one another. Professor Chandoke's essay reminds us of a very influential thinking line: Dependency Theory. The dependency school was characterised by a true world scholarship across the continents and regions of the globe. The contemporary global justice debate is yet to reach a global level scholarship as was the case with the Dependency Theory. The decline of dependency school may offer lessons for the growth a well-weighed comprehensive theory of global justice.

V. Conclusion

The long wait for a capacious beginning of challenging and taking a departure from the dominant western theoretical paradigms is over with Amartya Sen's capacious and innovative work. There is urgency for intellectual interventions to end the narrow base of global justice debate. The assertions —such as the existing worldviews may not be far from reasoning, the problems deemed as 'local' might have global dimensions, and all kinds of *unfreedoms* must end for realisation of justice— shall form a bedrock for a wide inclusive theoretical foundation of global justice. The parochialism must end for the development of a truly global theory of global justice. Justice is certainly more than a one-way moral help to poor. Fundamental to justice is that humans live a happy and flourishing life. I may conclude with a philosophic question raised by Thomas Nagel: 'Justice ... requires more than mere humanitarian assistance to those in desperate need, and injustice can exist without anyone being on the vergeof starvation.'[25] One does hope that it becomes a *part* of a beginning of a discourse of global significance.

References

1. Nagel, T. (2005). 'The Problem of Global Justice', *Philosophy & Public Affairs*, Vol. 33, No. 2, p. 113.
2. Rathore, A. S. (2012). 'The Romance of Global Justice: Sen's Deparochialisation and the Quandary of Dalit Marxism', Sebatiano Maffettone and Akash S. Rathore (eds.) *Global Justice: Critical Perspectives,* London: Routledge, pp. 165-166.
3. High abstract theory of global justice poses *no lesser* difficulty for speculating an *ideal* theory of global justice with the present international political structures (or realisable global institutional framework, in future) in place. A unique set of 'principles' of global justice which are universally acceptable and justifiable pose serious *methodological* problems both in conceptualisation and justification.

4. Parekh, B. (2000). 'Theorizing Political Theory', in Noël O'Sullivan (ed.) *Political Theory in Transition,* London: Routledge, pp. 242-259.
5. Chandoke, N. (2012). 'Who owes Whom, Why and to What Effect?' in Sebatiano Maffettone and Akash S. Rathore (eds.) *Global Justice: Critical Perspectives,* London: Routledge, p. 144.
6. Singer, P. (1972). 'Famine, Affluence and Morality', *Philosophy and Public Affairs,* Vol. 1, No. 1, pp. 229-243.
7. *Ibid*, p. 231.
8. The sub-title of the book captures it aptly: 'How to Do Your Part to End the World Poverty'. See Peter Singer (2009) *The Life You Can Save,* New York: Random House.
9. Nagel, T. (2005). 'The Problem of Global Justice', p. 119.
10. Pogge, T. (2005). 'Real World Justice', *The Journal of Ethics,* Vol. 9, No. 1/ 2, p. 31.
11. *Ibid,* pp. 30-31.
12. *Ibid,* p. 33.
13. Pogge, T. (2001). 'Priorities of Global Justice', in Thomas W. Pogge (ed.) *Global Justice,* Oxford: Blackwell Publishing, p. 6.
14. Pogge, T. (2005), p. 34.
15. Nagel, T. (2005), p. 119.
16. Hobbes, T. [1996, (1651)]. *The Leviathan,* Oxford: Oxford University Press, pp. 95-96.
17. Nagel, T. (2005), p. 115.
18. *Ibid,* p. 145.
19. Maffetone, S. and Rathore, A. S. (2012). 'Introduction: The Rawlsian Provenance of the Global Justice Debate' in Sebatiano Maffettone & Akash S. Rathore (eds.) *Global Justice: Critical Perspectives,* London: Routledge, p. 1.
20. Sen, A. (2009). *The Idea of Justice,* London: Penguin.
21. The contemporary means of communication technology has the very potential to transform the world society into a deliberative forum where marginalised can speak and articulate their view. The different worldviews are becoming *visible* and will broaden the very base of comparison. Going by this, comparative will become more *deliberative.*
22. Chandoke, N. (2012). 'Who owes Whom, Why and to What Effect?', p. 145.
23. *Ibid.*
24. *Ibid.*
25. Nagel, T. (2005), p. 118.

2

Decoding the Meanings of Development and Welfare in Indian Politics

— *K.C. Suri*

Development and welfare have been key terms in the vocabulary of Indian politics, as they are in many democracies of the world, especially in the "developing countries" also known by the name of the "Third World". Although very few would disagree on the need for development and welfare as the ideals for any society and also as a policy framework for any government, there is no agreement at any given point of time on the meaning of these terms and how they can be realised. Also, meanings of these terms kept changing from time to time, and context to context. While development and welfare can be treated as two processes that should happen in tandem, they are also understood as inimical to each other or at least in conflict with each other. If we understand the term development as a process of progress bringing the nation to an advanced condition compared to the earlier one, it need not necessarily come into conflict with the term welfare, understood as the well-being of people of a nation promoted by the financial and material assistance of the state to those facing hardship. But the shifting meanings of development and welfare posit a conflict between the two, especially in the wake of liberalisation policy framework adopted by the states in the developing countries. Understanding this tension between development and welfare, and the efforts to balance and combine the two by finding ways to resolve such a conflict is critical to the understanding of politics of India at the national and state levels over the past few decades.

Two principal and competing models of development prevailed at the time of decolonisation the world over. One was the capitalist model of economic development based on private enterprise and free market mechanisms actively supported and encouraged by the state. The other was the socialist model where the state exercised control through centralised planning of resources and distribution of goods and incomes. Having emerged from colonial rule, India did not adopt either the capitalist model or socialist model, but combined the two in what is known as mixed economy. In this, while the structure of the economy continued to be a capitalist one, the state was to play an active interventionist role in regulating industries and businesses. The objective of the state policy was to achieve rapid economic development, self-sufficiency through import substitution measures, and at the same time ensure well-being of its citizens, especially the workers and the socially disadvantaged sections. For this, rapid development of science and technology was considered imperative. Agrarian reforms that ended feudal control of land were initiated. Public sector, considered to be an important driving force of the economy, was vigorously developed. Thus, during the 1950s and 1960s, the emphasis was on economic development, in the way the industrialised western countries had achieved it over the past two centuries. The advocates of development in the west too prescribed a model of development to the Third World countries similar to the one that was experienced by the western countries. It presumed that the Third World nations too could develop through a series of stages of economic and political development — from a stage of backwardness to take off to prosperity.

But India did not have the all the time or conducive situation that the western nations had in their journey towards prosperity. Many of the western nations had gone through a long period of indigenous development of science and technology, industrialised under authoritarian states, established their rule over other nations from which they transferred wealth, and reaped the advantage of captive markets to their industrial goods in colonies. They became only gradually democratic with the introduction of universal franchise in the late nineteenth century and early twentieth century. Given their levels of industrialisation and overall prosperity, they could attend to the needs of the marginalised sections of the society and thus transformed themselves, especially in Europe, into welfare states in the first half of the twentieth century. But the context of independent India was different. It had to simultaneously address the issues of achieving industrialisation, eradication of poverty, and ensuring the well-being of the people which were hardly cared by the colonial state that was mainly interested in the development of its people in the imperial centre. These objectives, around which people were mobilised into the freedom movement, were to be achieved in a democratic political framework based on universal adult franchise and free and periodical elections. This was the key challenge of independent India, which continues even today.

The year 1967 saw the defeat of the Congress party in several states. Its position at the national level too became shaky with the rise of strong opposition parties. As political leaders had to secure popular support in election after election in order to retain or gain political power and as the economic growth rates were slow than expected, the leadership began to emphasise the need for welfare programmes. Thus, in the 1970s we see the introduction of welfare programmes and schemes that catered to the immediate needs of the disadvantaged and deprived. The emphasis was laid more on redistribution rather than mere economic growth. The Congress party under the leadership of Indira Gandhi and also several other regional parties that became contenders for political power in different states of India had introduced such schemes trying to outdo each other in the electoral arena. Development came to be understood as the development of the weaker sections, their increased participation in politics and their empowerment through effective implementation of reservation policies, redistribution of land to the landless, provision of basic needs such as food, housing, education and health. Critics of such welfare schemes and programmes castigated them as populism, saying that the political leaders resort to providing sops to people with a view to win elections. But populism may be seen as a way of according importance to welfare in a situation of limited economic growth.

The crisis and collapse of socialist states in Europe, and the introduction of economic reform policies in China had posed a big challenge to the model of economic development that was pursed in India after independence. Collapse of socialist states was widely interpreted as the end of an ideology that stood for centralised planning and social ownership of means of production and state controlled distribution. It also had practical implications for the Indian economy which hitherto heavily depended on socialist countries for trade, aid, transfer of technologies, and in defense matters. In the situation of seemingly no alternative to capitalist economic development, the arguments in favour of dismantling the centralised planning and public sector, opening up of the economy to multinational companies and foreign capital, and deregulation of the economy gathered force.

With the onset of economic reforms in 1991, development became synonymous with economic growth that warranted dismantling state controls of the economy, encouraging private enterprise, and integrating the Indian economy with the international economy. Critics of globalisation saw that it was only another term for the model of capitalist development hitherto prescribed by the developmentalists at the international level for the development of the Third World nations. Development now meant directing state resources into productive investment and giving fillip to market forces. Development implied the state yielding to the market and civil society. Welfare implied using up scarce resources in an unproductive way. In this sense, development is good for economic growth, while welfare is populism that hampers economic growth and overall health of the economy. Thus, development and welfare came to be seen as incongruent, as if they are two tracks that never meet. In the party political domain the contestation between a development agenda and a donative (welfare) agenda became vigorous. It appeared as if that the welfare discourse had been displaced by a development discourse.

In the initial euphoria surrounding economic reforms in the early 1990s, the role and responsibilities of the government were reappraised. A lower quantity of government and welfare spending was considered a necessary condition to ensure development that would result in a higher quality of governance. Governments at the national and state levels were called upon to concentrate on creating an environment for development by encouraging private initiative in much of the infrastructure building and businesses. Performance of the public sector enterprises was reviewed with reference to the productivity of capital invested in them. Public sector industries and businesses, where not profitable, were privatised. The model of development pursued by some of the South-East Asian nations was shown as the model for India's development.

Within a few years, however, a degree of skepticism began to creep in about the political consequences of economic reforms. Tension began to emerge between the logic of a market economy and that of the electoral market. Pressure to support the poor and the disadvantaged began to mount in the electoral market. Opposition parties started criticising the way in which a ruling party implemented reforms neglecting the poor and the marginalised sections. It was clear that India cannot proceed on the model of the South-East Asian nations or the model prescribed by the multilateral financial agencies such as the World Bank. India's political system is not authoritarian where the ruling elite could implement chosen policies for economic growth at will. India is a democracy like many of the nations of the west Europe, but its people are not as wealthy as the people of the western nations. In a country like India, where majority of the people are poor but its political system is based on periodically held free elections, it is not possible to implement policies that neglect the needs and demands of the majority of the population who have the power to decide the electoral outcomes. Such a situation posed serious dilemma to the political leaders. On the one hand, they operate in a democracy that is concerned with equality and welfare for all, and in which legitimacy for the government and governmental policies is derived through the consent of the majority. On the other hand, there was pressure to restructure the economy in a way that promotes the conditions necessary to facilitate the liberalisation process and strengthen market forces. This dilemma was manifest in the statements of political leaders about the constraints under which they had to operate. Actually, soon after the introduction of economic reforms, the then Finance Minister of India, Manmohan Singh, spoke of a two-track strategy, by which both the agendas of development and welfare can be pursued simultaneously.

There is also another aspect of the India's political economy that has gained ascendance in recent years. Corruption and crony capitalism have become intrinsic to all the regimes, whether they privilege welfare over development or development over welfare. Since election campaigns have become so costly, the dependence of parties and leaders on those who have money bags has increased over the years. At the same time, the personal greed of political leaders has increased. There are accusations that politicians amass wealth in huge quantity through quid pro quo deals, percentages in contracts and granting permissions. We notice a trend wherein the greater the levels of political corruption become, the greater the rhetoric of development and welfare becomes. There developed a symbiotic relationship between political leaders who seek to amass wealth by hook or crook, and those business interests, racketeers, and middlemen who seek to profit by their access to those in positions of power. This resulted in a sham promise of development, welfare and governance, while they are constantly undermined and sabotaged. This might be one of the sources of disaffection with the incumbent governments. This led to a situation where people think that all parties are corrupt, and so their vote decisions depend on who can deliver on the promise of welfare.

We also notice that parties change their positions vis-à-vis development and welfare depending on the situation whether they are in power or in opposition. It is not that a party is completely opposed to development or welfare. It is not possible for parties and leaders to operate with unadulterated models of development and welfare in electoral democracies ridden with problems of large-scale poverty and deprivation. Electoral compulsions act as a check on the government leaning excessively on the development agenda since the opposition party on the prowl projects itself as the champion of the interests of the weaker sections and the poor. Greater the frequency of elections, which come in India very often as elections take place for representative bodies at various levels, greater the pressure on the incumbent government to cater to the welfare needs. Thus, we see considerable degree of policy convergence between regimes and parties, although they differ in the accent they place on either of them and this could vary from time to time. What the parties have proposed in the 2014 elections was a kind of twining development and welfare, in what can be called welfare-oriented development. This we see in the election promises of the leaders and the election manifestoes of the major parties in 2014 election.

Tension between development, understood as allowing primacy to free market and emphasis on economic growth, and welfare, understood as state providing succor and support to the needy people, can be found in all nations of the world. But this tension is acute in democracies of the developing nations beset by generally low levels of income, industrial and economic underdevelopment on the one hand and high expectations of people from governments to meet their basic needs. This tension comes into light more fully during the times of elections as political leaders have to persuade people to vote in their favour, who in turn look at the performance of parties while in power or the promise they hold for future for the improvement of their living conditions. Thus, in the back and forth movement of leaders and parties between development and welfare or in the effort to combine development and welfare we discern the dynamics of democratic politics in developing societies. What we find is that a party or leader cannot harp upon or latch on to unadulterated model of development, and if they do so they are bound to come to grief. Chanting either the development mantra or the welfare mantra may not make governments last long in power. The tension between development and welfare does not go away by attempts at tight-rope walking between the two, but by integrating them in a way that simultaneously ensures economic growth as well as welfare, which together would lead to governance.

3

Trauma Theory in the Context of the Partition of Subcontinent

— Khan Touseef Osman

Sir Cyril Radcliffe arrived in what was still British India on 08 July 1947 with only five weeks to decide upon the boundaries of the two would be nations: India and Pakistan. It was not until 17 August, two days after the Partition of the subcontinent, that the boundaries were officially awarded. Meanwhile, uncertainty among people both in Punjab and Bengal provinces about the boundaries loomed to the extent that it sparked near genocidal violence. Between July and October 1947, around one million people lost their lives, ten to sixteen million people got dislocated and seventy-five thousand women were abducted and/or raped. Today we regard Radcliffe as synonymous with mayhem and atrocity in the popular history of the subcontinent. However, while doing so, we ignore the fact that Radcliffe was not the only person responsible for the territorial allocation of the two newly independent countries. Two border commissions were formed for Punjab and Bengal, both chaired by Radcliffe and included two representatives from Indian National Congress and two from Muslim League in each case. Seeing the unprecedented violence resulting from the division of the subcontinent, Radcliffe refused to accept the 40,000 rupees he was to receive for his job. ("Cyril John Radcliffe, 1st Viscount Radcliffe") I have started my discussion with this account to highlight the selective remembrance at work in the popular perception of history, often to absolve ourselves of our culpability.

Historiography on the event of the Partition took very different turns following the independence of India and Pakistan. In India, it was the Nehruvian narrative of the long struggle for freedom for a secular nation that dominated the official history, while Pakistan celebrated the achievement of a new country for Muslims that saved its population from assuming the minority status once the British left. Both meta narratives found their places in the text books of the respective countries, and several generations of Indians and Pakistanis were brought up on these accounts. Jinnah and his Muslim League were held solely responsible in India for the fracture of the subcontinent, even as a similar blame-game took place in Pakistan against the Hindu leadership of Congress and their supposed intension of communal domination over Muslims. Each country, at least officially, seemed triumphant against its imaginary windmill. What these celebratory meta narratives of independence did in effect was to drown the sufferings and cries of the people on whose lives the Partition wrought havoc. There was an uncanny silence on both sides of the Radcliffe line about the people who were murdered, dislocated or violated, almost always relegating their stories to a two-line description in history books. It would not be an exaggeration to say that there had not been any history of the Partition at all for a very long time, only the history of the Independence. But, the voices repressed by the celebratory meta narratives had eventually to come out and assert that the Independence everyone talks of with such jubilation had come at an enormous cost.

A decisive moment of shift in the focus of historiography on the Partition was the anti-Sikh riots in 1984 in Delhi and elsewhere following the murder of Prime Minister Indira Gandhi by her Sikh bodyguard. The mayhem against the Sikh population with indirect state complicity reminded many of the survivors and witnesses that this was not the first time they encountered communal violence of such nature; the first time was 1947. Indeed, a Sikh elderly said to Urvashi Butalia that it was like the Partition all over again (*The Other Side* 5). The resurfacing of communal violence enabled Butalia to discern the continuous presence of the past: "It took 1984 to make me understand how ever-present Partition was in our lives too, to recognise that it could not be so easily put away inside the covers of history books" (6). She was collecting oral narratives of the Partition at the time, which she later compiled in her seminal work titled *The Other Side of Silence: Voices from the Partition of India* (1998). A similar work of oral historiography was done by Ritu Menon and Kamla Bhasin titled *Borders and Boundaries: Women in India's Partition* (1998). Both works, the latter to a greater degree, are notable for their emphasis on the gendered dimension of partition violence. Subaltern historiography thrived at the same time as Butalia and others were collecting oral narratives, perhaps not too coincidentally as the two areas complement each other in many ways. Researchers like Gyanendra Pandey focused on the everyday affairs of common people during and around the time of the Partition rather than grand political events. A renewed enthusiasm in literary representation of the Partition has been seen since the 1980s not only in regional languages but in English as well. Salman Rushdie's *Midnight's Children*, Amitav Ghosh's *Shadow Lines* and Bapsi Sidhwa's *Ice-Candy-Man* best exemplify the proliferation of fictional writings in English in the 80s on this subject. The 50th anniversary of Independence in 1997 marked and in turn caused many instances of scholarly re-evaluation of the Partition in several research areas. This frequent looking back at the Partition since the mid-1980s till today has slowly, but decisively, eaten away the bases of the official meta narratives of independence, crumbling their established premises and casting doubts on their seemingly inviolable beliefs.

Today's scholarship on the Partition has taken a very curious turn: researchers have seen a possibility of treating oral narratives as testimonies of violence. Furthermore, literary representations, especially fictional ones, have begun to be considered as "'fictive' testimonies" or "testimonial fictions" (Saint 3, 5). These testimonies—both fictive and otherwise—are treated to be engaged in the ethical act of bearing witness to the atrocity perpetrated during the Partition. Put differently, they are widely being thought of as windows to the repressed past; being able to open them to negotiate with the violence of 1947 is, they seem to believe, a way to come to term with it. This novel approach to the Partition owes much to the researchers' awareness of the development in the field of trauma studies, which, despite having roots in Freud's deliberations on traumatic events, emerged as an independent area in its own right at the University of Yale in the 1990s.

Fortunoff Video Archive for Holocaust Testimonies, located at the Yale University, is a collection of approximately 4,400 video-taped accounts by Holocaust survivors and witnesses. Though it started as early as 1979, the project took its massive form only after it was taken over by the Yale University, where it became the centre of much scholarly work by Dori Laub, one of the earliest cofounders and a child Holocaust survivor, Shoshana Felman and Geoffrey Hartman. With Laub, Felman co-authored *Testimony: Crises of Witnessing in Literature, Psychoanalysis and History* in 1992, which brought testimonies to the forefront of Holocaust scholarship. ("Fortunoff Video Archive for Holocaust Testimonies") Cathy Caruth, a colleague of both Hartman and Felman, embarked on a project of creating a systematic model of trauma and its aftereffects. In 1995, her edited volume entitled *Trauma: Explorations in Memory* came out, for which she invited articles from researchers working in diverse areas—ranging from literature to psychiatry—on traumatic experiences. She published *Unclaimed Experience: Trauma, Narrative and History*, a seminal study in the field of trauma studies, in the next year. According to Caruth, trauma involves a violent experience or being witness to it which is too overwhelming for the survivor or the bystander to register in memory and cognition. The encounter with atrocity splits the self into two: the conscious and the dissociated selves. It is in the dissociated self that images of the actual event lie and, therefore, are inaccessible to active recollection. However, the apparently missing images of trauma come back to the survivor or witness in the forms of nightmares, flashbacks and other psychological intrusions with all their literality and exactness. (3-5) Two features of Caruth's model are particularly relevant to my discussion (both of which I object to, by the way): first, it is an event-based model, in which a single overwhelming event causes the dissociation of the self; secondly, it is a model that explains the effects of trauma on an individual, not the collective. In fact, psychoanalytic trauma theory quite unaccountably and uncritically assumes a similarity of traumatic pathology on both individual and collective levels.

Now, to come back to the first feature, thinking of the sub-continental experience of the Partition in terms of the event-based model poses a critical problem. In view of a quick survey of the history of the Indian subcontinent from 1947 till today, the Partition has never been a single 'unique' event; rather, any discourse about it naturally invokes the Partition's 'unfinished business' not exclusively with reference to Kashmir. The Partition has become a trope or a motif in the sub-continental history that cannot be left behind in the past. Instead, the communal violence we witnessed in 1947 resurfaces on the socio-political level every so often with a slightest nudge to our so-called religious feelings, as exemplified by the anti-Sikh riots in 1984, Gujarat pogrom in 2002, etc. Similar events have been reported from Pakistan and Bangladesh as well. Indeed, the most significant repetition of geopolitical fracture seen for the first time in 1947 was 1971 when the east wing of Pakistan got separated in the process of the bloody independence of Bangladesh. I would argue here that the event-based model of trauma is largely a result of trauma theory's overemphasis on the Holocaust, which has popularly been thought of as a unique rupture in the continuum of the history of human civilisation.

As for the second feature, that of trauma theory's insights into the effects of atrocity on the individual, not the collective, it may have happened because the theory itself has originated in the cultural milieu of the west. In the highly individuated Western culture—not that I consider it homogenous—it may be difficult to conceive of traumatic experience as a collective phenomenon rather than an individual one. However, the individual without reference to the community, to make a generalised statement, is unthinkable in the Indian subcontinent. Therefore, sub-continental traumatic experiences are collective ones, where the individual is positioned within the collective. In addition, the origin of trauma theory in Freudian psychoanalysis reveals a lot about its emphasis on the traumatic experience and its recovery of the individual. The 'talking cure' takes place between an individual and the therapist, and symptoms are medicalised and pathologised. Trauma theory has inherited this one-to-one therapeutic approach, where the recovery of the afflicted entails a narrative reconstruction of the traumatic experience. In the cultures such as the subcontinent, where trauma takes place on the social level rather than the level of the individual, treating specific members of the society holds very little prospect for a societal recovery.

The possibility of cross-cultural ethical engagement that Cathy Caruth envisioned in trauma theory, therefore, has not been realised as Stef Craps conclusively demonstrated in his book *Postcolonial Witnessing: Trauma out of Bounds* (2013). If anything, it has furthered the project of 'cultural imperialism' by attempting to apply its principles and practices to non-Western traumatic experiences. There is no easy solution to rid trauma theory of its Eurocentric bias, but taking cultural specificities into account might very well be the first step.

References

1. Butalia, Urvashi. *The Other Side of Silence: Voices from the Partition of India*. New Delhi, Penguin Books India Pvt Ltd, 2003. Print.
2. Caruth, Cathy. *Trauma: Explorations in Memory*. Baltimore: Johns Hopkins University Press, 1995. Print.
3. "Cyril John Radcliffe, 1st Viscount Radcliffe." *Wikipedia: The Free Encyclopedia*. Wikimedia Foundation, Inc. 29 July 2004. Web. 14 March 2016.
4. "Fortunoff Video Archive for Holocaust Testimonies." *Wikipedia: The Free Encyclopedia*. Wikimedia Foundation, Inc. 11 December 2011. Web. 22 July 2015.
5. Saint, Tarun K. *Witnessing Partition: Memory, History, Fiction*. New Delhi: Routledge, 2010. Print.

4

Changing Concept of Security

— Sangeeta Thapliyal

Security is a much-contested concept. What is to be secured, who will secure it and who threatens are some of the moot questions in the security discourse. While studying International relations, the concept of security changes with changing times and approach.

The realists understood it as employment of military means to achieve security from the territorial aggression or armed attack from other states. One of the most often quote on security of a state is by Walter Lippman who said that, "a nation is secure to the extent to which it is not in danger of having to sacrifice core values, if it wishes to avoid war, and is able, if challenged, to maintain them by victory in such a war" (Lippman, 1943: 51). Where as, Walt argued that security studies deal with "the study of the threat, use, and control of military force" (Walt, 1991:227). The main referent was the state, which had to be securitised in order to save it from external aggression. This could be done by strengthening armed forces, modernising them, alliances with other states either through military alliances or through collective or cooperative security. In the formative years of designing policies, India had to concentrate on internal and external security challenges. The armed aggression from Pakistan and later China had put place solidly the fear of territorial aggression. However, dislike to cold war politics, India did not prefer to join any of the ideological camps, alliances or pacts but preferred to be non-aligned and carve out a place in the international politics based on its experiences from colonial history. The realist understanding of security predominated Indian security perspectives.

In fact, the international politics at large has been influenced by the realist paradigm of territorial security, which believes that a state is secure if its territories are secured.

The statist discourse of security that gave emphasis to external aggression got more prominence during the cold war. To strengthen state's security, military was seen as a means to achieve political ends. Thus, national interest was the driving force that gave prominence to the state-centric concept of security-military in substance and external in nature. Thus, emerged the strategic studies, developed during the cold war, which gave emphasis to arms race, arms control, disarmament or nuclear deterrence.

Strategic studies came under scanner during the end of cold war. It was critiqued for not being able to predict the course and outcome of the Vietnam War or the end of cold war. The thrust of the studies was more on arms and armaments and external aggression threatening the regime and its ideology without giving due attention to the internal dynamics affecting states. The epistemological question, for whom the state exists, was not within the domain of the studies. People were not the focus of the strategic studies, where as they are affected by varied issues mostly internal in nature.

Barry Buzan, Ole Waever and others from the Copenhagen School of International relations tried to highlight issues emerging from within a country that could pose security challenge to a country. They widened the concept of security by bringing in political, societal, economic and environmental threats to a state. However, Security studies did not lose focus with the widening of the notion as not every concern qualified to be a security issue. Only those concerns arising from within the state that posed existential threat to the people qualified as securitised. "They have to be staged as existential threats to a referent object by securitising actor who thereby generates endorsement of emergency measures beyond rules that would otherwise bind." (Buzan, *et. al:* 5, 25). An issue had to reach a threshold beyond which it could lead to crisis like situation. The securitising actor, that is the state, had to acknowledge existential threats emanating from military or non-military issues and respond with alacrity and emergency measures. When an issue or situation reaches a crisis point beyond which the survival chances of the citizens are endangered, it reaches security domain. (Thakur and Newman, 2004:3) To take the debate further, especially in Third World, Ayoob (1995) argued that issues or situations reach security threshold when they produce political outcomes threatening the survival or effectiveness of the states and regimes.

The widening of the concept of security was within the statist perspective. The state was still the primary referent of security which had to deal with issues more than just confining to external aggression. State was the provider of security with added responsibility to deal with the issues emanating from within the state, between the states and related to international security. It has the power to negotiate on behalf of its people. (Smith, 2000: 83).

Inclusion of non-military issues within the domain of security is also identified by the nomenclature of non-traditional security. It implied military threats as traditional and other issues included with the widening of the concept as non-traditional, which went beyond the external aggression. It is considered multi-disciplinary, comprehensive and holistic approach to deal with people's welfare and well-being. It dealt with not only the issues of human insecurity but also their root causes and the ways to deal with them. However, it does not oppose the state and reposes in it the responsibility to provide security in non-military sectors as well.

It was the critical theorists that brought in a new dimension to the concept of security by asking questions whose security, for whom, by whom? Scholars like Lynn- Jones (1995), Ken Booth (1991, 2005), Wyn Jones (1995, 1999) challenged the notion of state as the primary referent of security and projected people as the primary referent. The utility of the state was not done away with but its role was changed. State was the guarantor and provider of security to its people but took into consideration people's voice on what affected their security. Through participatory approach, State had to take along people in its decision-making. Instead of top-down approach, the critical studies gave emphasis to bottom-up approach.

Related to the people centric notion of security is the concept of Human security. As the name suggests, it gives primacy to an individual as a referent of security rather than a state. An individual is the co-sharer of power with the state. It, however, did not ignore the state and its security but state had responsibility to provide security to its people. (Bajpai, 2002: 4) United Nations University defines the concept as "Human security is concerned with protection of people from critical and life threatening dangers, regardless of whether the threats are rooted in anthropogenic activities or national events, whether they lie within or outside states, and whether they are direct or structured." (Thakur and Newman, 2004: 4) In 1992, the United Nations Secretariat declaration recognised economic, social, humanitarian and ecological sources of instability as threats to peace and stability. In 1994, the concept was included in the UNDP report as "Human security is the freedom from worries about daily life. It includes physical safety from disease, hunger and protection of daily life patterns". Canada, Norway, Finland and Japan are a few countries, which have adopted human security in their national policies. Bhutan has embraced Gross National Happiness Index rather than Gross Domestic Product. Hence, the state is secure when its individuals' wellbeing is taken care of.

The Indian experience shows the state's responses to the changing dynamics in national and international politics. With its colonial experience and armed attack from the newly established Pakistan, India had to defend its territory from external aggression. The country had given emphasis to industrial development but the territorial aggression by Pakistan and China forced India to adopt the Third Five-Year Plan as the defence plan. The colonial experience of India had an influence on its policy of non-alignment from joining cold war camps or not joining any military alliances. The Indian strategic perception was based on denying external powers a foothold in the region and not to get involved in their global confrontationist designs. It was another matter that neighbours did develop relations with other countries. Pakistan was member of SEATO and CENTO*.

---

* South East Asian Treaty Organisation (SEATO) and Central Treaty Organisation (CENTO) were US led military alliances against the Soviet bloc.

India's neighbours have been apprehensive of the probable Indian interference in their domestic politics, national independence, territorial integrity and security. This perception was shaped and influenced by the geographical connectedness of the South Asian countries, their socio-cultural similarities, linguistic affinity and racial overlapping. As a result, domestic issue in one country can have trans-boundary ramifications such as refugees or cross-border terrorism. Hence, it is the non-military threats emanating from either within the state or with external linkages that have got focus of the contemporary security studies.

India's security has been threatened from within by the militants and armed movements in Jammu and Kashmir, Punjab or Nagaland. The complexities multiplied with external support to these movements. Various strategies from force, to coercion and negotiations were used to deal with the groups. Every militant group has its own history and complexities and the state deals with them accordingly. The issues involved are between the state and the people, between the state and the central government and at times involves the external actor. In all these state centricity, the voices and concerns of the people cannot be ignored. So the state's responsibility is enlarged to look after the issue in a holistic manner.

The end of cold war had an impact in highlighting other non-military issues within a country, which could threaten security. Such as, trans-boundary issues needed trans-boundary understanding of issues, for example, water resource. The state is the provider of water to the people, industries and agriculture sector and is responsible for procuring and distributing it. If it is a trans-boundary river within a country or between two countries then the government negotiates accordingly. State alone is not a sufficient actor for utilisation of water resource for its various uses and looks towards either financial institutions or corporate sector for aid and assistance. However, people are an important actor that cannot be ignored. To cite the ongoing water scarcity in the state of Maharashtra where it is scarce for drinking purposes and domestic consumption. It has reached a crisis point for the people who understood water usage for Cricket matches (IPL) in Maharashtra as misuse of the resource. Due to strong resistance from the people and Judicial intervention the matches are asked shift out from the water scarce state to other venue. This brings in the role of civil society in the state. Civil society ensures participatory role of the people in policy formulation. It reminds the state that people are co-sharer of power and the policies of the state have to be humane, centered around the well being of the people.

The concept of security has been both widened horizontally and deepened vertically by inclusion of more agendas and actors. The debates on security do not only revolve around the world, as it exists but also how it ought to be. Apart from what is to be secured, the concept has progressed towards what should be included how and why it should be secured. States are responsible to secure its people from external and internal threats. Through participatory approach states ought to look after the well being of its citizens and make them secure from fear and want.

References

1. Ayoob, Mohammad. 1995. *The Third World security predicament: State making, regional conflict, and the international system.* Boulder: Lynne Rienner.
2. Bajpai, Kanti. 2002. 'Beyond comprehensive security: Human security', in *Comprehensive security: Perspectives from India's regions*. Delhi: Delhi Policy Group.
3. Booth, Ken. 1991. Security and emancipation. *Review of International Studies*, 17(4), 313–26.
4. Buzan, Barry, Waever Ole and de Wilde Jaap. (1998). *Security a new framework for analysis*. Boulder: Lynne Reinner Pub.
5. Lippman, Walter. 1943. *US foreign policy*. Boston: Atlantic.
6. Lynn-Jones, Sean M. 1995. Security and emancipation. *Review of International Studies*, 17(4), 313–26.
7. Smith, Steve. 2000. 'The increasing insecurity of security studies: Conceptualising Security in the Last 20 years', in Stuart Croft.
8. Thakur, Ramesh and Newman, Edward. 2004. 'Introduction: Non-traditional security in Asia', in Ramesh Thakur and Edward Newman (eds), *Broadening Asia's security discourse and agenda: Political, social and environmental perspectives* (pp. 1–17). Tokyo: United Nations University Press.
9. Walt, Stephen M. 1991. The renaissance of security studies. *International Studies Quarterly*, 35(2), 211–39.
10. Wyn-Jones, Richard. 1995. Message in a bottle? Theory and praxis in critical security studies. *Contemporary Security Policy*, 16(3), 299–319.

5

Water Security in South Asia

— ***Pawan Bali***

Introduction

Asia is home to 3/4th of the world's population. This growing regional giant infamously has the lowest water efficiency in the world. Fears have been expressed that this increasing water distress will lead to international security strains and threats in Asia. The literature on water conflicts in Asia sounds an alarmist-warning bell that the region is sitting on a "water-time bomb", waiting to explode. The region's water crises have been exacerbated by rapidly expanding economies, growing population, rising per capita water consumptions and migrations. Scholars are looking at a future Asia, which will be drier, hotter and susceptible to wars over water. In analysing Asia's water crises, author Brahma Chellany in his book *Water-The New Battleground* argues that Asia has morphed into a flashpoint of water-wars and the region is ripe for rivalry. He also states that booming trade between the Asian states will not guarantee restrain and water will be the treacherous battle-ground. A report of the US senate in 2011 titled *Avoiding Water Wars* also states that the water scarcity in Central and South Asia is "fueling regional tensions which will have repercussions for regional security."

So in the light of these concerns, is a "war over water" in South Asia inevitable? Even if a full-scale war could be alarmist, the skirmishes and water disputes amongst the riparian South Nation nations need attention. For better water management and from a security perspective the South Asian nations need to work towards institutionalisation of water disputes and cooperation for better utilisation of resources.

Conflict and cooperation theories

The literature in hydro-politics and international relations is broadly divided into conflict and cooperation theories. While some arguments have pointed at increasing conflicts as water becomes scarce (offensive realist), the counter-view is that nations would increase cooperation if faced with acute scarcity. The International Water Management Institute (IWMI, 2007) has reported that approximately a quarter of the world's population lives in areas that are facing physical water shortages. The potential of water conflict is greater in developing countries since they lack mechanisms and tools for proper management of water resources (Brenann, 2008). Empirical studies have also shown that high level of water scarcity increases frequency of explicit claims over fresh waters, and chances of militarised conflicts over these claims (Hensel, Mitchell and Sowers, 2006: Homer and Dixon, 1994). Authors have argued that competition for limited supplies of water, will lead nations to see access to water as a national security issue (Gleick, 1993). A report by the Centre for Naval Analysis on National Security and Threat of Climate Change attributes environmental crises, water scarcity, soil depletion as causes of intensifying conflicts and contributors towards the national security issues.

There is another argument that the war between upstream and downstream countries is possible when the downstream country is highly dependent on the water for its national well-being and the upstream country threatens to restrict substantially the river's flow (Homer –Dixon, 1999). In this case, the downstream country has to be military powerful. Lowi (1994), while taking the examples of Middle East and South Asia, has argued that conflict is most likely when the most powerful country is in the upstream position and is a water-hegemon.

Literature on a cooperation scenario of water conflicts admits at the possibility of the conflict, but denies its inevitability (Kukk and Deese, 1996). This literature also points at cooperative arrangements for sharing river resources like treaties and joint river administration. Proponents of cooperative scenario have argued that water stress and degradation for resources can encourage joint efforts (Deudney, 1997) and environmental scarcities can be a starting point of cooperation (Dokken, 1997). On similar lines, literature on international relations over fresh water suggests overwhelming cooperation covering wide range of issues including water quantity, quality, joint management and hydropower (Yoffee *et al.,* 2000).

Historical perspective of water conflicts

The first recorded intra-state conflict over water can be traced back to 2500 BC between two Sumerian cities, Lagash and Umma, where disruption of water was used as a military tool. Conflict between Israel, Syria and Jordan in 1950s started over attempts by each side to divert the waters of Yarmuk and Jordan rivers. Skirmishes between Turkey-Syria and Iraq have ensued over the construction of a dam on Euphrates river. Water has been cited as the cause of "Six-Day" war between Israel and Arab neighbours in 1967. In that war, Israel destroyed Jordanian dam on Yarmouk river. In 1979, Egyptian President Anwar Saddat announced that the only matter, which could take Egypt to war again, was water. Saddat was referring to Ethopia, where majority of waters of Nile originate. In 1990s, King Hussein of Jordan issued warlike declarations targeted at Israel over water. Similar concerns were voiced in 1988 by Boutrous Gali who said that the next wars in the region will be over waters of the Nile, and not politics. If not a war, water has been a cause of several skirmishes and political disputes between countries.

South Asian water conflicts

Amongst the Asian nations, barring Japan, South Korea and Burma, water-stress is looming large. In 1951, India's annual water availability per person was 5,277 cubic meters. In the 1990s, it fell to 2,464 cubic meters. By 2025, it is projected to fall dangerously close to the 1,000 cubic meters level (Shiva, 2003). As for China, its water availability per person was 4,597 in 1950 and 2,427 in the 1990s – slightly above the sufficiency threshold level. However, by 2025, it is assessed that China's water availability will plummet to 1,818 cubic meters – an alarming number for an approximate population of 1.5 billion (Charles Wolf *et al,* 2004). Finally, Pakistan's water availability per person in 1950 was 10,590 cubic meters. It fell drastically to 3,962 in the 1990s and is projected to level out at 1,803 by 2025. Authors like Falkenmark, (Fallenmark, 1992) have argued that when water scarcity falls below 1000 cubic meters per capita per year, the problem is acute and conflicts are probable. Given these examples of acute water stress, some scholars have predicted an outright conflict amongst the South Asian states. But the region has had a history of water disputes and political skirmishes, though none of them have threatened a full-fledged war.

India and Pakistan have been long entangled into a political battle over shared rivers ever since both countries gained Independence. In the absence of water sharing treaty in 1948, India decided to stem the flow of Indus River flowing into the Dipalpur Canal and the main branches of Bari Daab Canal. This was seen as the move on part of the Indian state to establish sovereign control over the river or pressurize Pakistan over Kashmir. After negotiation started in 1951, both countries signed the Indus Water Treaty in 1969 for sharing rivers. The treaty has stood tests of three wars between both countries and often political tangles. Pakistan has often objected to India's decision to construct Baghliar dam on Chenab River and has stalled the Kishenganga Dam project on Jhelum river, contesting that these dams violate the Indus Water Treaty.

India and Bangladesh had been entangled into a water dispute over water resources of Ganges. Despite a Joint River Commission set up in 1972, India's decision to build the Farakka Dam on the Ganges affected Bangladesh severely. Even as both countries signed a 30-year treaty for water sharing in 1996 , water flow to Bangladesh has decreased by 51 per cent ever since the Farraka Dam was constructed (Tazneema and Faisal, 2003). The water-ties between both countries hit a low in January 1976 when India unilaterally diverted the waters at Farraka without consulting Bangladesh. The latter responded by approaching the UN, NAM, Islamic Foreign Ministers Conference.

Water issues have existed between India and Nepal over Kosi river. Both nations signed a Kosi Agreement in 1954 for flood management and to regulate the waters of the river. In 2008, a devastating flood in Kosi displaced over 3.5 million people on both sides. Nepal blamed India for the lack of maintenance of the embankments of the barrage, which led to the floods.

In South East Asia, Cambodia, Vietnam, Laos and Thailand rely mainly on the Mekong River, which courses through heartland of South East Asia. In 1957, Mekong Committee was set up for regional initiatives to develop the basin. The Asian Development Bank supported development of Greater Mekong Sub Region Committee for economic cooperation of countries that share Mekong River, including China. Backed by ASEAN, Mekong Basin Development Corporation was formed in 1995. A year later, Mekong River Commission was set up, which China refused to join. China's argument was that "whatever action it takes to exploit the Mekong potential is an internal matter". China wants to use the Mekong River for transportation and also, as an outlet to Indian Ocean. The ties between MRC members have also been strained after Laos bid to construct a dam on Mekong in Xayuburi province, which other MRC members are objecting to.

India and China, the two Asian giants, are on a volatile ground over water sharing of Brahmaputra or Yarlong Tsango, which originates in the Tibetan Plateau. Both countries have no bilateral agreement on water sharing. In 2000, India had accused China of not sharing flood data of the river, which had led to India's failure in anticipating floods and later, deaths of 40 civilians on the Indian side. In 2002, a Memorandum of Understanding was signed between both countries to coordinate data sharing pertaining to flood water level, discharge and rainfall. The situation between both countries once again worsened in 2009 after reports that China was planning to construct a massive 40,000 MW dam on the great bend of Brahmaputra, before it enters India. This dam has been worrying India since it will majorly deplete the waters of its main river, the Brahmaputra.

Water Hegemony and Realist View

The South Asian water politics exhibits more of a realist view, where the upstream states try to gain from water usage and downstream state suffers losses. Realists contend that the states are often compelled to acquire resources through force, especially if resources are essential for maintaining a state's security and survival. The acquisition of resources by one state is view antagonistically by another in most of the water disputes in South Asia, like between India-China, India-Pakistan, India-Bangladesh and the partner states of Mekong River Basin. Attempts to construct dams, or harness waters by states are objected by the other riparian states.

The border tensions between India and China were high in 2009 over China's decision to construct a colossal Motuo dam on Brahmaputra. After denying several times, China's foreign minister in 2009, finally admitted to India that China was constructing a dam on the river, even though not as colossal. Author Brahma Chellany argues that at the cost of its riparian states, China is excessively making efforts to harness potential of Tibetan Plateau, which is Asia's main fresh water repository and largest water supplier. Since water woes have intensified in Central and Northern China, the state-run hydropower industry is lobbying in China for the inter-river and the inter-basin river transfer project to divert water from Tibetan Plateau towards the heartland. The diversion project is aimed at reviving the depleted Yellow or the Yangstse River. China's relentless pursuit of water is reflected in the mushrooming dam building projects. According to Chellany, China has dammed every river in Tibetan Plateau including the Mekong, the Brahmaputra, the Salween, the Yellow, and the Indus. On the Brahmputra's great bend, China is considering a mega project whose map includes the Daduqai region-which is along it's disputed territory with India. China's attempts to harness the resources of the Tibetan Plateau at the cost of other states, reveals its design to be a water-hegemon in the region. The rivers originating from the plateau are lifeblood for countries like India, Bangladesh, Burma, Bhutan, Cambodia, Vietnam, Laos, Nepal, Pakistan and Afghanistan. China has avoided signing the Mekong River Agreement citing it as a "internal matter". It has not entered into any water sharing agreements with its other riparian neighbours like India and Nepal, Bangladesh. China's realist approach was supported by its former minister of water resources Wang Shucheng, who stated, "To fight for every drop of water or die, that is the challenge facing China." Shucheng's narrative is not new to China. The country's water management has been historically related to politics. As per a popular myth, the first King of Xia Dynasty harnessed flood-waters in 22 BC and established nine new states. China's Maoist era was characterised by Mao Zeodang insistence that "man must conquer and tame nature".

Reacting to China's excessive dam building and South North Water Diversion Project, India had proposed the River Linking Project, to divert waters from North East to the South. India is also constructing dams in Arunachal Pradesh, making Brahmaputra a water hotspot of the region (Wirsing, 2012). India has risen to balance power against China's hegemonic designs, with regular objections and a strong monitoring of China's dam building progress. Between India and China, a bilateral balance of power has been maintained, but offensive behaviour has been limited. Even as water is regarded as a core reason behind the territorial dispute in Arunachal Pradesh, both Asian powers have shown restraint and have tried to protect the status quo.

India-Pakistan have also been caught in Realist battle over water, with disputes over the Baghliar Dam project on Chenab and Kishenganga on Jhelum. Any attempt by one nation to harness water resources are viewed antagonistically by the other. Pakistan's objection have halted the Kishenganga project and delayed the Baghliar dam project several times. The dispute over the 330-MW Kishenganga dam over Jhelum has now been taken to the International Court of Justice for arbitration by Pakistan, who is arguing that the dam will affect its own projects on the Neelum river. The realist perspective can be traced back in 1948, when India decided on a hegemonic move and stopped the flow of Indus river to Pakistan. Besides this sole incident, both countries have avoided an "offensive" behaviour over water, which could have triggered a war.

India and Pakistan have fought three wars over Kashmir, but it is hard to conclude that water was the core reason for it. Infact, despite the wars, the Indus Water treaty, was never withdrawn, terminated or explicitly violated. While authors like Chellany argue that the territorial dispute over Kashmir is embedded in fight for water resources, it is difficult to ignore the political-historical reasons to the dispute. In 2011, the US Senate in 2011 defined the water stress in realist term by stating, that "the cumulative effect of [many dam] projects could give India the ability to store enough water to limit the supply to Pakistan at crucial moments in the growing season." It also added that dams are a source of "significant bilateral tension". The bilateral tensions continue, but a bilateral balance of power is also being maintained between both the countries.

India and Bangladesh share 54 rivers between them. Their water ties touched a low in 1976 when India unilaterally diverted the water at Farraka Dam without consulting Bangladesh. India's decision again could be seen as "power maximizing technique", but a full drawn conflict was avoided. Bangladesh cried foul and approached the UN, the NAM, to counter India's hegemonic designs. Even as both nations have entered into a 30-year-old bilateral agreement, India being the upper riparian state has been a more dominated power. Bangladesh has attempted to balance India's hegemony by seeking external help. Bangladesh also opposed India's plans to dam the Teesta and Barak rivers in the North-East region. The bilateral relationship between both nations reflects more of realist tendencies, where a full-drawn conflict has been avoided.

Offensive Vs Defensive Realism

Proponents of offensive realist view on water politics, like Fred Pearce, Chietigi Bajpaee, Vandana Shiva, Brahma Chellany argue that full scale water wars will break out in Asia in near future as countries like China would want to "maximize" its water potential at the cost of downstream nations. Even though Asian countries are realist when it comes to water-policy and politics, this offensive realist view is alarmist and largely pessimistic. It misses the point that when the nations will not be able to sustain their populations with the available resources, they will consider cooperation with neighbours to fix the problem. For now, Asian states are harnessing resources within their territorial boundaries and the skirmishes over water resources are attempts to maintain their status-quo over this precious commodity.

Cooperation start with institutionalisation

The institutionalisation framework for water disputes has been weak in South Asia. This is sharp contrast to Europe, which has regional organisations to oversee disputes of Danube and Rhine and US-Canada, who are members of International Joint Commission and of Rio Pact which stresses on peace negotiations. Several attempts at cooperation, however, have been made over time like the Mekong River Committee (1957) or Mekong River Commission (1999), Treaties of Sarada (1920), Kosi and Gandak between India and Nepal (Bilateral), Indus Water Treaty between India and Pakistan (1969) and Ganges Waters Treaty between India and Bangladesh (1977). These treaties have been largely considered weak due to the unwillingness of its signatories to modify them with changing times and due to a lack of enforcement agency in most cases. The most successful of all has been the Indus Water Treaty, which is being moderated by the World Bank. The Mekong River Commission, which is a multilateral treaty has failed to bring China on board. The weakness of MRC was highlighted again when Laos went ahead with its decision to construct a dam on Mekong, despite objections by other three MRC signatories, Cambodia, Vietnam and Thailand.

The weak institutionalisation can be attributed to the fact that most of the riparian states have chosen to deal with water issues at a bilateral level. Also, South Asian nations, who had been struggling with developing economies and nascent democracies, are slowly getting into the process of recognising water scarcity as a security issues. Environmental and water issues have not been a security priority till now.

Growing signs of cooperation and interdependence

As South Asian states shed off their baggage of colonialism and are coming to terms with their own growth story, they are recognising the salience of the environmental and water issues in regard to the larger security scenario. The South Asian states are attempting new collaborations and institutionalisation over water issues. In 2006, the Asia Pacific Water Forum was set up as a small step towards multilateral cooperation over water disputes. Besides focusing on water management, the forum also published a framework policy document on water for leaders and policy makers. It also organises summits for water ministers of the Asia-Pacific nations. Even as Chinese government had been reluctant to relate environmental and security issues, and had opposed UN's effort to link climate change with security debates in Security Council, its attitude towards agreements and institutions is slowly changing. China has refused to sign the MRC, but has now agreed to share flood data with the Mekong river basin countries. It is even sharing flood-water data with Bangladesh, and India. China has concluded agreements with countries like Russia and Kazakhstan, regarding sharing and protection of trans-boundary rivers. The Chinese government in 2008 released the national Framework For Medium to Long Term Food Security, which emphasises water-saving agriculture and conversation. It is a strong sign of Chinese government is keen to link water to security issues now. China's need to domestically manage its water resources is further laying stress on the importance of maintaining water relations internationally. In 2003, India and China signed a Memorandum of Understanding to share floodwater data. As per the MoU, any plans of China to divert the Brahmaputra will have to be known to the Indian Water Ministry. The MoU was further extended in 2008 to include Brahmaputra's two other tributaries, the Parlung Tsnagpo and the Lohit. Both countries are also exploring possibilities of further cooperation like on joint water management.

The Shanghia Cooperation Organisation is further promoting water security cooperation amongst Asian states. The SCO's 2004 meet was focused on water security cooperation and in 2005, the organisation signed a pact with ASEAN to broaden cooperation on water resources.

India and Bangladesh, who have signed a 30-year water sharing treaty over Ganges are close to signing another historic treaty on sharing waters of Teesta river. In 2011, India liberalised its markets to Bangladesh and has offered commercial power or related benefits from hydro-project on shared rivers to Bangladesh. If India-Bangladesh agree to share mutual benefits of dam projects, this could set precedent of water-resource cooperation and interdependence. In 2011, India and Nepal also set up a Joint Ministerial Commission on Water Resources to focus on shared water resources and to strengthen cooperation over water issues.

Over the years, the constructivist approach to water management has become more relevant in regard to the role of epistemic communities (non-official and semi-official expert groups) in managing environmental and water issues.

They are strongly influencing the domestic water policies in India and slowly, in China too. The role of epistemic communities in managing international disputes is also gaining significance. According to Dinar, the epistemic communities played an important role the negotiations of Ganga-Brahmaputra-Meghna river basin between India-Bangladesh. In the Mekong River negotiations, the UNDP provided a critical feedbacks and assistance to finally forge cooperative agreement between the countries. Non-state actors, environmental NGOs and scientific groups, like Inter Governmental Panel on Climate Change, (IPCC), have expressed concerns over depleting water resources in South Asia, and have suggested measures to avoid acute scarcity, conflict and forge cooperation.

Be concerned, but not alarmist

Just as an alarm was being raised over China's design to harness water of the Brahmaputra, which could trigger conflict with India, the Indian Prime Minister Manmohan Singh told the Parliament in 2011 that China's dam projects were no threat to India. He said what was being alleged as a massive diversion of water, was just a "run of the river dam". Singh's comments allayed the alarmist fears that water wars in South Asia had begun. Even as water stress is leading to domestic tensions, and international political disputes, it is difficult to see South Asian nations going to war over water like in the Middle East. As economic and political interdependence increases, water problems of one state will become the concern of the other. The South Asian nations have managed to avoid a full drawn conflict with bilateral ties and agreements. A realist approach has been successful so far in maintaining security order in South Asia. Like the literature on cooperation suggests, as water supplies decline acutely, the states will realise the need towards cooperative measures to handle environmental crises jointly. The initial trends of cooperation, and institutions are been seen with sharing flood-water data, drawing up new treaties and collaborative projects for water utilisation. The cooperative mechanism is still weak and needs to travel a long way, but the South Asian nations are fast recognising the need for it. South Asia is staring at water stress, domestic tensions over water, political disputes and skirmishes, but not really at a war over water.

References

1. A Crisis to Come? China, India, and Water Rivalry. (n.d.). *Carnegie Endowment for International Peace*. Retrieved November 28, 2012, from http://carnegieendowment.org/2011/09/13/crisis-to-come-china-india-and-water-rivalry/54wg
2. A dam on the Mekong: Opening the floodgates. (2012, May 5). *The Economist*. Retrieved from http://www.economist.com/node/21554253
3. Baylis, J., Smith, S., and Owens, P. (2010). *The Globalisation of World Politics: An Introduction to International Relations*. Oxford University Press.
4. Biswad, A.K., and Seetharam K. E. (2008). Achieving Water Security for Asia. *International Journal of Water Resources Development*, *24*(1), 145–176. doi:10.1080/07900620701760556
5. Brennan, L., and Binney, W. (2008). Concepts in Conflict: Social Marketing and Sustainability. *Journal of Nonprofit and Public Sector Marketing*, *20*(2), 261–281. doi:10.1080/10495140802224951
6. China admits to Brahmaputra project. (n.d.). *The Times of India*. Retrieved November 28, 2012, from http://articles.timesofindia.indiatimes.com/2010-04-22/india/28126091_1_zangmu-brahmaputra-india-and-china
7. China Will Have Mastery of Asia's Water Tap by 2020. (n.d.). *The Huffington Post*. Retrieved November 28, 2012, from http://www.huffingtonpost.co.uk/catriona-luke/china-will-have-mastery-o_b_917158.html
8. China's tourism plan quells Brahmaputra dam fears. (n.d.). *The Hindu*. Retrieved December 8, 2012, from http://www.thehindu.com/news/international/chinas-tourism-plan-quells-brahmaputra-dam-fears/article3566337.ece
9. *Conflict Management of Water Resources*. (n.d.). Retrieved from http://www.bn.com/w/conflict-management-of-water-resources-manas-chatterji/1100915015
10. Deudney, D. (1990). National Security. *Millennium-Journal of International Studies*, *19*, 461.
11. Dinar, S. (2002). Water, Security, Conflict, and Cooperation. *SAIS Review*, *22*(2), 229–253. doi:10.1353/sais.2002.0030
12. Dokken, K. (2001). Environment, security and regionalism in the Asia-Pacific: is environmental security a useful concept? *The Pacific Review*, *14*(4), 509–530. doi:10.1080/09512740110087311

13. Falkenmark, M., Lundqvist, J., and Widstrand, C. (1989). Macro-scale water scarcity requires micro-scale approaches. *Natural Resources Forum*, *13*(4), 258–267. doi:10.1111/j.1477-8947.1989.tb00348.x

14. Gleick, P. H. (1993). Water and Conflict: Fresh Water Resources and International Security. *International Security*, *18*(1), 79. doi:10.2307/2539033

15. Grover, V. I. (2007). *Water: a source of conflict or cooperation?* Science Publishers.

16. Hensel, P. R., McLaughlin Mitchell, S., and Sowers II, T. E. (2006). Conflict management of riparian disputes. *Political Geography*, *25*(4), 383–411. doi:10.1016/j.polgeo.2005.11.001

17. Homer-Dixon, T. F. (1994). Environmental scarcities and violent conflict: evidence from cases. *International security*, 5–40.

18. India reassures Bangladesh on Teesta water treaty and border deal - Hindustan Times. (n.d.). *Http://www.hindustantimes.com/*. Retrieved December 8, 2012, from http://www.hindustantimes.com/world-news/RestOfAsia/India-reassures-Bangladesh-on-Teesta-water-treaty-and-border-deal/Article1-921530.aspx

19. Jasparro, C., and Taylor, J. (2008). Climate Change and Regional Vulnerability to Transnational Security Threats in Southeast Asia. *Geopolitics*, *13*(2), 232–256. doi:10.1080/14650040801991480

20. Joy, K. J., Paranjape, S., Gujja, B., Goud, V., and Vispute, S. (Eds.). (2009). *Water Conflicts in India: A Million Revolts in the Making*. Routledge India.

21. Kukk, C. L., and Deese, D. A. (1996). At the Water's Edge—Regional Conflict and Cooperation over Fresh Water. *UCLA Journal of International Law and Foreign Affairs*, *1*, 21.

22. Lies, dams and statistics. (n.d.). *The Economist*. Retrieved November 28, 2012, from http://www.economist.com/blogs/banyan/2012/07/mekong-river

23. Lorey, D. E. (2003). *Global Environmental Challenges of the Twenty-First Century: Resources, Consumption, and Sustainable Solutions*. Rowman & Littlefield.

24. Lowi, M. R. (1999). Water and Conflict in the Middle East and South Asia: Are Environmental Issues and Security Issues Linked? *The Journal of Environment & Development*, *8*(4), 376–396. doi:10.1177/107049659900800403

25. Moore, S. (2009). Climate Change, Water and China's National Interest. *China Security*, *5*(3), 25–39.

26. Ohlsson, L. (Ed.). (1995). *Hydropolitics: Conflicts Over Water as a Development Constraint* (illustrated edition). Zed Books.

27. Rahaman, M. M. (2012). Hydropower ambitions of South Asian nations and China: Ganges and Brahmaputra Rivers basins. *International Journal of Sustainable Society*, *4*(1), 131–157. doi:10.1504/IJSSOC.2012.044670

28. Shambaugh, D., and Yahuda, M. (2008). *International Relations of Asia*. Rowman & Littlefield Publishers.

29. Shapiro, J. (2012). *China's Environmental Challenges* (1st ed.). Polity.

30. Shiva, V. (1991). Ecology and the politics of survival: conflicts over natural resources in India. Retrieved from http://www.cabdirect.org.proxyau.wrlc.org/abstracts/19920659616.html;jsessionid=D352B721A503B719406E75D85AC713FA?freeview=true

31. South Asia's water: Unquenchable thirst. (2011, November 19). *The Economist*. Retrieved from http://www.economist.com/node/21538687

32. Swain, A. (2004). *Managing Water Conflict: Asia, Africa, and the Middle East*. Psychology Press.

33. Tanzeema, S., and Faisal, I. M. (2001a). Sharing the Ganges: a critical analysis of the water sharing treaties. *Water Policy*, *3*(1), 13–28. doi:10.1016/S1366-7017(01)00004-6

34. Tanzeema, S., and Faisal, I. M. (2001b). Sharing the Ganges: a critical analysis of the water sharing treaties. *Water Policy*, *3*(1), 13–28. doi:10.1016/S1366-7017(01)00004-6

35. Why the time for a China-India water treaty is now. (n.d.). *CNN*. Retrieved November 28, 2012, from http://articles.cnn.com/2012-07-23/opinion/opinion_china-india-water-scarcity_1_zangmu-three-gorges-project-water-treaty

36. Wolf, A. T. (1999). The Transboundary Freshwater Dispute Database Project. *Water International*, *24*(2), 160–163. doi:10.1080/02508069908692153

37. Wolf, C. (2004). Fault lines in China's economic terrain. *Asia-Pacific Review*, *11*(1), 58–72. doi:10.1080/13439000410001687751

38. Yoffe, S., Fiske, G., Giordano, M., Giordano, M., Larson, K., Stahl, K., and Wolf, A. T. (2004). Geography of international water conflict and cooperation: Data sets and applications. *Water Resources Research*, *40*(5), W05S04. doi:10.1029/2003WR002530

Regional Development in South Asia

6

"Neighbourhood First": A Reality Check

— S.D. Muni

The Great Initiative

Prime Minister Modi's enthusiastically launched out of box foreign policy initiative of 'neighbourhood first' seems to have hit the realm of scepticism and anxiety within two years of its execution. Recall the excitement and enthusiasm when all the heads of South Asian neighbours were invited to be a part of Prime Minister Modi's swearing-in ceremony. The Bangladesh Prime Minister Mrs Hasina Wajed could not come owing to her prior commitment in Tokyo but she sent the Speaker of Parliament Mrs Sirin Chaudhury, to adequately represent her. The one on one talks between Modi and his South Asian guests generated hopes that the South Asian region would soon become a region of harmony, greater mutual understanding and cooperation. This has not happened. Contrary to the claims of success made by Modi's suave foreign minister Mrs Sushma Swaraj and the articulate and energetic foreign secretary Dr S. Jaishankar, expectations aroused by the initiative and the energy invested in driving it seem to be losing their momentum.

Relationship Status

The real challenge of India's neighbourhood policy has always been in dealing with China and Pakistan. Both these relationships look as confused, uncertain and daunting as ever. China being in a category beyond immediate neighbours was not formally a part of Modi's initiative, but on Pakistan, in some ways, Dr Manmohan Singh perhaps did better. He, through back channel parleys with Gen. Musharraf, brought the Kashmir issue closer to a resolution at some point. The back channel efforts could not be converted into a firm deal as Musharraf had to vacate his presidency and the democratic parties informally pleaded with India not to conclude any deal with a military dictator. They even threatened that such a deal would not be honoured by any succeeding civilian government in Pakistan. Ignoring his earlier and pre-election campaign rhetoric on Pakistan, Modi was warm and friendly to Nawaz Sharif in his first meeting in New Delhi. He promised to resume the Composite Bilateral Dialogue for which dates were worked out very soon. But this dialogue has not yet been resumed in any meaningful way despite several contacts between India and Pakistan at various levels, of the Prime Ministers, Foreign Ministers, National Security Advisers and Foreign Secretaries. The dialogue has passed through a process of repeated scheduling, cancelling and rescheduling, thanks to India's shifting redlines of contacts between Pakistani diplomats and the Kashmir based Hurriyat Conference separatist leaders, Pakistan's lack of adequate progress on prosecuting the culprits of cross-border terrorism, and new cross-border terrorist attacks against India like the one on Pathankot air force base in January 2016.

As for other neighbours, India stands quite alienated in Nepal; from the hill people due to its cold and undiplomatic response to the new constitution followed by the coercive diplomacy of 'undeclared' but carefully calibrated trade 'blockade'; and from the Madhes and Janjati groups by half-hearted support to their cause. India's sympathies in Maldives oscillate between the ousted President Nasheed and the new regime led by President Abdulla Yameen. Relationships with Bhutan, Afghanistan, Bangladesh, and Sri Lanka are generally friction free but without any new significant development under Modi, except for the change of regime in Sri Lanka and ratification of Land Boundary Agreement with Bangladesh. SAARC remains a slow and uninspiring instrument of regional integration. Efforts to activate sub-regional mechanisms to enhance connectivity are being made, but results look far and few. An area of growing concern for India is the keen interest and willingness on the part of all its immediate neighbours, to help

China consolidate its fast expanding economic and strategic presence in the region. China's loud promise of support for the independence and sovereignty and attractive economic offers under its Belt and Road Initiative (BRI) to all of India's neighbours have been enthusiastically welcomed by the latter, while India looks confused and diffident about China's BRI and the strong Chinese push into South Asia for economic and strategic presence. Only a few like Myanmar and Sri Lanka have displayed some caution regarding the strategic costs and economic liabilities underlying their possible long term and deeper engagement with China.

It would be unfair to blame any lack of sincerity and efforts on the part of Prime Minister Modi and his team in pursuance of the neighbourhood initiative. He travelled to them, including surprise visit to Lahore in December 2015, talked to them at various levels and assured them of his commitment to their developmental aspirations. A soft loan window of 1 and 2 billion US dollars respectively has been created for Nepal and Bangladesh to help build their infrastructure. Many of the pending and stalled Indian projects are being activated in neighbouring countries. Modi also succeeded in mitigating reservations of some of India's regional leaders like Mamta Banerjee of West Bengal in promoting cooperation and understanding with the adjacent neighbouring country. When the neighbours were in distress, India was the first to reach out to them. Recall the support for Nepal when hit by a strong earthquake in April-May 2015. Not only the supplies and immediate rescue were rushed but a billion US dollars have also been committed for the reconstruction. For Maldives, five plane loads of drinking water was rushed to meet the unusual scarcity. Naval ships and a plane load of relief material was rushed to help meet Sri Lanka's flood affected people when cyclone 'Roanu' struck the Island republic in May 2016. Security cooperation with Myanmar and Bangladesh has been strengthened and maritime security cooperation has been expanded in the Indian Ocean by reaching out not only to Sri Lanka and Maldives but also to Mauritius and Seychelles.

The Fault Lines

In spite of these efforts, the neighbourhood initiative has slipped because of three critical factors. To begin with, when launched, the initiative lacked adequate preparation and a credible road map. The MEA was initially not fully on board for the initiative. The first big visit of all the South Asian leaders at Prime Minister's swearing-in was hurriedly prepared as was disclosed by the outgoing foreign secretary Sujata Singh in a TV interview with Karan Thapar in January 2015. There did not appear to be any firm plan or strategy to back the initiative. It was an idea that had to be flashed out. An attempt to work out a coherent new approach towards the neighbours, the Heads of Missions in neighbouring countries were called by the Ministry of External Affairs in August 2014. This meeting helped prepare a "3-C *mantra* of commerce, culture and connectivity".[1] But the diplomacy employed in pursuing this *mantra* was full of knee-jerk reactions and flip-flop moves. For instance, the Hurriyat redline for cancelling talks with Pakistan was imposed in July 2014, but this redline was unceremoniously dropped subsequently. To express displeasure with Nepal's new Constitution that did not accommodate the Madhesi demands, first an undiplomatic move was made, of sending foreign secretary Jaishankar as Prime Minister's special envoy to delay the promulgation of the constitution two days after the constitution had been adopted by the Constituent Assembly in September 2015. This was followed by an undeclared but carefully calibrated blockade of the supplies of essential goods like petrol, cooking gas, medicines and food items. This hurt common Nepalese and raised the anti-Indian sentiments in Nepal to its height. The effigies of Prime Minister Modi and the Indian national flag were burnt in officially sponsored protests in Kathmandu. Again, Prime Minister Modi's visit to Maldives was cancelled at the last minute to show displeasure for harsh treatment to the former president Nasheed by the Abdulla Yameen administration. None of these moves could be sustained and India had to retreat on them fully or partially.

The second area is of "delivery deficit" on promises made and agreements concluded. This is a serious flaw in India's foreign policy as a whole. As noted earlier, Modi has tried to narrow this deficit in relation to neighbours, and other foreign policy areas as well, but has not been able to succeed to any effective level. The question of "delivery deficit" in foreign policy is systemic. It needs economic resources to be invested strategically in diplomatic moves. Delivery deficit is also linked to coordination among various decision-making and decision-executing agencies. With the growing centralisation of decision-making in the Prime Minister's office under Modi, there are serious coordination issues with the Ministries of External Affairs, Finance, Home and Defence. All these ministries and their related departments impinge decisively on implementation of foreign policy related issues regarding neighbours. Various state governments bordering India's neighbours are also critical stake holders in neighbourhood policy as we mentioned earlier about West Bengal in relation to Bangladesh. Some of the sensitive bilateral issues with Bangladesh like Teesta waters or illegal migration may not be easy to resolve because of the states like West Bengal and Assam standing up as strong stake holders. Same may be true regarding Tamil Nadu in policies towards Sri Lanka and regarding Jammu & Kashmir and Punjab in policies towards Pakistan. It is increasingly being realised that federal imperatives of neighbourhood policy have not been properly addressed.[2]

Under Modi's 'neighbourhood first' initiative, thrust has been placed on the projection of India's soft power. In this projection, civilisational dimension, specially religion and culture, is being specially emphasised. However, there has been a disconnect between the ruling party's (BJP) civilisational agenda and the other aspects of official policy. For instance, the parallel moves from the ruling party's interested constituencies to push for a Hindu state and Monarchy's revival along with the official policy supporting a republican, federal and inclusive constitution have sent confusing signals in Nepal, raising questions as to what India really wants. It may be kept in mind that large sections of the republican constituencies are strongly opposed to either the revival of Monarchy or for designating Nepal a Hindu State. Both these issues remind them of the 1960s when Monarchy had become authoritarian and in order to secure legitimacy for the King's autocratic rule, character of the Nepali state was constitutionally given a Hindu identity in 1962 for the first time. The communal debate within India that often drags Pakistan in, has invoked sharp reactions from across the western borders. Then there are strong BJP allies like Shiv Sena and religious fronts like *Vishva Hindu Parishad* that have preferred a hard, non-compromising approach towards Pakistan. Similarly moves like stopping of cattle export to save cows and grant of citizenships to migrant Hindus have ruffled sensitivities in Bangladesh. A clear emphasis on Hindu and Buddhist identities in Modi's civilisational approach has also not given any comfort to the neighbouring Muslim countries like Pakistan, Maldives and Bangladesh. It has alienated common people and reinforced jihadi forces in these countries. The holding of Sufi International Conference in New Delhi in March 2016 and Modi's inspiring and balanced address to this conference are welcome indicators that the Government of India is fully cognisant of India's composite culture and diversified civilisational harmony, but such indicators are poor cushions against reckless political rhetoric periodically emanating out of the ruling party.

External Factors

The foregoing discussion should not lead us to the conclusion that the responsibility for the lack of success in India's neighbourhood policy lies with India alone. There are two other challenges emanating from outside India that have impinged adversely on this policy and Indian policy has been found wanting in coping with them adequately. One is of internal political turbulence within each of the neighbouring countries where India is perceived as an inevitable divisive factor. As a result, there has not been any viable national consensus in any of the neighbours on what should be its relationship with India; how close is too close and how far is too far? In Pakistan, whenever the civilian regime has responded positively to Modi's initiative, the Jihadi forces and section of military establishment, including the Inter-Services Intelligence (ISI) have tried to sabotage it. In Nepal, rivalries and differences between different social groups like hill elites and marginalised Madhes and Janjatis, or between Nepali Congress, Maoists and the Communist Party-United Marxist Leninist (UML) have not allowed a credible and consistent engagement with Modi's initiative. Internal political polarisation in Maldives, Sri Lanka and Bangladesh have also come in the way of India's concerns and cooperation in these countries. It is unfortunate that policy managers in New Delhi have failed many times in properly assessing the internal dynamics in these countries and deal with the possible implications of this dynamics on bilateral and regional relations.

The second challenge is of China's aggressive push into South Asia under its economic and strategic compulsions. China wants to have a strong presence in South Asia to fend for its vulnerabilities in Tibet and Xinjiang; for addressing its Malacca dilemma of trade dependence on unfriendly sea lanes and to create opportunities for its over grown infrastructure companies and financial assets.[3] China's Belt Road Initiative (BRI) is a major economic and strategic platform to facilitate China's drive into South Asia and its vision to connect with Europe through land and sea routes. Any tension or disagreement between India and its South Asian neighbours has been aggressively exploited by China to its advantage through the offer of political support and of generous economic assistance. All of India's neighbours have found it economically attractive and politically comforting to engage with China, more so whenever they run into difficulties with India. Chinese competitive edge has seriously dented the appeal and promise of Modi's initiative.

The Prospects

It has only been two years of operation of India's 'neighbourhood first initiative'. It would be unfair to conclude that its shortcomings will eventually lead to its collapse. There are indications that the Modi government is acutely aware of the shortcomings and is trying to address them. Though the dialogue between India and Pakistan has not been resumed, and Pakistan is complaining about it saying that "India is running away from talks"[4], India has kept the channels of communication with Pakistan open. Prime Minister Modi talked to Prime Minister Nawaz Sharif on the eve of his open heart surgery on May 31, 2016, to wish him successful operation and speedy recovery, and India continues to say that it is open for talks that have now been renamed as "Comprehensive Bilateral Dialogue". India has applied a course correction in Maldives and assured support for president Yameen. India's Nepal policy has also been moderated since the damage control exercise done by lifting the partial blockade in January 2016 and by making Prime Minister Oli's visit to India in February as a special one.

The neighbourhood initiative, will however, continue to move with a sluggish pace unless its major bottlenecks are cleared. Modi administration will have to apply drastic correctives to improve India's "deliver deficit" and bridge the gap between promise and performance in relation to the neighbours. Prime Minister Modi will also have to insulate the direction and thrust of his policy from the deviations emanating from the political agenda of his party, the BJP, or some of its powerful Hindu constituencies. Many countries other than India's immediate neighbours, such as even the US, are expressing concerns about the communal and divisive agenda of India's ruling party. And last but not the least, India's diplomatic establishments will have to gear up and cope with, on the one hand with the spill-over of internal political turbulence within the neighbouring countries and on the other, China's determined economic and strategic push into the South Asian and Indian Ocean region. These are formidable tasks and only time will tell if Modi's India will be able to stand up to them.

7

Liberalisation, Peace Process and India-Pakistan Trade

— Dr. Sajad Padder, Prof. Gull Wani

Abstract

Historically, the Indian sub-continent was well connected as one integrated economic entity. At the time of partition in 1947, India and Pakistan formed not only one political entity but also one integrated economy. Greater Punjab was one economic entity for centuries before partition bi-furcated it between India and Pakistan in 1947. Karachi and Bombay were closely tied sister cities on the sea under the same administrative unit of Bombay Presidency of the British Raj. Today these regions are all but severed. Earlier, these regions enjoyed trade complementarities and thus interdependence between them. A salient feature of this interdependence was that Pakistan produced raw materials while India processed them thus earning a much higher rate of return. After 1950's, both countries tried to minimise their trade interdependence. Thereafter, trade volume witnessed a steep decline. The India-Pakistan war of 1965 brought to a halt even the limited amount of trade that was there at the time. This was followed by the Bangladesh War in 1971. Trade on a limited scale resumed only in 1975. In 1996, India and Pakistan became signatories to the South Asia Preferential Trade Agreement requiring member states to reform tariffs and increase intra-regional trade. In the same year, India granted to Pakistan the Most Favoured Nation status and Pakistan decided to expand its positive list (imports from India) to include 596 items. The positive list went on expanding till 2012 when it was finally replaced by a negative list of 1209 items. The present volume of official *bilateral trade hovers around US$ 2.3 billion. But the bilateral trade balance is heavily in favour of India. Greater India-Pakistan trade will increase the prospects of peace in South Asia.*

Keywords: *Trade, positive list, Kashmir, composite dialogue, peace.*

Introduction

Ever since their independence in 1947, the relations between India and Pakistan have been in a state of flux. They have had overt military conflicts on differing scales and close military confrontations in 1948, 1965, 1971, 1986-7, 1999, 2002 and 2008. There have been numerous unsuccessful attempts and meetings between the two countries at the highest levels to resolve the conflicts. Although they resolved the Indus Waters dispute in 1960 and the Rann of Kutch dispute in 1968 through negotiations, there was no agreed mechanism to navigate their enduring conflictual relationship. In the 1980s the two sides began to confer on the Siachen, Sir Creek and the Tulbul/ Wullar disputes and put in place a series of confidence building measures pertaining to conventional and nuclear weapons power. These negotiations had no set time table and were held on need to meet basis.

In was in May 1997 that the then Indian Prime Minister Inder Kumar Gujral and his Pakistani counterpart Nawaz Sharif met at Male and floated the idea of a structured dialogue or the Composite Dialogue Process (CDP).[1] The dialogue process is composite being focused on making progress simultaneously on all the major issues of bilateral dispute. The Foreign Secretary level meeting of June 23, 1997 agreed to constitute Joint Working Groups (JWGs) on eight issues that were identified to be discussed between India and Pakistan.[2] Based on a compromising approach, the peace process enabled the two countries to discuss all issues including Jammu and Kashmir simultaneously. It was a compromise in the sense that while India agreed to include Kashmir in the agenda for talks, Pakistan relented to include terrorism—the two major irritants in bilateral relations.[3] The Lahore Agreement of February 1999 had reiterated the desire of the two countries to move forward on the path of dialogue. The Kargil War in June-July 1999, the failed Agra Summit in July 2001, the attack on Indian Parliament on December 13, 2001 and the subsequent mobilisation of troops on the border led to the difficult phase in the bilateral relations. This phase saw active US and British mediatory efforts whose significance cannot be under-estimated. A joint statement issued on 27 March 2003, after a Bush-Blair summit at Camp David laid down a detailed road map which both India and Pakistan followed. It bears recalling:

> "The United States and the United Kingdom condemn all terrorism wherever it occurs and whatever its purported justification, we will continue to work with our partners to eliminate this scourge, violence will not solve Kashmir's problems. Pending the resolution of these problems, the LoC should be strictly respected and Pakistan should fulfill its commitments to stop infiltration across it. Pakistan should also do its utmost to discourage any acts of violence by militants in Kashmir. Both sides should consider immediately implementing a ceasefire and taking other active steps to reduce tension including by moves within the SAARC context. The differences between India and Pakistan can only be resolved through peaceful means and engagement."[4]

Revival of Composite Dialogue process

India and Pakistan agreed to revive the process of Composite Dialogue in February 2004.[5] This became possible only after the then President of Pakistan General Pervez Musharraf assured Indian Prime Minister Shri Vajpayee that he would not allow any part of the territory under Pakistan's control to be used to support terrorism against India.[6] In a significant move, troops along the border disengaged following the cease-fire along the LoC, International Border (IB) and the Actual Ground Position Line (AGPL)[7] in November 2003.[8] The 12th SAARC summit of 2004 saw a change in the history of this conflict. Specific suggestions were made by the PM of Pakistan Zafarullah Jamali in the context of India-Pakistan relations to resume civil aviation links, road and rail links, sports events etc.[9] Subsequently, the foreign secretaries of the two countries met on February 18, 2004 to restart the process of Composite Dialogue. The Composite Dialogue Process (CDP) dealt with eight issues:

1. Peace and Security including CBMs;
2. Jammu and Kashmir;
3. Siachen;

4. Wullar Barrage Project/Tulbul Navigation Project;
5. Sir Creek;
6. Terrorism and Drug Trafficking;
7. Economic and Commercial Cooperation, and
8. Promotion of Friendly Exchanges in various fields.[10]

Each round of dialogue is initiated and reviewed by the foreign secretaries and the overall progress is reviewed at the Ministerial level. The first four rounds of Composite Dialogue were smoothly conducted from 2004 to 2007. The fourth one was started in March 2007 and completed in August 2007. The fifth round was in progress when it was paused in the wake of the Mumbai terrorist attacks in November 2008. Apart from dialogue on the eight issues mentioned above, technical and expert level talks on Nuclear CBMs, Conventional CBMs, Cross Line of Control CBMs, Cooperation between Coast Guards, Narcotics Control Agencies, Civil Aviation, etc., were also held regularly.[11]

Trade cooperation between India and Pakistan was a direct outcome of the partition of Indian sub-continent on August 14, 1947. At that time, India and Pakistan were highly dependent on each other for trade. Thereafter, both resorted to deliberate measures to minimise their trade dependence. Thus, in spite of the close interdependence of the two countries in respect of many commodities, we find a declining trade between them. The percentage of imports into India from Pakistan to India's total imports decreased gradually from 9.3 in 1951-52 to 3.03 in 1952-53, 1.3 in 1961-62 and 1.0 in 1964-65. The percentage of exports from India to Pakistan to India's total exports decreased from 6.3 in 1951-52 to 4.2 in 1952-53, 1.5 in 1953-54 and about 1.2 in 1964-65.[12] From 10th September 1965 the trade between India and Pakistan was suspended because of the war. In fact, the period between 1965 and 1971 witnessed two wars between India and Pakistan. Immediately after the war, Pakistan imposed official embargo on her trade with India. The trade relations between the two neighbouring countries remained suspended for nine years and created problems for both the countries. The resumption of trade relations between them took place with the signing of bilateral trade agreement on January 23, 1975.[13] But the flow of trade was restricted to government levels.

This trade agreement expired on January 22, 1978 and, thereafter, trade has continued without any agreement.

In March 1983, India-Pakistan Joint Commission (IPJC) was established to build co-operation in different areas of inter-state relations.[14] The Joint Commission held its first meeting in Islamabad from 1 to 4 June 1983. The Indian delegation was led by the Minister of External Affairs Shri P. V. Narasimha Rao.

The Joint Commission consisted of four sub-commissions dealing with:

(i) Economic Matters;
(ii) Trade;
(iii) Information, Culture and Social Sciences; and
(iv) Travel, Tourism and Consular Matters.[15]

Several proposals were made by both sides for improving relations in these fields, including those relating to the signing of a Tourism Protocol, a Cultural Agreement, relaxation of visa formalities and increase of commercial exchanges on a non-discriminatory basis. Suggestions were made for improvements in telecommunication facilities, reduced postal rates, and increased cooperation in areas such as health, family welfare, science and technology, education, archaeology, social sciences, agriculture and the performing arts.

In July 1989, India-Pakistan Joint Business Council was set up in the aftermath of third meeting of India-Pakistan Joint Commission. After the Lahore Declaration, India-Pakistan Chamber of Commerce and Industry was established on April 10, 1999 to identify the major roadblocks to economic co-operation and to broaden their economic engagements to include collaboration in the areas of banking, insurance, medical, travel and human resource development.[16] However, despite all these efforts, the overall extent of bilateral trade between India and Pakistan remained abysmally low.

Economic Reforms and Impact on Trade

Despite the overall economic liberalisation and globalisation in both India and Pakistan, bilateral trade relations have been highly "managed." Official trade stood at US$ 129 million in the fiscal year 1996 and reached an average of less than US$ 250 million during fiscal years 2001-03. In comparison, merchandise trade between India and the rest of the world increased from close to US$ 70 billion to US$ 101 billion during the same period.[17] It is only after the two countries revived the Composite Dialogue process in January 2004 that there has been a sizable increase in bilateral trade. The Commerce Secretaries of the two sides met on 11-12 August 2004 in Islamabad to discuss various proposals to expand their economic and commercial relationship. The India-Pakistan Joint Study Group (JSG) which has been constituted to discuss trade and economic issues in a detailed manner met on 22-23 February 2005. The Indian delegation was led by Mr. S.N. Menon, Commerce Secretary, Govt. of India and the Pakistani delegation was led by Mr. Tasneem Noorani, Commerce Secretary, Govt. of Pakistan.[18] The JSG constituted two Working/Sub Groups on Customs Cooperation and Trade facilitation and Non-Tariff Barriers (NTBs) and mutually agreed upon the Terms of Reference (TOR) for the Sub Groups. The two sides identified issues relating to bilateral trade and deliberated upon the future roadmap in order to enhance trade and commercial cooperation. The second round of talks on Economic and Commercial Cooperation was held on 9-10 August 2005.[19] The two sides agreed that the aeronautical talks would be held in Pakistan in September 2005 to review the existing Air Services Agreement, bilateral meeting to review the Shipping Protocol of 1975 would also be held in Pakistan in September 2005 and the second meeting of the Joint Study Group (JSG) would be convened at an early date in Islamabad. The JSG meeting would be preceded by the meeting of the Sub-Groups on Non-Tariff Barriers and Customs Cooperation and Trade Facilitation to formulate recommendations for consideration by the JSG.[20]

The third round of Economic and Commercial cooperation meeting was held on 28-29 March 2006 at Islamabad. A broad range of issues were discussed from opening of scheduled branches of banks in each country, tea trade, shipping procedures, problems of transportation of goods to enlargement of export items from India to Pakistan and the feasibility of trade in IT-enabled medical services. Both sides expressed satisfaction over the ratification of the South Asian Free Trade

Agreement (SAFTA) by all SAARC member states which can potentially boost intraregional trade to a great extent.[21]

Subsequently, the fourth round of India-Pakistan talks on Economic and Commercial Cooperation within the framework of the Composite Dialogue was held on 31 July - 1 August 2007 in New Delhi. The Indian delegation was led by Commerce Secretary, Shri G.K. Pillai and the Pakistani delegation was led by its Commerce Secretary, Syed Asif Shah.[22] The talks were held in a cordial and constructive atmosphere.

The two sides agreed on the following:

- To allow two banks from both countries to operate branches across the border by December 31, 2007. State Bank of India and Bank of India had applied for opening branches in Pakistan while United Bank and National Bank of Pakistan are keen on starting operations in India;
- To facilitate import of cement from Pakistan, the Indian side informed that India will complete all statutory certification related formalities on a fast track. The Indian side informed that it is also in the process of making appropriate policy changes to accept third party certification;
- To facilitate import of tea from India it was agreed to facilitate and encourage the trading of tea through rail. Pakistan side noted the request for providing duty concessions on import of Indian tea;
- Pakistan will nominate representatives to the Joint Working Group to discuss the issues relating to joint registration of Basmati rice as Geographical Indication (GI) and the first meeting of the Group will be held at an early date. The Pakistan side raised the issue of Notification issued by India declaring 'Super Basmati rice' as an approved variety for export. India agreed to look into this issue;
- The Indian delegation handed over a list of 484 tariff lines for inclusion in the Positive List of items importable from India. The Pakistan side agreed to examine the request in consultation with stakeholders;

- The Indian side informed that a Task Force comprising of representatives from various ministries and departments of Government of India has been constituted to address the issues of Non-Tariff Barriers (NTBs) and para-tariffs. The Task Force will make recommendations in a time bound manner for removing these barriers to provide greater market access to all members of SAARC;
- In order to address the issue of imbalance in bilateral trade, the Indian side invited the Pakistan side to identify twenty products of its export interest so that India could inform Pakistan about the detailed import regime on these products with a view to facilitating their import into India;
- Both sides will facilitate holding of trade exhibitions in each other's country. The Indian side invited Pakistan to organise a "Made in Pakistan" Trade Fair in India;
- A delegation from Pakistan was invited to visit India to see some of the IT-enabled tele-medicine facilities, with the objective of exploring avenues of cooperation in this field;
- Both sides noted with satisfaction the initiative to allow cross border movement of trucks, up to designated points at Wagah/ Attari, for unloading/reloading of cargo. It was decided that the first technical level meeting to work out modalities would be held on 20th August 2007 at the Wagah border on the Pakistan side;
- Indian side also proposed that in order to reduce pressure on Attari-Lahore Rail route and to improve trade, the Munabhao-Khokrapar route should be opened for freight movement. Pakistan side noted the proposal; and
- Both sides agreed to constitute a Joint Group headed by Joint Secretaries of Commerce of both countries to monitor and coordinate the decisions taken during the fourth round of talks on Economic and Commercial Co-operation within the framework of Composite Dialogue.[23]

After a long pause, the fifth round of India-Pakistan talks on Economic and Commercial Cooperation was held on 27-28 April 2011 in Islamabad. The Indian and Pakistani delegations were led by their

Commerce Secretaries, Rahul Khullar and Zafar Mahmood respectively. Both sides agreed that increase in trade and economic engagement would help not only in the mutual quest for national development, but also contribute to building trust between the two countries. The discussions were guided by the mutual desire to realize the full potential of bilateral trade. To facilitate this objective, they agreed to make efforts to create an enabling environment for trade on both sides. The two sides also agreed to encourage greater engagement between the private sectors of the two countries. They agreed that in order to promote trade, both tariff and non-tariff barriers (NTBs) need to be reduced and finally removed. It was decided to establish a Working Group, specifically dedicated to address and resolve clearly identified sector specific barriers to trade.

Both sides agreed to expand trade through Wagah-Attari by, *inter-alia,*

(a) Increasing trading hours taking advantage of the new infrastructure;
(b) Expeditious clearance of cargo; and
(c) Facilitating movement of large vehicles and containerised traffic.[24]

It was also agreed that Pakistan side would remove its present restrictions on trade by land route as soon as the infrastructure to facilitate mutual trade is completed. Currently, Pakistan allows only 137 items to be traded through Attari-Wagah border. During the fifth round of talks both sides also agreed that the cooperation in the IT sector would be encouraged through the private sector route. Pakistan recognised that grant of the MFN status to India would help in expanding the bilateral trade relations. Both sides agreed that facilitating the grant of Business Visas was essential to expansion of trade.

The Commerce Ministers of India and Pakistan met in September 2011 and gave a clear political mandate to the respective Commerce Secretaries to lay down specific timelines for full normalisation of the trade relationship, dismantling of remaining non-tariff barriers, and full implementation of the legal obligations under the SAARC Agreement on South Asian Free Trade Area (SAFTA). Both sides appreciated that the visit of Commerce Minister of Pakistan to India after a gap of 35 years in September 2011[25] and the political ownership of leaders of both the countries has not only given the trade normalisation process further strength and direction but a great hope and confidence to the business community also. They expressed hope that positive developments in the trade track would encourage similar progress in other components of the dialogue process.

The Prime Ministers of India and Pakistan met on the sidelines of the 17th SAARC Summit held in Maldives from 9-11 November 2011. Building on positive momentum generated by Pakistan granting India Most Favoured Nation (MFN) status in principle, Indian Foreign Secretary Ranjan Mathai said that the two countries are now planning to move towards a preferential trade agreement as part of the shared vision to significantly expand bilateral trade.[26] During the meeting, the Pakistan side informed that its Cabinet has given a mandate to the Commerce Ministry for complete normalisation of trade with India. It appreciated India's support in World Trade Organisation (WTO) for the European Union (EU) concession package for Pakistan which would give the Pakistani business community confidence and create an environment of trust and cooperation. The Indian side welcomed the Cabinet decision and reiterated its support for the normalisation process and building trust.

Within the framework of Composite Dialogue process, the sixth round of India-Pakistan talks on Commercial and Economic Cooperation was held during 14-16 November 2011 at New Delhi. The delegations were led by Commerce Secretaries of India and Pakistan Rahul Khullar and Zafar Mahmood respectively. Both sides agreed that the momentum of work and the determination to move forward had transmitted positive signals about advancing the bilateral trade agenda. In this context, India welcomed the decision taken by Pakistan to accord Most Favoured Nation status to India and to the mandate given for full normalisation of the bilateral trade relations, as also meeting of all legal obligations.

During the sixth round of talks the following decisions were taken on the trade front:[27]

(i) The move to full normalisation of trade relations shall be sequenced. In the first stage, Pakistan will make a transition from the current Positive List approach to a Negative List. The consultation process on devising this Negative List is almost complete. A small Negative List shall be finalised and ratified by February, 2012. Thereafter, all items other than those on the Negative List shall be freely exportable from India to Pakistan. In the second stage, the Negative List shall be phased out. The timing for this phasing out will be announced in February 2012 at the time the List is notified and it is expected that the phasing out will be completed before the end of 2012.

(ii) In terms of the clear mandate given by the political leadership, both sides agreed to move towards enhancing the preferential trading arrangements under the SAFTA process. As agreed earlier, bilateral trade can be significantly expanded by extending tariff concessions on products of commercial interest. Both sides designated the Joint Secretaries in their respective Ministries of Commerce as Chief Negotiators for working on how to improve preferential trading arrangements under SAFTA.

(iii) The first meeting of the Joint Group of Experts to examine feasibility of trade of electricity was held on 20th October 2011 at New Delhi. Central Electricity Authority and Power Grid Corporation of India Limited have been designated as the nodal technical agencies from the Indian side. They are interacting with National Transmission and Dispatch Company Ltd of Pakistan to work out the optimal technical solutions for grid connectivity between both countries. A broad understanding has been reached on possible grid connectivity between Amritsar-Lahore to enable trade of up to 500 MW of power.

(iv) To boost bilateral business confidence for enhanced bilateral trade, both sides agreed to encourage greater interaction amongst the business entities. It was noted with satisfaction that Apex Chambers of Commerce and Industry on both sides have formed a Joint India-Pakistan Chamber at the apex level (FICCI and FPCCI). Similarly, arrangements have been worked out for regional-level Chambers between Bombay and Karachi.

It is expected that a similar joint arrangements between the Lahore and Punjab-Haryana-Delhi (PHD) Chambers would also be worked out.

(v) Both sides agreed that the present visa regime for businesspersons was a significant barrier to the rapid expansion of trade. It was agreed that best efforts would be made by the respective Commerce Secretaries to push for further liberalisation of the business visa arrangements.

(vi) On the opening of bank branches in each other's countries, it was agreed that the Central Banks of both countries need to discuss this issue further.

The seventh round of India-Pakistan talks on Commercial and Economic Cooperation was held during 20-21 September 2012 at Islamabad. The delegations were led by the Commerce Secretaries of India and Pakistan Mr. S R Rao and Mr. Munir Qureshi respectively. The transition towards full normalisation of trade relations with India was initiated by moving from a 'positive list' regime to a 'negative list' regime. Following the visit of Commerce Minister Shri Anand Sharma to Pakistan in February 2012, Pakistan side notified its negative list on 20th March 2012.[28] The understanding at the previous Ministerial level talks has been that after the approval by the Cabinet this negative list would be dismantled before the end of 2012.

During these talks Commerce Secretaries showed satisfaction that Commerce Ministers of India and Pakistan as well as the Chief Ministers of Punjab on either side of the border had jointly participated in the inauguration ceremony of the new Integrated Check Post (ICP) at Attari on April 13, 2012.[29] Commerce Secretaries appreciated that better trading opportunities provided through land route would enhance mutual prosperity of the business communities and consumers on both sides of the border. They, however, noted that there is need to further strengthen infrastructure on both sides. They directed the customs and the port authorities to resolve all the issues through mutual cooperation, harmonisation of customs procedures, provision of laboratory facilities, scanners, weigh bridges, cold houses, containerised services and automation of the business processes. The need for more trade traffic to be carried through the Railways was also emphasised.

On exploring the possibilities of opening new land routes for trade, Pakistan side informed that a working group on Munabhao-Khokrapar has been constituted. It was agreed that meeting of the JWG on Munabhao-Khokrapar would be held in the 4th week of October, 2012 at New Delhi. Both sides appreciated the signing of the new liberalised bilateral visa regime in September 2012. This fulfills a long pending demand of the business communities of both sides to ensure a better enabling environment for bilateral trade.[30]

On the issues relating to the removal of Non-Tariff Barriers, Commerce Secretary of Pakistan highlighted that certifications/ licensing/ lab testing/ are not the only NTBs but issues like delays in customs clearance, non-availability of railway wagons for cargo transport, absence of direct flights or any problem which delays the clearance of goods with no end results or change, faced by importer/ exporter amounts to NTB. While noting the views expressed by the Commerce Secretary of Pakistan, his Indian counterpart emphasised the need for elimination of such NTBs on both sides. Both sides expressed satisfaction on signing of the three agreements i.e. Redressal of Trade Grievances Agreement, Mutual Recognition Agreement and Customs Cooperation Agreement and directed the relevant authorities to frame rules and procedures to fully implement these agreements. These agreements are expected to substantially facilitate bilateral trade mechanisms.

The Pakistan side expressed appreciation of the steps taken by India to reduce its SAFTA sensitive list by 30 per cent from 878 tariff lines to 614 tariff lines as agreed earlier during the sixth round of talks. The Indian side explained that out of 264 tariff lines which have been removed from India's SAFTA sensitive list, 155 tariff lines pertain to agricultural commodities and 106 tariff lines relate to textile items.[31] It was agreed that after Pakistan has notified its removal of all restrictions on trade by Wagah-Attari land route, the Indian side would bring down its SAFTA sensitive list by 30 per cent before December, 2012 keeping in view Pakistan's export interests. Pakistan would transition fully to MFN (non-discriminatory) status for India by December 2012 as agreed earlier. It was agreed that before the end of 2017, both India and Pakistan would have no more than 100 tariff lines in their respective SAFTA sensitive lists. Before the end of year 2020, except for small number of tariff lines under respective SAFTA sensitive lists, the peak tariff rate for all other tariff lines would not be more than five per cent.

The Commerce Secretaries also reviewed the progress on other issues, such as enhanced trade for petroleum products, trade in power and reciprocal opening of bank branches. Based on this review, the Commerce Secretaries exhorted the relevant stakeholders on both sides to speed up the mutual consultations so that concrete progress is achieved within the next six months. During this review, Indian side informed its willingness to consider export of gas up to 5 million cubic metres per day for an initial period of five years. Pakistan side informed that India's offer has been received and is under active consideration. The Bharat Heavy Electricals Limited BHEL (an Indian PSU) made an offer to cooperate with the Pakistan side in setting up 500–2000 MW capacity in coal/hydro or gas power plants as per their requirements. Indian side also made an offer for meeting the requirements of Pakistan Railways for up to 100 locomotives.

As a part of this round of talks, representatives of the Civil Aviation Authorities of both the countries undertook discussions to ensure better air connectivity between New Delhi and Islamabad. It was noted that against an average of about 23 flights per week between New Delhi and other important national capitals of the SAARC countries, there is as yet no direct air connectivity between New Delhi and Islamabad. It was agreed that a Joint Working Group (JWG) would be formed before 15th November 2012, which would work out a more liberalised regime of reciprocal bilateral rights for commercial flights, to ensure economic viability of this air route. This JWG would also explore mechanisms for more efficient courier services.

Trade in energy can bring about a quantum leap in India-Pakistan trade. The opening of a US$ 4 billion plant in April 2012 on the northern border with Pakistan at Bhatinda by Mittal Energy Investments and Hindustan Petroleum was expected to gain significantly from the energy talks. The slowdown in the process of strengthening trade and economic relations between the two countries was reversed on August 1, 2012 when India's Department of Industrial Policy and Promotion (DIPP) notified changes in the consolidated FDI policy to allow investment from Pakistan in sectors/activities apart from defence, space and atomic energy through government route and made the requisite amendment. Following this, India has removed Pakistan from the negative list under the Foreign Exchange Management Act, paving the way for investment from Pakistan. Pakistan, on the other hand, has maintained a liberal investment policy with no restrictions on inward investment from, and outward investment to India. In this context, the circular issued by the Reserve Bank of India (RBI) allowing Indians to invest overseas in Pakistan under the "government" route is an important confidence building move.[32] This opening up of investment opportunities has been hailed by businesses on both sides and is likely to open up other multi-dimensional opportunities. There is no doubt that encouraging two-way investments will enhance business confidence on both sides. An enabling business environment between the two countries will promote joint ventures and allow firms to access technologies, which in turn will lead to productivity improvement, generating growth and employment opportunities.

The private sector is expected to step in to assess bilateral investment possibilities. At the moment it appears that investment possibilities for Pakistani investors are limited. If we look at the year 2011, Pakistan's total outward FDI flow was only US$ 62 million, while India's was US$ 14.8 billion. Further, Pakistan's inward FDI flow for 2011 was US$ 1.3 billion, while that of India was US$ 31.6 billion.[33] The chambers of commerce in the two countries have identified clothing, clothing accessories, fabric, surgical instruments and cutlery as some of the possible sectors for Pakistani investment.[34] There are larger possibilities for Indian investors in Pakistan in sectors, such as chemicals, pharmaceuticals, automobile components and information technology. In the seventh round of talks on Economic and Commercial Cooperation, the Pakistani side recognised efforts by India to remove restrictions on inbound and outbound investment to Pakistan. However, they raised concerns about the "government" route and its implications for Pakistani investors in India. Under India's FDI policy, an Indian company can receive foreign direct investment under two routes – automatic route and government route. According to the RBI guidelines, under the automatic route, investors do not require any prior approval from either the government or the Reserve Bank of India. On the other hand, under the government route, investors require prior approval from the Foreign Investment Promotion Board (FIPB), Department of Economic Affairs and Ministry of Finance.[35] The FIPB is the government body that provides a single window clearance for foreign investment proposals into the country that is not permitted via the automatic route. This agency discusses and examines proposals for investments in sectors that are not allowed via the automatic route under FDI policy. For investors from Pakistan and Bangladesh, the "government route" applies to all sectors. The investors from these countries are concerned on two fronts – transparency and time taken for approvals.

Another important issue that needs to be addressed in facilitating bilateral trade and investment between the two countries is allowing banking operations on a reciprocal basis. This would also promote further economic interaction. Action on this front has already been initiated with the commencement of talks between the Reserve Bank of India and the State Bank of Pakistan in 2012. As India moves towards completing the important task of liberalising investment flows, it will reinforce its commitment to the trade and investment agenda laid down by the two countries in April 2011.[36] Stronger and deeper economic ties will not only benefit the two countries but will also facilitate the greater regional integration in South Asia.

India's Bilateral Trade with Pakistan (2005-06 to 2012-13)

(Value in US $ Million)

Year	*Exports*	*Imports*	*Total Trade*	*Balance of Trade*
2005-06	689.23	179.56	868.79	509.67
2006-07	1350.09	323.62	1673.71	1026.47
2007-08	1950.53	287.97	2238.50	1662.56
2008-09	1439.88	370.17	1810.05	1069.71
2009-10	1573.32	275.94	1849.26	1297.38
2010-11	2039.61	332.51	2372.12	1707.10
2011-12	1534.72	421.85	1956.57	1112.88
2012-13	2064.79	541.87	2606.66	1522.92
2013-14	2274.26	426.88	2701.15	1847.38
2014-15	1857.18	497.31	2354.49	1359.87

The yearly data is from April to March e.g. 2012-2013 means April 2012 to March 2013.
Source: Annual Reports, Ministry of Commerce & Industry, Government of India.

The revival of Composite Dialogue process coincided with a steady upward trend in Indo-Pak trade. 'Economic and Commercial Cooperation' was one of the pillars of the dialogue process. It was the first step towards delinking trade negotiations from political issues. Since 2004, any major political event between India and Pakistan has neither met with any major impact on trading relations nor an imposition of a ban on trade. Rather, bilateral trade has only been rising over the years.

At the invitation of the Commerce and Industry Minister of India Shri Anand Sharma, the Commerce and Textile Industry Minister of Pakistan Mr. Khurram Dastgir Khan visited India from 16th to 18th January 2014 to attend the 5th SAARC Business Leaders Conclave in New Delhi. The Ministerial meeting on the margins of the Conclave was preceded by consultations at the level of the Commerce Secretaries of the two countries on matters related to economic and trade relations between India and Pakistan. Both Ministers reaffirmed the commitment of their governments to expeditiously establish normal trading relations and in this context to provide Non-Discriminatory Market Access (NDMA) on a reciprocal basis. They decided to intensify and accelerate the process of trade normalisation, liberalisation and facilitation and to implement the agreed measures before the end of February 2014. The Ministers noted with satisfaction that arrangements have been implemented by both sides to keep the Wagah/Attari Land Customs Station operational on all seven days of each week. The Ministers emphasised the importance of trade facilitation measures and directed their respective Ministries to work out modalities for containerisation of cargo, allowing all tradable items by land route at Wagah, liberalisation of business visa regime and enhancing operational hours at Wagah/ Attari and to consider such other measures as deemed necessary by the business communities of the two countries.[37]

The Ministers agreed that both sides will convene the meetings of the technical working groups of Customs, Railways, Banking, Standards Organisations and Energy to devise the modalities for effective implementation of all requisite measures. The Ministers noted with satisfaction that there has been enhanced interaction between the business communities of both countries. Several trade delegations have been received on either side. A Joint Business Forum of Chief Executive Officers in different sectors has also met twice after the formation of present Nawaz Sharif led Government. Several sub-groups have been formed by this Joint Business Forum to enhance trade cooperation in diverse sector such as textiles, tourism, energy, light engineering, pharmaceuticals and others.

With the objective of enhancing bilateral trade opportunities, FICCI and the Trade Development Authority of Pakistan have coordinated an "India Show" in Lahore from 14-16 February 2014. Around 120 stalls have been set up to exhibit different Indian products including textiles, gems, jewellery, embroidery, herbal medicine, electric products, paint, designing and engineering. The "India Show" aimed at:[38]

- Boosting bilateral trade and investment between the two countries with fresh vigour;
- Highlighting the possibilities of a huge potential market in the region;
- Showcasing the finest and latest Indian products, technology and equipment's in the focus sectors;
- Exploration of investment and joint-venture opportunities; and
- Excellent networking opportunities with business counterparts and others.

Modi-Sharif Bonhomie and Trade

The SAARC ambition for greater economic cooperation has been suffering serious jolts due to bilateral rivalry between the two regional giants, India and Pakistan. The Indian Prime Minister Narendra Modi's invitation to Pakistan Prime Minister Nawaz Sharif to his inauguration ceremony and the latter's acceptance along with other SAARC leaders presence can be seen as a welcoming gesture for a possible step towards stability in the region. Except Maldives, Mr. Modi has visited all SAARC countries including a stopover at Lahore. Many believe the pro-business approach of both Modi and Sharif can make a France-Germany or Brazil-Argentina – each of which share significant trade relations despite a past of political hostilities – possibly by keeping economic ties independent of 'other' issues.

Commenting on the India-Pakistan trade relations, former President of the Karachi Chamber of Commerce and Industry in Pakistan, Majyd Aziz, who has been very emphatic of his views on liberalisation of trade and investment within SAARC and primarily between India and Pakistan, says,

"I have been very vocal when it comes to trade and investment between both the neighbours. Yes, I do agree that the process is not easy. My assertion has always been that trade and investment should never remain a hostage to other contentious issues or even the usual accusations that emanate out of the hallowed halls of officialdom in New Delhi and Islamabad."[39]

He further adds,

> "Examples galore among countries where trade and investment have been shielded from getting overpowered by troublesome issues that are the domain of diplomats, military or bureaucracy. China-India, China-Taiwan, China-Japan, China-USA, France-Germany, just to name a few."[40]

In fact, India-China trade presently stands at around US$ 80 billion, despite both countries being arch rivals. Most certainly then Indo-Pak trade which today stands at less than US$ 3 billion with a possibility of reaching US$ 40 billion is a huge potential that needs to be exploited.[41] Modi is riding the wave of his success on promises of economic development. For him to come across as a leader committed to greater investment, infrastructure and job creation, he needs to have a secure and peaceful region apart from using foreign relations to create more businesses at home. Modi's invitation to SAARC members is probably a sign of his intent to have long term economic alliances in the region.

Belonging to a business family Nawaz Sharif seems to share the same sense of economic diplomacy. He is seen as a leader keen on eliminating roadblocks towards trade liberalisation and creating friendlier environment for investment. In fact, a few days after the Modi-Sharif meeting in New Delhi, Pakistan's Commerce Minister Khurram Dastgir Khan told the media that India would be granted Non-Discriminatory Market Access status[42] despite issues like Kashmir, Siachen, Afghanistan and Sir Creek.

Majyd Aziz is very optimistic about the future of India-Pakistan trade. He says,

> "The advent of a Corporate Prime Minister in New Delhi and the business-oriented thinking of Nawaz Sharif coupled with their commonalities have enforced the hopes and aspirations of the Pakistani businessmen who see a new paradigm in the bilateral relations and, by extension, in the intra-SAARC trade and investment scenario."[43]

Will trade and investment then be the necessary game changer to bring about the long awaited and often thwarted peace between India and Pakistan?

Mr. Aziz Ahmed Khan, the former Pakistan High Commissioner to India, also shows optimism that the future holds good for India-Pakistan trade. But he puts a caveat that the talks must continue to find for amicable solutions to the unresolved bilateral issues. He said,

> "As for trade relations during Modi's era, I am quite confident that the regime of Non-Discriminatory trade relations will be established soon and the trade relations will grow and be mutually beneficial. Of course India would need to address Pakistan's concerns about non-tariff and par-tariff barriers. Good trade relations will be beneficial for the promotion of peace. However, it is absolutely essential that for peace to be durable serious political issues like Kashmir, Siachen etc. need to be resolved justly and amicably. Non-resolution of Kashmir can trigger tensions and even hostilities and thus threaten peace."[44]

Shri Mani Shankar Aiyar, Member of Parliament (Rajya Sabha) and former Consul-General in Karachi from 1978-1982, favours the cause of uninterrupted and uninterruptible dialogue between India and Pakistan. He is of the opinion that trade in itself is not a panacea to all problems, but it can create a favourable atmosphere for bilateral dialogue process. He said,

> "As Modi represents the business class, and it is in the interest of the business class to trade with Pakistan, it is possible that trade will increase, but for such trade to reach its full potential, the BJP will insist on the fulfillment of several preconditions before it

engages in an uninterrupted and uninterruptible dialogue with Pakistan, without which untoward incidents will upset the dialogue process and adversely affect the realisation of the full potential of Indo-Pak trade and economic relations."[45]

On the issue of Kashmir, he added,

"The Kashmir issue is not the cause but the symbol of the unstable India-Pakistan relationship. The way forward on Kashmir was signaled in the Simla Agreement of 1972 and the back-channel discussions between Ambassadors Satinder Lambah and Tariq Aziz during the Manmohan Singh-Pervez Musharraf period. The bottom line was that the outstanding issues will be resolved without exchange of territories and population and the softening of the LoC to the point that it does not inhibit intra J&K exchanges of every kind. But the Nawaz Sharif Government is in denial of the progress made under Musharraf and it is entirely possible that the Modi government will take the same line. In that case, we will have to start all over again. I believe greater trade engagement is desirable in itself but cannot, of its own accord, make an adequately constructive contribution to the resolution of outstanding issues, including the "final settlement" provided for in the Simla Agreement".[46]

The initiative of inviting the SAARC leaders by Mr. Narendra Modi at his swearing-in ceremony is taken as a good omen by the people of South Asia. There is a lot of optimism that the new government in India will take bold steps on the trade front. Professor Maya Chadda, Professor of Political Science at William Paterson University, New Jersey, US, maintains that Modi has an ambitious plan to use South Asia as a path to bolster India's interests in larger Asia. She says that Modi is keen on developing an investment and trade corridor from Northeast to Bangladesh and beyond, so also with Myanmar.[47] Pakistan is, however, a different order of challenge. Not only the instability in Pakistan is an impediment but also the level of distrust between the two countries. Even the events such as the militant attack on the Karachi airport on June 8, 2014 have raised anxiety in India.[48] These episodes make India cautious and reluctant to implement a roadmap to peace.

The gesture to invite PM Nawaz Sharif was sincere and a first step in India's and Modi's larger design to build connections to Central Asia. But, as Prof. Chadda puts it, trade will always take back seat to security imperatives in India's book. Trade relations have the best chance of taking off under Modi if other things hold but will not do so until Pakistan can restore a degree of confidence in the longevity of its government.

To the question whether trade can bring peace between the nuclear weapon states of India and Pakistan Prof. Chadda believes that the Nuclear weapons put a damper on war or escalation of clashes for sure. If Pakistan can reciprocate India's 'no first use' promise, things will move in the right direction. But Prof. Chadda questions the possibility of trade building a pathway to friendship. As she said,

> "China and India have substantial trade ties and they are growing but that has not reduced the anxieties and sensitivities in New Delhi to hostile or considered to be hostile gesture China might make on the border or in collective security and trade organisations. However, if in the future, Indo-Pak trade assumes large proportions, the chances of negotiated resolution of most conflicts are not impossible. The most important question is the strength and breadth of peace and business constituencies in each country. Traders want to make money as business lobbies but there needs to be a perception of benefits beyond trade among the larger populous. This constituency can be built only if there is an end to anxieties over buttressed by thicker ties of interdependence."[49]

Professor Madhu Bhalla, an expert on 'East *Asian Studies*' at the University of *Delhi* thinks on similar lines. She holds that greater trade engagement is not a guarantee for durable peace between India and Pakistan. She cites the example of Germany and England who were good trade partners before the World War-I. Similarly, although China and India have bilateral trade of the order of US$ 60 billion but it has not stopped China from displaying territorial assertions vis-à-vis India.[50]

Both Modi and Sharif enjoy majority in their respective national legislatures. However, the context in both countries is different. As

Michael Kugelman, Senior Program Associate for South and Southeast Asia, at the Woodrow Wilson International Center puts it,

> "Even though Pakistan's government was elected on a strong mandate, it is difficult for it to act with carte blanche given the power of the military. By contrast, India's new government will truly be unencumbered, because there is no larger institutional player behind the scenes that can constrain—or attempt to constrain—its actions and policies."[51]

Kugelman suggests the recent developments be taken with a 'generous dose of pragmatism'. While Modi's initial focus will be on economic diplomacy with Pakistan, he feels this will continue only as long as there is no provocation such as a terrorist attack in India traced back to Pakistan. He observes,

> "And once this provocation occurs, all bets are off and we can expect Modi will revert to his more hard-line, security-focused side. After all, while Modi is an economic pragmatist, he is above all a nationalist. And as a nationalist, he will not let his country stand idly by if it is provoked by its long-time nemesis."[52]

Modi is more likely to resort to a muscular foreign policy on the eve of any border provocation. In the recent past, his party has been very vocal in criticizing inaction from the UPA government over the alleged beheading of Indian soldiers by Pakistani troops. During the bilateral meeting after his swearing-in, Mr. Modi asserted that Pakistan brings those accused of 26/11 attacks and other terrorism in India to task. Even if the Modi government would like to pursue an economic diplomacy independent of security issues pressure will mount from various factions in India to take tough actions.

This is the tragedy of India-Pakistan relations. Regardless of how much progress is made, and regardless of the various diplomatic efforts to inject momentum into a peace process, all it takes is one big terror attack in India traced back to Pakistan that can dissipate all of the goodwill. It is important for the two sides to generate sufficient goodwill and trust so that the bilateral relations can survive a traumatic act such as a Pakistani-hatched terror attack on Indian soil.

References

1. The Composite Dialogue is a type of structured dialogue process between Indian and Pakistan. Under this dialogue process eight issues of bilateral dispute are being discussed. The eight issues are: (i) Peace and Security including CBMs (ii) Jammu and Kashmir (iii) Siachen (iv) Wullar Barrage Project/Tulbul Navigation Project (v) Sir Creek (vi) Terrorism and Drug Trafficking (vii) Economic and Commercial Cooperation and (viii) Promotion of Friendly Exchanges in various fields. The Composite Dialogue process was originally started in 1997 but due to the Kargil war it was halted. It was only in 2004 that the dialogue process was revived by Pakistan President General Pervez Musharraf and Indian Prime Minister Shri Vajpayee in Islamabad.
2. Wirsing, Robert (2004). *Kashmir in the Shadow of War: Regional Rivalries in a Nuclear Age*. Gurgaon, India: Spring Books, p. 17.
3. The two foreign secretaries agreed to discuss 'all outstanding issues of concern including, inter alia: (a) Peace and security, including CBMs, (b) Jammu and Kashmir, (c) Siachen, (d) Wullar Barrage Project/Tulbul Navigation Project, (e) Sir Creek, (f) Terrorism and drug-trafficking, (g) Economic and Commercial Cooperation (h) Promotion of friendly exchanges in various fields. It was decided that the first two issues would be dealt with at the level of Foreign Secretaries who will also coordinate and monitor the progress of work of all the working groups.
4. Noorani, A. G. (2008). India-Pakistan Peace Process. *Institute of Regional Studies*, Seminar Papers, Islamabad, 20-21 Oct. 2008, pp. 136-137.
5. Pattanaik, S and Arpita Anan. (2010). Cross-LoC Confidence Building Measures between India and Pakistan: A Giant Leap or a Small Step towards Peace?. *Institute for Defence Studies and Analyses,* Issue Brief, February 12, 2010.
6. For details, see Joint Statement: President Musharraf and PM Vajpayee, Islamabad, January 6, 2004. Retrieved from:

   http://www.satp.org/satporgtp/countries/india/document/papers/indo_pak-6jan04.htm
7. The Actual Ground Position Line refers to the existing position that divides Indian and Pakistani troops in the Siachen Glacier region. The line extends from the northernmost point of the LoC to Indira Col. The AGPL is about 110 kilometers long.
8. On the eve of Id ul Fitr, Pakistani Prime Minister Zafarullah Jamali announced a ceasefire offer to India along the International Border (IB) and the Line of Control (LoC) on 23 November, 2003. India proposes extension of the ceasefire along the Actual Ground Position Line (AGPL) in Siachen. Formal ceasefire between India and Pakistan along the

International Border (IB), Line of Control (LoC) and the Actual Ground Position Line (AGPL) in Jammu and Kashmir began at the midnight of 25th November, 2003.

9. The Composite Dialogue process between India and Pakistan has been replacing enmity with amity. The peace process between India and Pakistan has been on a cordial path. Since the rapprochement began in April 2003, significant progress has been made in normalising relations between the belligerent neighbours. This began after then Indian Prime Minister A.B. Vajpayee's Srinagar statement in April 2003. The goodwill gesture was well received by the then Prime Minister of Pakistan, Zafarullah Jamali. He responded positively not only rhetorically, but he also took practical initiatives to materialise the goodwill gesture. Consequently, diplomatic representation at the two capitals has been restored; a ceasefire declared at the Siachen and LoC; road, rail and air links have been revived; delegations of businessmen, Members of Parliament, artists and poets have exchanged visits, and cricket ties resumed after a break of nearly a decade and a half. Above all, both sides' rulers and higher government officials met number of times to ameliorate India-Pakistan relations.
10. Noorani, A.G. *op.cit.,* p. 132.
11. Behuria, Ashok. (2011). Pakistan-India Relations: An Indian Narrative. *Pakistan Institute of Legislative Development and Transparency,* (PILDAT), Background Paper, January 2011, p. 9.

    Retrieved from: http://www.pildat.org/publications/publication/FP/PakistanIndiaRelations-AnIndianNarrative.pdf
12. Vakil, C.N. & G. Raghava Rao. (1968). *Economic Relations between India and Pakistan: Need for International Cooperation,* Bombay: Vora & Co., 1968, pp. 156-57.
13. For details, see India-Pakistan Trade Agreement, 23 January 1975. Available at: http://www.commonlii.org/in/other/treaties/INTSer/1975/5.html
14. Bajpai Kanti et al. (1995). *Brasstacks and Beyond: Perception and Management of Crisis in South Asia,* New Delhi: Manohar, pp. 9-10.
15. Annual Report 1983-84, MEA Library, Ministry of External Affairs, Government of India, p. 3.
16. *The Hindu,* April 11, 1999.
17. Naqvi, Zareen. (2009). Pakistan-India Trade Potential and Issues, *The Lahore Journal of Economics,* Lahore: Lahore School of Economics Vol. 14, September 2009, p. 179.
18. Misra, Ashutosh. (2007). An audit of the India-Pakistan peace process. *Australian Journal of International Affairs,* Volume 61, Issue 4, 2007, p. 520. Retrieved from: http://www.tandfonline.com/doi/pdf/10.1080/10357710701684955

19. Manjunath, KS, Seema Sridhar and Beryl Anand. (2006). Indo-Pak Composite Dialogue 2004-05: A Profile. Institute of Peace and Conflict Studies (IPCS), New Delhi, Special Report 12, February, 2006.

    Retrieved from: http://www.ipcs.org/pdf_file/issue/1372586579IPCS-Special-Report-12.pdf
20. *Ibid.*
21. Joint Statement, Third Round of Pakistan-India Talks on Economic and Commercial Cooperation, Islamabad, 29 March, 2006.

    Retrieved from: http://mea.gov.in/bilateraldocuments.htm?dtl/6078/Joint+Statement+Third+ Round+of+PakistanIndia+talks+on+Economic+and+Commercial+Cooperation

22 Joint Statement on the Fourth Round of India Pakistan talks on Economic and Commercial Cooperation, New Delhi, August 1, 2007.

    Retrieved from: http://mea.gov.in/bilateraldocuments.htm?dtl/5589/Joint+ Statement+on+ the+Fourth+Round+of+IndiaPakistan+talks+on+Economic+and+Commercial+Cooperation

23. *Ibid.*
24. For details, see "Joint Statement of the 5th round of talks on Commercial and Economic Cooperation between Commerce Secretaries of India and Pakistan". Available at: http://www.indiapakistantrade.org/data/jointstatements/Joint%20 Statement%2028%20April%202011.pdf
25. In September 2011, Pakistan's Commerce Minister, Makhdoom Amin Fahim met his Indian counterpart, Anand Sharma to kick start talks to normalise trade. Fahim became Pakistan's first Commerce Minister to visit India in 35 years and the trade ministries of both nations made a joint statement to lay out a timeline for removing all non-tariff barriers.
26. Yousaf, Kamran. (2011). SAARC summit: PMs Pledge 'new chapter' in ties. *The Express Tribune,* Pakistan, November 10, 2011. Retrieved from:

    http://tribune.com.pk/story/289627/saarc-summit-gilani-singh-eye-future-progress-at-talks/
27. For details, see "Joint Statement of the 6th round of talks on Commercial and Economic Cooperation between Commerce Secretaries of India and Pakistan", November 16, 2011. Available at:

    http://commerce.nic.in/trade/Minutes14-16Nov2011.pdf
28. Joint Statement of the 7th Round of talks on Commercial and Economic Co-operation between Commerce Secretaries of India and Pakistan, 21 September 2012.
29. NDTV News. (2012). New checkpost opened at Attari, to boost sub-continental trade. April 13, 2012. Available at: http://www.ndtv.com/india-news/new-checkpost-opened-at-attari-to-boost-sub-continental-trade-476526

30. For more details, see "Joint Statement of the 7th round of talks on Commercial and Economic Cooperation between Commerce Secretaries of India and Pakistan", September 21, 2012. Available at: http://www.pib.nic.in/newsite/erelease.aspx?relid=87891
31. Raihan, Selim and Prabir De. (2013). India-Pakistan Economic Cooperation: Implications for Regional Integration in South Asia. A Report, *Commonwealth Secretariat,* London, UK, April 2013, p. 46.
32. Taneja, Nisha and Samridhi Bimal. (2012). Liberalizing India-Pakistan Investment Flows. *India-Pakistan Trade Newsletter,* Indian Council for Research on International Economic Relations (ICRIER), October 2012, p. 2.
33. *Ibid.,* p. 3.
34. Taneja, Nisha and Samridhi Bimal. (2012). FDI-a major milestone in Indo-Pak ties. *The Hindu Business Line,* August 22, 2012.
35. Taneja, Nisha and Samridhi Bimal. Liberalizing India-Pakistan Investment Flows. p. 3.
36. For details, see "Joint Statement of the 5th round of talks on Commercial and Economic Cooperation between Commerce Secretaries of India and Pakistan". Available at:

    http://www.indiapakistantrade.org/data/jointstatements/Joint%20Statement%2028%20April%202011.pdf
37. For details see, "Joint Press Statement of the Commerce Ministers of India and Pakistan", 18 January 2014, New Delhi. Available at:

    http://www.commerce.gov.pk/Readmore/Pak_India_Ministers_Joint_Statement_18012014.pdf
38. For details see, "The India Show: Land of Limitless Opportunities", Ministry of Commerce and Industry, Govt. of Indian & FICCI, February 14-16, 2014. Available at: http://www.ficci.com/events/21770/Add_docs/India-show-Pakistan-2014.pdf
39. Chowdhury, Jhinuk. (2014). Can trade be the game changer in Indo-Pak relations? *RT Network,* June 12, 2014. Retrieved from: http://rt.com/op-edge/165324-india-pakistan-relations-trade/
40. *Ibid.*
41. *Ibid.*
42. The principle of non-discrimination stipulates that a member of the WTO shall not discriminate between "like" products from different trading partners (giving them equally "most favoured-nation" or MFN status, GATT Article I); and between its own and like foreign products (giving them "national treatment", GATT Article III).
43. Chowdhury, Jhinuk, loc.cit.
44. E-mail conversation with the researcher, 6th June 2014.

45. Conversation with the researcher on 9th June 2014.
46. *Ibid.*
47. E-mail communication to the researcher, 10th June 2014.
48. Haider, Mateen. 2014). Modi condemns Karachi airport attack in letter to Nawaz. *The Dawn,* Pakistan, June 13, 2014. Retrieved from: http://www.dawn.com/news/1112499
49. E-mail communication to the researcher, 10th June 2014.
50. Personal conversation with the author, 29th June 2014, University of Kashmir, Srinagar.
51. Chowdhury, Jhinuk, loc. cit.
52. *Ibid.*

8

Gender, Equality and Governance in South Asia

— *Seema Kazi*

Introduction

Democracy in South Asia: An Overview

A study of democracy in South Asia must begin with a delineation of the region's geographical and political contours. Initially, the term South Asia was coterminous with the Indian subcontinent including Afghanistan on the west and Myanmar – a province of British India till 1935. The idea of South Asia as a distinct geographic and political entity is a recent, roughly six decades old construct formalised by the adoption of the South Asian Association for Regional Cooperation (SAARC) Charter by the heads of state of India, Pakistan, Bangladesh, Sri Lanka, Nepal, Bhutan and Maldives in 1985. These seven-member states constitute the geographical and political entity presently referred to as South Asia. For reasons of scope and analysis, the term South Asia in this paper is restricted to India, Pakistan, Bangladesh, Sri Lanka and Nepal.

Despite a shared sub-continental cultural heritage, post-colonial South Asian nation-states have charted different political trajectories. India became a parliamentary democracy even as the decline of a post-independence secular-nationalist consensus paralleled a fragmentation of the polity; ethnic rebellions against the central government, and increasing demands by newly politicised social groups on the state. These challenges coincided with the rise of Hindu nationalism and a weakening of India's secular fabric. India's economic growth paralleled the persistence of high levels of poverty and human deprivation. Much remains to be achieved in terms of ensuring equality, liberty and justice for the majority of Indian citizens.

The state of Pakistan was an outcome of the 1947 partition of the subcontinent, with the new nation-state of Pakistan divided into two (East and West) territorial halves. In 1956, Pakistan adopted a constitution to become a republic based on Islamic principles. After a period of political uncertainty and martial rule, a new constitution (1962) established a presidential form of government with a single National Parliament (Assembly). The refusal of West Pakistan to respect the electoral mandate precipitated Bengali resistance culminated in the secession of East Pakistan and the establishment of the independent nation-state of Bangladesh. Pakistan has been subject to prolonged periods of martial law (1977-1988). National elections in 2008 restored a civilian government. As Pakistan battles to consolidate civil authority within, and defend its borders against extremists without, it has a long way to go towards providing security and justice for the majority of its citizens.

Bangladesh is South Asia's youngest nation-state. The country plunged into political turmoil soon after its establishment in 1971 with the assassination of Prime Minister Sheikh Mujibur Rahman and an extended period of martial law. Bangladesh's subsequent drift towards an Islamic state was in contradiction to its original self-identification as a secular country. The rise of Islamist forces precipitated violence against Hindu, Christian and Buddhist minorities. Opposition to martial law began with student protests in 1983 ending with the restoration of democracy. National elections in 1996, 2001 and 2007 voted in civilian governments whose democratic record was marred by allegations of violence, corruption and authoritarianism. Bangladesh faces enormous challenges in terms of ensuring equitable development and protecting the democratic rights of citizens and minorities.

Sri Lanka gained independence from the British in 1948 to adopt a constitution providing for a parliamentary form of governance. The rise of Sinhalese nationalism, its repudiation of Tamil (Sri Lanka's largest minority) concerns, and its opposition to moves for political decentralisation precipitated a brutal civil war between government forces and Tamil rebels led by the Liberation Tigers of Tamil Eelam (LTTE). Sri Lanka's bicameral parliamentary democracy was replaced with a presidential form of government (1978) headed by a powerful president, the replacement of a federation by a unitary state, and the abolishment of crucial safeguards for minorities. The civil war drew to a close in 2009 with the defeat of the LTTE and widespread allegations of indiscriminate killings of civilians by Sri Lankan security forces and by the LTTE. Sri Lanka's tragic ethnic conflict undermined its notable achievements in social and human development. Much depends on the Sri state's Lankan willingness to address the concerns of Tamil and other minorities, and uphold citizens' democratic rights before Sri Lanka can emerge from its war-ravaged past.

Historically, Nepal was a monarchy since the eighteenth century when Gorkha King Prithvi Narayan Shah forged the warring kingdoms of the Kathmandu Valley into a single political entity, thus laying the foundations of modern Nepal. A 1923 Anglo-Nepalese treaty affirmed Nepalese sovereignty and its present territorial borders. Nepal came to be subsequently dominated by the *Rana* dynasty that ruled as hereditary prime ministers with the King as titular head. Popular discontent and opposition to the *Rana* autocracy began to be articulated during the 1930s and 1940s. The Nepali Congress and the Communist Party of Nepal led a successful struggle against the *Ranas* who were eventually overthrown. A referendum endorsed a parliamentary form of government and a new democratic Constitution with a bicameral Parliament and fundamental rights. A Congress-led government was established in 1991 after Nepal's first democratic elections. Parliament was subsequently dissolved in 1995 as Maoists began an insurrection aimed at abolishing the monarchy and establishing a people's republic. After a prolonged civil war, Nepal became a secular and democratic republic in 2006 with a Constituent Assembly (CA) voting to abolish the monarchy. Maoists joined the government yet political tensions continue in the wake of Nepal's transition to democracy as it struggles to maintain its fledgling democracy and ensure equitable development and justice for its citizens.

The political record of South Asian nation-states presents an ambiguous picture. India and Sri Lanka have retained their formal democratic systems since independence, albeit with restrictions on human rights and civil liberties. Pakistan and Bangladesh, on the other hand, witnessed frequent and prolonged disruption in civilian rule by the military and restrictions on civil rights. Nepal's struggle for democracy that began in the last decade of the twentieth century was realised in 2006 after an extraordinary mass mobilisation. Notwithstanding these divergent histories and trajectories, South Asian nation-states share certain paradoxes and challenges distinguishing them from Western democracies.

Presently, all five states are democracies with elected governments. At the same time, however, South Asia is one of the world's poorest, least developed, and profoundly unequal societies. The disjuncture between constitutionally guaranteed formal equality and widespread socio-economic inequality is an enduring contradiction underpinning democracy in South Asia. Integral to, and symbolic of, this great contradiction is the condition of female citizens for whom inequalities across caste, class, ethnicity and region intersect with those of gender. With the exception of Sri Lanka, South Asia fares poorly with reference to the UNDP Gender-related Development Index (GDI) and Gender Empowerment Measure (GEM) that measures gender inequality. A report on gender equality in 2009 ranked India – South Asia's pre-eminent democracy – 114th among 134 countries – behind Bangladesh, Sri Lanka and Nepal. The South Asian region is also home to the world's largest number of poor and illiterate citizens – a majority of whom are female – with notable gender gaps in primary development indicators such as health, education, employment and political participation. The marginalisation of women in politics and policy-making, and in structures of power and governance flows from, and is influenced by, the structural inequalities of gender across the region. For the majority of economically underprivileged and politically marginalised South Asian women, the formal rights of equal citizenship are yet to translate into equal access to basic social services or the equality of social and economic opportunity crucial for transformative change.

In addition to the overarching inequalities of, among others, gender, caste and class, South Asian states share a poor record of protecting the rights of ethnic, linguistic and religious minorities. In India, powerful dissident movements by ethnic minorities in Kashmir, Punjab, Assam, Nagaland and Mizoram in support of greater autonomy have been subject to coercive repression by the state; Muslim, Christian and Sikh religious minorities have been targets of violence by right-wing forces – in many instances with the consent or active collaboration of state agencies. The period of state-backed Islamisation in Pakistan coincided with violence against *Ahmediyya* and *Shia* religious minorities; the record of secular parties like the Pakistan's People's Party (PPP) is not much better: Christian, Hindu and *Ahmediyya* minorities in Pakistan have been targeted by Islamist forces during civilian rule even as a blasphemy law is routinely used to legitimise violence against minorities; popular demands for greater provincial autonomy in the province of Baluchistan have been negotiated through military means. In Bangladesh, the rise of right-wing Islamist parties fuelled violence against Bangladesh's Hindu, Christian and tribal minorities. Sri Lanka's failure to protect its Tamil minority precipitated a brutal civil between state forces and the LTTE that ended with grave breaches of human rights by both sides. In Nepal, the long-drawn struggle for democracy that began in the 1990s claimed thousands of lives with hundreds of disappeared citizens and a deeply damaged social fabric.

South Asia's domestic crises and civil wars have had far reaching effects on state, politics and society. They have weakened the moral authority and secular credentials of the state, eroded the federal mechanisms crucial for governing South Asia's diverse societies, damaged the socio-cultural fabric and exacerbated grievance within social groups. The nature of intra-state violence in South Asia is deeply gendered: the disappearance of male kin members, an increase in widows and female-headed households, displacement and dislocation, women's vulnerability to sexual violence, and enhanced levels of poverty among female survivors of war are some of its common features; its gendered contours exemplify the dismal record of governance in South Asian states. Women remain poorly represented or altogether absent from decision-making bodies and mainstream politics in conflict zones.

Women's movements in South Asia are part of wider civil society mobilisations that emerged in response to popular disillusionment with the state and its inability to administer democratic governance and ensure distributive justice. The women's movement in India was forged around the issue of state violence against women that informed its 1970s and 1980s campaigns against dowry deaths, domestic violence, and the rape of women by state forces. The electoral arena was not a site for struggle until much later. The present engagement between women/feminist groups and political parties in India around the specific issue of reservation for women in local legislatures and the national parliament has, as this study subsequently illustrates, yielded partial albeit important gains. The women's movement in Pakistan emerged during an extended period of martial law during the 1970s and 1980s; its implications for women were particularly severe. The issue of women's representation in governance bodies surfaced initially during the 1970s – a gain subsequently neutralised during ensuing periods of military rule that relegated the issue of women's representation into the background. Much like Pakistan, the energies of the women's movement in Bangladesh during the 1980s were initially focused on opposing military rule and state-sponsored Islamisation. Martial law in Bangladesh was not, however, as explicitly women-centred as in Pakistan. The reservation of seats for women in local bodies and the national parliament was among the major issues addressed by the women's movement in Bangladesh, with women's groups mobilising for an increase in the number of reserved seats for women at both levels. Compared to its neighbours, Sri Lanka has a notably higher Gender Development Index (GDI) – a singular achievement greatly undermined by a tragic civil war that has been especially detrimental for women. The war polarised women on ethnic and ideological lines making it that much more difficult to forge a collective vision and struggle for women from different ethnic and religious groups. The 1990s witnessed greater engagement of women's groups with political parties in Sri Lanka; women and feminist groups have called upon political parties to address women's concerns and enhance women's participation in politics.

In general, South Asia's feminist movements against state violence, authoritarianism, religious chauvinism and equitable development sought to advance the goals of gender equality and women's democratic rights. The class dimensions of this struggle cannot be underestimated: a large majority of South Asian women are poor, illiterate, undernourished and unemployed. Democracy in South Asia has heightened public awareness of rights though it is yet to alter the socio-economic and realities of a very large underclass of female citizens. Given the region's cultural and ethnic diversity, and the multiplicity of challenges confronting individual states, these cross-cutting factors are part of the wider context against which the issue of women's rights and governance must be framed and analysed.

Critical Issues

State

With the exception of Sri Lanka, much of South Asia is characterised by widespread poverty and socio-economic deprivation. At the turn of the new millennium South Asia had the most distorted sex-ratio in the world and was identified as the world's least gender sensitive region. The disparities of class that flow from poverty and socio-economic inequality overlap with those of gender: the outcome of this convergence for underprivileged women is particularly severe. South Asia's paradox of democracy and deprivation mandates need for active and concerted public intervention to redress this incongruity. The state has a vital role to play in terms of ensuring the provision of basic social services and implanting inclusive and equitable development policies, and eliminating the structural inequalities of class and gender that are especially detrimental for a large number of South Asia's poor female citizens. Quite the opposite, however, is presently the case: governments across the region have slashed public spending and investment, imposed cuts on the provision of essential services, frozen public sector/formal employment, and evinced little interest in regulating the increasingly skewed relationship between the state and the market. Despite the political rhetoric emanating from different political parties within states, there is implicit acquiescence, if not outright endorsement across the political spectrum for privatisation, deregulation and liberalisation across the region – the costs of which are largely and disproportionately borne by the large majority of

South Asia's poor. Declining formal sector employment, the emergence of a large and unregulated informal economy, the erosion of workers' rights, dispossession and displacement wrought by corporate-led industrialisation, and the transformation of rights into commodities willed by a rapidly retreating state have deepened class and gender inequalities across the region. This is the backdrop against which women's demand and mobilisation for political gender equality and greater political participation has been articulated – a conjuncture that raises important questions for the women's movement.

Women's Movements and Political Parties

The women's movement in South Asia is among a variety of social movements that emerged in response to popular disillusionment with the state. Although politics in South Asia has historically been a male domain, this trend is punctured by a paradoxical regional record of having the largest number of female heads of state than any other region in the world. The political eminence of South Asia's female heads of state, however, derived from more from their association with privileged male politicians than from opportunities afforded to women by male-dominated and patriarchal polities. Political parties, on the other hand, have engaged with women and sought their support, even as they have exhibited a manifest reluctance to yield to women the institutional space and resources necessary for political participation – a reluctance informed by social constructions of gender, fears about potential erosion in established male power and patronage networks, and an implicit rejection of the principle of gender equality. The cultural notion that men are better equipped to enter politics and public life has fair resonance across the South Asian region making it that much more difficult for women – especially in rural settings where patriarchy is more entrenched – to breach the status quo. In addition to political and cultural factors, the degeneration of political parties, increased levels of corruption, and the threat of violence are among the factors that inhibit women's participation in mainstream politics in South Asia.

For the past two decades, there has been growing concern among women across the region regarding the absence of women in governance and political decision-making bodies. Aiming to halt and reverse this trend, women's groups in South Asia have engaged with political parties on the issue of women's presence and participation in legislative bodies. While this engagement has secured a greater presence of women in local and national governance bodies, it has also, simultaneously, raised several questions. Women's demand for greater political participation in South Asia must be weighed against the paradox of a receding state (coterminous with increasing gender inequality) and its simultaneous attempt to garner women's support for legislation favouring gender quotas for women. Can women's legitimate demand for gender equality in politics be meaningfully or substantively addressed by a state that is increasingly disinclined to eliminate the structural roots of gender inequality in society and economy? Will a 'politics of presence' serve the interests of South Asia's large majority of poor, underprivileged women with little power or influence? The women's movement has historically been characterised by an autonomous politics and mobilisation: what may be the implications of a contemporary emphasis on numerical parity and the attendant proximity of a section of gender equality advocates to the institutions of power, in contrast to an earlier emphasis on voice, participatory democracy, and an anti-system politics? Will engendering parliament and local governance bodies engender policy-making and democracy in South Asia? These are the questions this paper seeks to address.

Equality Strategies: Gender Quotas

For almost three decades, the principle of gender equality has been the stated goal of governments across the world. Equality between men and women is widely accepted as a positive value and a core component of struggles for social justice; governments world-wide have endorsed institutional measures for advancing women's equality. The mechanism of gender quotas is among the measures that have come to define the commitment of states to gender equality in the political sphere. The argument for a greater presence and participation of women in the political sphere is legitimate and compelling even as it raises questions regarding equality, representation and democracy. Four key issues are foregrounded, namely, interest, representation, the limits of representative democracy, and neo-liberal economic policy - against which the demand for gender quotas must be assessed. The suggestion here is that women's struggle for equality in politics is inextricably linked with issues of representation, democracy, the fulfilment of citizens' rights, and equal access to basic services for marginalised groups, especially women.

Interest

Central to the strategy of gender quotas for women as a means to achieve political equality is the assumption that women are best placed to represent women's interests. This seemingly self-evident assertion is, however, fraught with a fundamental contradiction. The term 'women' is not a self-evident or homogenous category. A consensus among women regarding their putative interests can hardly be assumed – least of all in a South Asian setting characterised by, among others, profound class, caste and gender disparities. Given the variety of women's perspectives on political issues (including representation) it is neither practically possible nor politically prudent to reduce a diversity of (different) views and interests derived from different *locations* to an objective, commonly shared 'women's' perspective that may end up obscuring material and ideological differences among women.

Also implicit in the women-for-women approach is the assumption that women would, and do follow different policies than men. A brief appraisal of the record and performance of South Asia's erstwhile female heads of state, or the performance of female legislators and provincial leaders within South Asian states does not, however, validate this claim. Female politicians and legislators in South Asia are not known for raising specific issues concerning women's rights or interests; nor do they share a record of shifting public policy in favour of women. If issues such as state violence against women, women's reproductive health, female literacy, dowry deaths, or women's marginalisation in politics do not figure in mainstream political debate or policy-making, the problem lies more with a polity and political class that has consistently failed to prioritise gender issues or undertake institutional measures to redress gender-based violence and discrimination, than with the gender composition of legislative bodies.

Representation

A further dilemma concerns the tension between the logic of representative democracy and women's claim to best represent women's interests. The contradiction between women's demand for equal representation in political institutions, and their simultaneous insistence on a special identity and role as women begs the question as to whether women can claim a special mandate beyond the confines of party politics within a democratic set-up by virtue of their sex. If the response to this dilemma is in the affirmative, it would be prudent to reflect upon Anne Phillip's (1991) reminder that the marker of legitimacy in representative democracy is elections, not nature. The 'representation' of women's special interests derives from public recognition and prioritisation of these interests by political parties, legislative bodies and state agencies, not from women's individual identity or experience as women. Women are not endowed with a special mandate beyond party and political system constraints. In other words, women's claim to represent women's interests cannot be viewed in isolation or outside of the mechanisms of democratic functioning and control, nor can this claim simply rest and rely upon an implicit (and as yet unsubstantiated) trust in female capability. From the point of view of justice, South Asia needs more women in politics. However, whether the interests of all women shall be best served by female legislators and whether a greater numerical presence of women in governance institutions is coterminous with greater democratisation of institutional practice is far from clear.

Limits of Representative Democracy

South Asia's cultural diversity foregrounds the limits of a representation defined by numerical presence. If the demand for political justice privileges numerical parity between men and women in national parliaments and assemblies, what about the representation of marginalised minorities across the rubrics of class, caste, religion, tribe, or region? Must a proportional number of poor, lower caste, minority or tribal women be elected to parliament in order to ensure justice for these women? To pose this question is not to deny the legitimacy of minority women's demand for equality in politics but to underscore the limits of representative democracy in a context where elected representatives may not necessarily reflect the multiple interests of female citizens within it. While the interests of South Asia's large majority of underprivileged women may, arguably, be advanced by a representative presence, it is far from clear whether presence alone shall guarantee policy implementation.

Neo-liberalism and Gender Equality

Over the decades, there has been a fragmentation of the women's movement due to a parting of ways between those who emphasise economic and class inequality while remaining committed to an anti-system politics as against those who prioritise political equality within mainstream politics with the aim of increasing the number of women in political parties and legislatures. The focus on political equality within the normative system diminishes the political significance of South Asia's enduring class inequalities. A women's movement activism focused exclusively on political equality within the existing institutional framework is therefore unlikely to challenge the injustices of neo-liberalism or its attendant logic of economic efficiency that seamlessly appropriates the feminist demand for political equality.

Equality between women and men within the context of a neo-liberal policy paradigm does not challenge or dislodge the structural inequalities of gender and class within which women's inequality in politics is rooted. Uncritical acceptance of the neo-liberal paradigm begs the question as to whether a greater or 'equal' numerical presence of women in political institutions is necessarily synonymous with greater public recognition and policy intervention on women's issues, or the creation of a gender-inclusive egalitarian polity. There are no easy answers to these dilemmas. It is necessary, however, to place them in reference to the demand for gender quotas in order to arrive at a more nuanced understanding of the complexities underpinning women's mobilisation for equality in politics in South Asia.

South Asia: Women's Representation in Governance Institutions

The gender gap in politics in South Asia is attributable to a combination of historical, political and cultural factors. South Asia women have been historically marginalised from politics and public life; in the post-colonial period women's marginalisation in politics has been shaped by political developments within the state and by state policy even as cultural notions regarding gender roles, discrimination within the family and community, greater domestic responsibilities for women, ignorance of electoral procedures, and family/patriarchal/religious constraints on mobility are among the major cross-cutting factors inhibiting women's political participation. Although there has been an overall increase in women's representation in South Asian parliaments and local bodies, the goal of gender equality in public life is far from being realised.

Mobilising for reserved quotas for women in governance bodies is one of the strategies adopted by feminist and women's groups to redress the gender imbalance in politics. While women's *access* to governance institutions is the first step towards this goal, of equal if not greater importance is the need to effect change *within* these institutions and ensure the entitlements of women affected by lack of rights and influence. The picture in terms of women's representation in governance bodies is not positive: although women's share in South Asia's national parliaments has increased over the decades, they are still far from achieving equal representation in governance bodies. A ten-year review of human development in South Asia noted:

India

India - South Asia's largest and pre-eminent state – is a parliamentary, multi-party democracy. Sixteen of the last 50 years were occupied by a female in the executive office; women hold 11 per cent of the total number of seats in parliament and 10 per cent of ministerial level positions. Paradoxically, however, India has consistently returned a small number of women to the national parliament; women's presence in parliament or the emergence of influential female political personalities like Sonia Gandhi at the national level, or chief minister Mayawati at the state/provincial level, has not made any discernible difference to the policy agenda of incumbent regimes, or evoked greater public articulation of women's interests. India's female politicians lack power in their own right since almost all of them owe their political eminence to powerful political families or kinship links with male politicians. There is an absence of cross-cutting political alliances between female politicians, even as differences in social class, political backgrounds and party positions prevent them from forging a collective vision for Indian women. Other reasons behind women's low participation in representative structures is the reluctance of political parties to nominate women or their tendency to field women from constituencies where they are likely to lose, or where male candidates are reluctant to contest. Female parliamentarians often have to toe the party line with little freedom to formulate or implement their own agendas. While the women's wing of some political parties does interact with the party leadership, there is no channel linking non-party women with members of parliament (MPs) or political parties that focus on women's rights.

Over the years, political parties have increasingly sought the support of women and included women's concerns in party manifestos. The outcome of this engagement has been mixed. A proposed Bill reserving one-third of seats for women in the Indian parliament has been repeatedly stalled for years. At the time of writing, the Rajya Sabha passed the 108th Amendment Bill reserving 33 per cent of seats for women in the national parliament and state legislatures; it is expected to be placed before the Lok Sabha for approval. By way of contrast, in response to growing demands for decentralisation and greater representation of women in politics, the passage of the 73rd and 74th Amendments in parliament in 1993 was relatively smooth. The continued stalling of the 108st Amendment indicates there is much more is at stake at the national level for male politicians and mainstream political parties. Reserved quotas for women in higher governing bodies (parliament and state assemblies) has proved more difficult as the threat to male dominance at the policy-making (parliament), rather than policy implementation (village and local council) level, is more direct.

Generally speaking, India presents a mixed picture: at the national level, there is no notable increase in the percentage of women parliamentarians (8 per cent in 1984 and 8.3 per cent in 2009 being the highest). Female members of parliament and state assemblies are drawn from different political parties and subscribe to divergent ideologies: as a result they do not share a common politics or a common vision for Indian women. Women MPs lack the power to set their own agendas; in many cases they need to defer to male authority. There is almost a complete disconnect between women's groups and female parliamentarians due to which the specific interests of underprivileged women rarely figure in party politics or parliamentary debate.

Pakistan

Pakistan has been interrupted by prolonged periods of martial law. The entrenchment of the military and its consistent hold on politics in Pakistan weakened civilian institutions and authority. Benazir Bhutto's ascent to power (1988) was imbued with symbolic and political significance for women. Yet, even as Benazir pledged to empower women and end gender discrimination, her regime was unable to implement the party (PPP) manifesto in any substantive measure – a failure that had much to do with the contradiction between her party's commitment to women, the poor and the disenfranchised, and the interests of a large number of PPP party members – mainly (male) feudal (to which Benazir herself belonged) and wealthy elites. The weakness of political parties, prejudice against women, a patriarchal and feudal environment, and opposition from family and local male elites explain the marginalisation of women in politics in Pakistan. In general, political parties have tended to treat women as a passive vote bank subject to the dictates of men in the family or clan.

Pakistan's first constitution (1956) provided for three per cent reserved seats for women in national and provincial legislatures: there were ten reserved seats for women for a period of ten years, a provision that was utilised as and when the political situation permitted with a total of six female legislators in Pakistan during 1956-1972. After the establishment of Bangladesh, the 1973 constitution provided for ten reserved seats for women in the lower house of parliament, later doubled to 20 (out of a total of 237) in 1985. Although the number of directly elected women in Pakistan's parliament has increased, and female parliamentarians have voiced their opinion on gender and national issues, they remain beholden to their respective parties for their political position and the indirect manner of their election. The reserved quota (17.5 per cent) for women has been extended to the state/provincial assemblies though it falls well short of the demand for 33 per cent demanded by women's groups. A (2000) legislation provides for 33 per cent reservation for women in local government (in urban areas and districts).

The women's wing of provincial parties like the Mohajir Qaumi Movement (MQM) and the Sindhiani Tekrik has been used by parties to consolidate their own political base rather than address women's interests. Pakistan has the highest proportion of female parliamentarians in South Asia though as mentioned earlier, most parliamentarians are drawn from the upper-crust of society. At the local level, the barriers for rural/poor women are greater. Women are discouraged from entering electoral politics and often forced to stand as independents in the absence of nomination from political parties; elected women councillors at the local (village) are frequently obliged to depend on influential male members, forced to defer to men in order to receive funding, and are often not in a position to oppose policy set by men.

Sri Lanka

Sri Lanka has a better record of gender equality than other South Asian states, though this has not translated into greater political participation of Sri Lankan women. Much like in India and Pakistan, Sri Lanka's female presidents owed their political eminence to their association with male political leaders. Apart from gender, class plays an important role in the selection of political leaders in Sri Lanka: male leaders are preferred to females unless the latter are from prominent, upper class and politically influential families. In 2000, Sri Lanka's parliament had nine women out of a total strength of 224; the cabinet had 42 men and 2 women.

Sri Lanka is the only country in South Asia not to have reserved quotas for women at any level. Although the number of women running for electoral office has increased over the years, this has not translated into a greater number of women being elected. Women and feminist groups have lobbied with political parties on the issue of including women's interests in party manifestos – an engagement that produced significant shifts in party positions regarding women. Women's groups in Sri Lanka have demanded a 25-30 per cent quota of nominations by political parties for women candidates as a means to redress the gender imbalance in politics. On the eve of the 2010 national elections, women's groups and NGOs shared a platform with political parties to voice concern at the under-representation of women in politics (11 women in Parliament out of a total strength of 225) and suggested the likelihood of a less violent and less fractious politics with the entry of a greater number of women in local and national governance bodies. In general, women's engagement with political parties around the issue of political participation remains paradoxical: political parties are known to have co-opted the women's movement to advance their own interests. Time and future elections shall indicate whether there is any shift towards a greater role of women in Sri Lankan politics.

Bangladesh

The women's movement in Bangladesh emerged during the national liberation struggle (1970-71) and was part of the civil society response to political developments in the 1980s – not the least of which was the politicisation of Islam and the subversion of democracy by the military. The women's movement played a key role in opposing martial law and attempts by the military leadership and the Islamist right-wing to alter the secular identity of the state: there was a high turnout of women voters in the 1996 national parliamentary elections that ended the military dictatorship. During the 1980s, a group of 20 women's organisations demanded, among others things, the ratification of the Convention for the Elimination of All Forms of Discrimination against Women (CEDAW) and an increased female quota in the civil services. Bangladesh has had two female prime ministers who have dominated national politics in the post-1991 period: both Khaleda Zia (Bangladesh National Party or BNP) and Sheikh Hasina (Awami League, current prime minister) owe their political prominence to their close links with male political leaders; their respective regimes are not known for advancing women's rights or gender-friendly governance.

One of the areas of mobilisation for the women's movement in Bangladesh has been around the issue of women's representation in parliament. A constitutional provision provided for 15 reserved seats for women in the national parliament, a quota that was doubled to 30 in the second national assembly (1979-1982) and eventually lapsed in 2001. Confining women to reserved women-only quotas has been counter-productive: it has left male-dominated political parties with little incentive to field women candidates in the open/general category. For exactly this reason, the women's movement in Bangladesh has opposed the policy of reservation and mobilised in favour of a greater number of reserved seats for women to be open for direct election.

At the local level, there have been efforts by the government to include a greater number of women in governance bodies. The 1997 Local Government Second Amendment reserved three seats for women in the Union Parishad (village council) through direct election. The number of women candidates, however, has remained disappointingly low. Restrictive gender roles within the home and community; gender stereotypes regarding the role of women; discrimination within existing institutional structures, limitations on mobility and lack of resources to contest elections are the intersecting factors constraining women's political participation at the local level in Bangladesh; successful women candidates are known to have faced threats by male opponents. Bangladesh presents a paradox whereby an increase in reserved seats for women through indirect election in parliament has not translated into political advantage because women-only quotas do not enhance women's autonomy or agency and serve to reinforce male monopoly in politics.

Nepal

After a prolonged civil war and the abolishment of a 240-year old monarchy, Nepal became South Asia's youngest democracy in 2008. Women were crucial to the movement for democracy during which they were victims of rape and sexual abuse, and deprived of the benefits of education, health, access to productive resources, and reproductive rights. With support from the United Nations (UN) and other international agencies, women's groups in Nepal succeeded in securing a reserved quota of seats in the newly established Constituent Assembly (CA) where women constitute just over 33 per cent of the total number of seats – a huge jump from the previous figure of 6 per cent. Nepal's interim constitution (2007) provides for 33 per cent reservation for women in governance structures. In the 2008 elections, there were 32.8 per cent women (197 out of 601) in Nepal's national parliament: parties nominated 167 women while 30 were elected directly. Women parliamentarians formed an inter-party alliance and have pressured the government for 50 per cent reservation for women in all policymaking positions. Women's lobbying forced the government to pass bills decriminalising abortion, allowing women to inherit property at birth, and women's right to give their children citizenship rights. At the same time, however, it has been difficult for women to voice other gender-related issues through parliamentary channels because gender issues were not deemed important.

At the local level, the Act on Local Election mandates representation of women at the district and village level as a result of which more than 100,000 women stood as candidates for Village Development Committees (VDCs) with more than 36,000 elected to Village Assemblies. In 2007, a women's NGO alliance promoted a list of 3000 rural and urban women for peace and electoral processes including in the CA even though there was no direct participation of women in the 2006 agreement between political parties. There exists a high degree of political awareness among Nepali women with the potential for carving out a greater political role for women in collaboration with women's groups. Whether democracy in Nepal can ensure a more substantive role for Nepali women in politics and governance remains to be seen.

Key Issues

Several key points emerge from the above trends. From the point of view of justice and legitimacy, a greater numerical presence of women in national parliaments subverts the established gender hierarchy, alters the political culture, and imparts greater legitimacy to the political system. Women's increased political presence in national and local governance bodies is an essential first step towards redressing the gender imbalance in politics; it opens up the possibility of challenging established policy-making and reorienting development agendas.

At the same time, however, a greater *numerical* presence of women may not necessarily secure the representation of the diverse *interests* of women – especially those of South Asia's very large constituency of underprivileged women with little influence or resources. From a class perspective, existing trends are not optimistic: in India for instance, the majority of female members of parliament are from upper class/ caste backgrounds, as is also the case in Pakistan, Bangladesh and Sri Lanka where female legislators come from feudal or elite backgrounds. In an overview of the 1991-1996 Indian Parliament, academic Shirin Rai noted that the majority of women in the Indian parliament were elite women from upper caste and class backgrounds allowing them a far greater range of options than are available to poorer women. The class origin of female MPs is a major determinant of women's entry into parliament and is also the reason why a large majority of underprivileged women lack the education, access to resources, institutional support or wealth necessary for entering governance institutions. In such a context, the anticipated engendering of parliament may achieve little more than the engendering of elites. The privileging of gender must not be at the cost of South Asia's great class disparities. The inclusion of women in political institutions process is an important first step towards altering a male-dominated polity; it nevertheless remains an insufficient condition for challenging the political status quo unless the class disparities flowing from socio-economic inequality are addressed simultaneously.

Further, an examination of the record of female parliamentarians in South Asia indicates that a greater presence of women does not necessarily translate into a better representation of women's interests. Most Indian female parliamentarians, for instance, as Shirin Rai noted "did not have women's issues high on their list of interests. Rather, they wanted to be on committees relating to economy, international relations and trade. As ambitious women these MPs want to be where power and influence converge". While the pursuit of power and influence is not a characteristic confined to female MP's from South Asia, it does indicate that women MPs may not necessarily pursue a different politics and agenda than men. Accordingly, even as there is a strong case in favour of women's entry in greater numbers into parliament, there is no way of knowing or predicting how women shall behave once they are there. The evidence suggests a need to engender policy rather than focusing on the gender of policy-makers.

A related concern is the representation of women from minority/ ethnic groups. As mentioned already, the record of South Asian states regarding the protection of (ethnic, religious, tribal) minorities is poor. The fact of discrimination against minorities translates into a legitimate defence of quotas for minorities, though this would necessarily come with the assumption that the 'interests' of minorities are clearly defined and consensually agreed upon by the group. This may not, however, be practically achievable, given the gender, class, sect, and regional differences within the minority group itself. This does not mean that the claim for minority representation should be surrendered or discarded for want of representatives; rather, it may be more prudent for women and the women's movement to demand institutional measure to protect and advance the rights of minority women.

The record of political parties in South Asia in relation to gender issues is not particularly impressive. Women and women's groups have a crucial role to play in terms of facilitating the articulation of gender issues within political parties and their integration into public policy. Further, the importance of the state in South Asia cannot be overstated: it has the resources, the institutions and the mechanisms to fulfil the democratic rights of citizens and marginalised social groups i.e. freedom from want, hunger and fear, and the provision of basic social services to *all*, that in turn, shall invest women with the skills, capability, confidence and opportunity to compete for electoral office on an even footing with men. The removal of social inequality is thus an essential pre-requisite for deepening democracy in South Asia. Democratic governance in South Asia is therefore not merely not only about closing the gender gap between women and men in political institutions; it is, more fundamentally, about eliminating social inequality and the absence of distributive justice that creates and reinforces the gender gap in politics.

Finally, the women's movement in South Asia needs to reflect upon the paradoxes, contradictions and challenges generated by the retreat of the state in the region and its pursuit of a neo-liberal economic agenda. If a citizen-centric concept of democracy and governance is premised on an active engagement of female citizens with the state and the opening up of development agendas and policymaking to political contestation, the neo-liberal version of democracy and good governance rests on a minimal, non-political technocratic state geared towards the goal of economic efficiency.

Conclusion

Three broad issues emerge from the discussion. First, the issue of women's political marginalisation must be framed against South Asia's great paradox of democracy and social and economic inequality that has particular salience for the bulk of poor, economically underprivileged women in the region. There is a clear class dimension to the issue of women's political marginalisation relatively unaddressed in the literature on gender and governance in South Asia. The institution of the welfare state – so crucial towards developing a gender-just society – is presently in the process of being actively dismantled in South Asia. Poor, underprivileged women are far more vulnerable to the outcome of state withdrawal than their upper-class counterparts; state withdrawal in South Asia spells an end to the struggle for social equality; widening class disparity can only heighten gender inequality.

Second, even as the women's movement has addressed the under-representation of women in local and national decision-making bodies, it has been unable to exert much influence over political parties that seek women's votes but are largely indifferent to gender concerns. Women's groups need to deepen and broaden their engagement with political parties and female politicians in order to integrate gender concerns in party manifestos and government policy. The South Asian experience demonstrates that an increased presence of women in parliaments and legislatures is not necessarily coterminous with the advancement or realisation of gender equality in politics. Democratic governance is best advanced by the affirmation of women's *individual equality* with men in formal politics, a realisation of distributive justice for *all* citizens, and public recognition and protection of women's rights.

Finally, even as women's access to structures of governance has been facilitated by a greater engagement of women with political parties, this engagement is also fraught with dilemmas for the women's movement in general, and feminists in particular. Empirical examples from India, Pakistan, Bangladesh and Nepal suggest that a feminist activism informed by a shared understanding of gender interests can effectively subvert male dominance in politics.

9

Regional Organisations: A Theoretical Perspective

— Dr. Sanjeda Warsi

Regional organisations are institutional mechanisms for regional cooperation and integration on the basis of collective action to promote common security and welfare. Regional organisations have come to assume increasingly important role in the contemporary world and regionalism has become a pervasive feature of international affairs. There is a global trend towards the establishment of regional mechanism of cooperation as regional arrangements are one way in which states in different parts of the world respond to the challenges of globalisation. By providing a framework for cooperative problem-solving amongst states, International Organisations have modified traditional power politics in some regions like European Union. There are of course challenges to these cooperative institutional arrangements in the form of rising tide of populism, right-wing nationalism and immigrations but we consider it a phenomenon yet to provide definite direction.

After the First World War, the field of IR focused on International Organisations, an era often referred to in academic international relations as idealism. Realists dubbed those who promoted these organisations as idealists who ignore true nature of international politics, rooted in power and interest. Yet following the Second World War, there was even more emphasis by great powers to construct International Organisations. With the birth of United Nations Organisation, there was a brief resurgence of liberal sentiment, although the return of Cold War power politics ended this beacon of hope. After the end of Cold War, neo-liberal Institutionalists have the greatest impact on academic discourse in US and elsewhere. International Organisations and regional integration are today, established sub-fields of International Politics. Before 1980, the study of International Institutions was descriptive and lacking an overarching analytical framework. This situation changed with the publication of two important works; Robert O Keohane book *After Hegemony* (1984) and *International Regimes* (1983) by Krasner. With these works this subfield became less normative and increasingly theoretical. Today, we have so many analytical constructs that can be applied to our understanding of regional organisations.

Neo-Liberalism and Regional Organisations

Liberal Institutionalists believe that the spirits of war and commerce were mutually incompatible. Free trade and removal of barriers to commerce as in case of regional economic integration in Europe was inspired by the belief that the likelihood of war between states would be reduced by creating a common interest in economic cooperation amongst members of same geographical region. Earlier David Mitrany (1966) and Earnst Haas (1958) also argued that in the beginning cooperation between states would be achieved in technical areas where it was mutually convenient but once successful it could 'Spillover' into other functional areas. An ambitious attempt to set forth a general theory of interdependence was made by Robert Keohane and Joseph Nye, Jr, in Power and Interdependence (1977). They argued post-war interdependence is qualitatively different from earlier and simpler kind of interdependence. It is 'Complex Interdependence'. Complex interdependence is the term that according to these thinkers describes a world in which actors other than states, significant non-state actors participate directly in world politics, in which a clear hierarchy of issues does not exist as envisaged by neo-realist thinkers (they prioritise 'high politics' over 'low politics') and in which force is an ineffective instrument of policy. They strongly argue that military force is not of decisive relevance to all aspects of International relations. These neo-liberals are critical of the naïve assumptions of the nineteenth century liberals that commerce will automatically breed peace. Transnational cooperation, open economy and free trade provide incentives for peace and cooperation but do not guarantee it. To engineer cooperation, planning and negotiations are two important pre-requisites and existence of international institutions will help in achieving cooperation. Neo-liberal Institutionalists claim that these international institutions foster international interdependence and cooperation.

In this Context, regional organisations, are important determining features of the international anarchic structure. These organisations provide forum in which states can mitigate collective action problems that threaten stable patterns of cooperation. Regional organisations can perform monitoring functions, providing assurance that others are living up to the terms of their commitments. They are forums for negotiations to resolve coordination problems, and to learn about the preferences and constraints facing other governments. They create Structures for enforcement and dispute resolution, although actual enforcement powers crucially remain in the hands of member states. Globalisation has introduced states with new problems that states are unable to deal unilaterally. New global political problems require global solution through global and regional governance mechanism. For these neo-liberal institutionalists, the focus on mutual interests extends beyond trade and development issues. Now states need to address new security concerns like the threat of global terrorism, Intra state civil and ethnic conflicts, problems related to environment and proliferation of radiological, chemical, biological and nuclear weapon that threatened regional and global security. That's why; successful responses to security threats require the creation of regional and global institutions that promote cooperation among states and the coordination of policy responses to these new security threats. This does not mean that international institution can take precedence over state role in world politics. For neo-liberal institutionalist states remain the key actors in world politics but not the only important actors. States are rational actors and seek to maximise their interest in all issue areas. States seek to maximise absolute gains through cooperation and are less concerned with gains or advantages achieved by other states in cooperative arrangements. The greatest obstacle to cooperation is non-compliance or cheating by states. States by and large comply with the agreements they make. Though compliance is not easy to ensure and is related to the convergence of expectations achieved by an institution, occurred even without enforcement mechanism. In this competitive environment cooperation is never without problems, but states will cooperate with such organisations if they provide states with increasing opportunities to secure their national interests.

Neo Realism and Regional Organisations

Neo realism emphasises importance of states as unitary actors in international politics, if there are other actors they are less significant. All these actors operate and interact in an anarchic structure of international system. This means there is no overarching central authority to enforce rules and norms to safeguard the interest of global community. The structure of international system determines behaviour of the actors and constrains their choices. States have acquired self-help mechanism to achieve their national interest in this anarchic competitive system and always favour self-help over cooperation. In this structural anarchy they have security dilemma and they prefer to see all other states as potential enemies to their national security. Though their primary motive is to maximise security but it creates an anarchic competitive environment.

Grieco., J.(1988) in *'Anarchy and the Limits of Cooperation: a Realist critique of the Newest Liberal Institutionalism'* focuses on the concepts of relative gains and absolute gains. He is critical of neo-liberal institutionalists who claim that states are mainly interested in absolute gains in any cooperative arrangements. He claims that states are interested in increasing their power and influence and to increase their capabilities they will cooperate to achieve these absolute gains. However, how gains are distributed is an important issue and how much power and influence other states might achieve, that is relative gains, in any cooperative endeavour is more important issue. States may abandon any regional arrangement if they see other neighbouring states are gaining more from such organisations. As anarchy requires states to be preoccupied and more concerned with relative power, to be sure about their security and survival, it is wrong to exaggerate the impact of regional organisations on state behaviour. Such institutions donot mitigate the constraining effects of anarchy on cooperation. Powerful states may determine outcome of such regional arrangements by manipulating rules and decision-making processes. Whenever a choice is to be made between national interest and regional cooperation, national interest certainly would take precedence over regional cooperation. Moreover, membership of such organisations is not binding on member states; they may withdraw any time from such regional arrangements if these become a hindrance in achieving their goals of high politics.

Critical Perspectives on Regional Organisations

In the late twentieth century, neoliberal institutionalism and neo-realism have come under challenge. Mainly critical theorists question the rationality of these theories. They suggest a deep understanding of the illiberal nature of such institutions and putting them to critical scrutiny. There is massive democratic deficit in such institutions as it is evident that issues of international peace and security is determined by only fifteen member states in Security Council, of whom only five has power to veto any decision. Always there is danger of a hegemon to overpower such institution to achieve its interest as USA ensured smooth operation of post-World War-II liberal institutions. Robert Cox (1981) also discusses the nature of the theory in his very famous article *'Social Forces, States and World Orders: Beyond International Relations Theory'*. He claims that 'Theory is always for someone, and for some purpose. He challenges the claim of timeless, objective knowledge of neo-realist thinkers. Subjectivity is central to any theoretical endeavour. From the selection of a problem, deciding ontology and choosing of particular methodology to the epistemology, it is theoretical preferences of those who create knowledge, dominate over them. Their use of particular methodology (Scientific methodology) is biased as they try to justify a political order, which according to them is perfect and desirable. He distinguishes between problem solving theories and critical theories on the basis of the purpose of such theories. No theory can be objective or value free as theory never exists in void. This can be easily understood, if we analyse who are benefitted and what purpose is served under such political order. A problem solving theory is a status quo theory. It legitimizes and reinforces existing political order. It does not challenge it. Only powerful states derive all the benefits and poor suffer. When realism claims that 'history is the same damn thing over and over again' it serves the interest of those who prosper under the prevailing order. This is also true with neo-liberal institutionalism, as it also accepts the parameters of the present order, and thus helps legitimate and manage an unjust order through some undemocratic liberal institutions. For critical theorists, it is not required to manage and maintain such unjust political order through certain institutions rather need is to challenge existing world order and transform it accordingly. Critical theory does not take institutions and social and power structures as timeless but calls them into question by analysing their origins and how and whether they might be in the process of transformation, and, where possible, assisting social processes that can potentially lead to emancipatory change. Once an emancipatory transformation is achieved, just institutions would be created.

Globalisation and role of regional organisations

Globalisation is understood as a process of increasing interconnectedness between societies in such a way that events in one part of the world have effects on peoples and societies far away. Hyper globalists argue that it is bringing about the demise of Westphalian sovereign nation-state as states and governments are no longer in control of their own social and economic processes. Their actions are conditioned by the forces of globalisation and at times they are helpless in achieving their larger ends. To manage the effects of globalisation, states from some particular regions are coming closer to create some regional cooperation. Not all the time they are successful in achieving regional integration but some regional cooperation is established through formal regional organisations. States alone are not capable to protect their national economy, so a different form of protectionism is being exercised to regulate uncontrolled movements of capital through collective regional control over global market forces- and to counter the more negative social consequences of globalisation.

The most successful model of regional integration by far is the European Union. Though, Brexit shows even that success is only partial.

Different member states of European Union, many a times, had to deal with the issues related to sovereignty like how far regional integration could go and how much sovereignty to cede to a regional government. The European Union represents an ongoing and dynamic experiment in international relations and its members continue to negotiate on several issues. After the enlargement of European Union in 2004, 2007 and 2013 when Croatia joined as its twenty-eighth member, many states especially Britain were concerned about the enlarged union, if not reformed would find it difficult to take decisions. On June 23, 2016 British voters chose to leave the European Union through a referendum. What is unclear is the impact that Brexit will have on those states and regions moving towards regional integration. So far EU has served as a model for successful regional integration, Brexit may encourage revisionist states to review their own regional policies and many states may lose their commitment in such organisations. Neo-realist certainly will look at this development in terms of national interest taking supremacy over regional interest. It is pertinent to mention here that regional arrangements like SAARC could never deliver because of rivalry between India and Pakistan and both the states are more concerned with security and other strategic issues. Cancellation of SAARC summit in 2016 is not a new thing. Almost 12 summits could not take place because of political problems in the region. As all the regions throughout the world witness different impact of the process of globalisation, they also follow different pattern of regionalism, based on their historical and cultural contexts.

Conclusion

This chapter has shown briefly how regional organisations have become a pervasive feature of world politics and what are the different perspectives available to provide a theoretical understanding of regional organisations as international institutions established to foster cooperation between the states. State-centric writers have two different lines of arguments where neo-liberal institutionalist are highly optimistic about the role of such institutions in establishing cooperation in different areas from terrorism to environment, neo-realists are more concerned about security and self-help and do not look at regional institutions disconnected from the distribution of power. They would site Brexit as an example to prove their stance, while neo-liberal institutionalist may talk about issues like trade, terrorism and environment that have moved from margins to an increasingly central place on the international agenda. If some island may vanish by submerging due to increase in sea level because of global warming then it is better to redefine the concept of security and it would be better to interact and cooperate. Regional organisations can prove to be important forum for interaction, discussion and cooperation. Third perspective discussed in the chapter is critical perspective that questions all existing knowledge on the basis of distribution of gains, made in the society. For them all theoretical understandings are biased if these do not lead us towards emancipation of humanity. Need, according to them, is to bring social transformation to bring emancipation and to establish institutions those may create just political order. The process of globalisation is promoted and directed by the powerful states and promote their interest. It should not be a surprise that USA has been one of the foremost proponents of globalisation. Finally, regional organisations as a global phenomenon are here to stay with the differences between the kinds of regional arrangements that are being developed in different parts of the world. Some states may be more integrated some less, some arrangement may be an expression of local attempts to accommodate and respond to the challenges of globalisation, there is no denial of the significance of these institutions.

References

1. Cox, R. (1981). Social Forces, States and World Orders: Beyond International Relations Theory, *Millennium: Journal of International Studies,* 10/2: 126-55.
2. Grieco, J. (1988). 'Anarchy and the Limits of Cooperation: A Realist Critique of the Newest Liberal Institutionalism' *International Organisation*, 42 (August): 485-507.
3. Haas, E. B. (1958). *The Uniting of Europe: Political, Social and Economic Forces 1950-1957.* (Stanford: Stanford University Press).
4. Keohane, R. O. (1984), *After Hegemony cooperation and Discord in the World Political Economy*, (Princeton: Princeton University Press).
5. Keohane, R. O. and Nye, J.S., Jr (1977), *Power and Interdependence: World Politics in Transition,* (Boston: Little, Brown).

6. Krasner, S. D. (1983) (ed). International Regimes (Ithaca NY: Cornell University Press).
7. Mitrany, D. (1966). *A Working Peace System*, (Chicago: Quadrangle).
8. Waltz, K. (1979). *Theory of International Politics*, (New York: Random House).

10

Dynamics of India-Pakistan Relations: Implications for South Asia

— Wajahat Qazi

India and Pakistan- the centre of gravity of the South Asian region- appear to be in the throes of transitions. It could be stated that both countries are at an "inflection point- a business term which denotes a turning point or significant change. This has a bearing on the ideational rubric of these two South Asian neighbours. The very "Idea(s) of India and Pakistan" appear to be evolving and there appears to be a concomitant change in the nature of their polities, societies and economies. While there is disagreement over both the conventionally accepted "Idea of India" and to some extent that of Pakistan, our peg and predicate for the essay would be these very Ideas. Given the rather indelible link between Ideas and politics and their import on "practical" life, institutions and quotidian practices of people where these get reified, the central puzzle of our essay would be:

> "What is the nature of transitions that are occurring in core South Asia-India and Pakistan- and what implications and consequences follow from these for the two nations in contention, the South Asian region and the world at large?"

Our focus is on ideas because Ideas are important in politics and political lives of nations. We, therefore, privilege ideas and ideational change over instrumental and rational view of politics. The former presupposes radical change and the latter the path dependent variety. According to Beland and Cox, "Ideas are a primary source of political behaviour (2010:2). Cox and Beland define ideas as causal beliefs, ideas posit connections between things and between people in the world" (ibid). The authors add, "Ideas are also causal beliefs, or ideas, provide guides for action. Ideas help us to think about ways to address problems and challenges we face, and therefore are the cause of our actions (Beland and Cox, 2010:21). In a nutshell, ideas shape political behaviour.

Ideas are also inextricably linked or even enshrined in the design of institutions. "From this perspective, ideas are the foundation of institutions. At the core of politics is the way ideas are packaged, disseminated, adopted, and embraced. The muddle of politics is the muddle of ideas" (Beland and Cox, 2010:14).

Methodology

Our research is more qualitative than quantitative. This is not to demean the quantitative method but the nature of our enquiry militates against a "full blown" quantitative analysis. Our research design and data analysis to the extent our study warrants will be to tease out the validity of our arguments and our theoretical. The aim, to repeat, is not to validate our theory or arguments but to tease out their validity and "truth". In lieu of this, we will rely more on secondary sources. We will conduct a study of secondary sources with an interpretive and heuristic focus that could allow us to arrive at the import of these sources and their consequence.

From the perspective of qualitative research, we will attempt to understand the nature of India and Pakistan by examining respectively the nationalisms of the two countries. We will then examine the post-Independence nature and trajectories of India and Pakistan- political, economic and cultural. This will be overlaid by a synoptic view of the foreign, security and defence policies that the two states either chose or were compelled to choose under given circumstances. We will cull why the respective nationalisms of the two countries were "negative nationalisms"? Why did each country become each other's "Other"? And what implications followed from this –politically, security-wise and in terms of the foreign policies of each country? We will also examine the nature of the state of each country and its evolution thereof from a Weberian perspective overlain by the political economy of the state and state formation in both India and Pakistan.

Ideas, Nations and Nationalism

Juxtaposing ideas and Ideational change or changes in the respective "Ideas of India and Pakistan" and the super and substructure of the two nations then will have significant, far reaching, wide and deep consequences on their respective polities, the region and the world at large. Specifically and in reified terms, what would ideational change mean in terms of India and Pakistan? In this ideational churn, which of the two nations is affected more?

We will invert the order of these questions to arrive at an answer(s).

Nations and nationalism, in the Andersenian schema, are essentially ideas and/ or imagined constructs (Andersen:1982). Both India and Pakistan- both formatively and consequentially- correspond to what Benedict Andersen called "imagined communities" (1982). Pakistan or the Idea of Pakistan was premised on the notion of a separate homeland for South Asian Muslims (Cohen S, 2004); this came to be the two nation theory and concomitantly became the predicate of partition of British India. India, on the other hand, latched onto an Idea of a composite, plural and secular nation. It needs to be said that these foundational ideas of both India and Pakistan were what is termed in academic jargon as "ideal types". That is, while both nations jealously promoted and grafted these self definitions and constructs onto their respective institutional super and sub-structures, neither corresponded strictly and purely to these self definitions. However, for the purposes of this essay, we will take these constructs and, to twist Andersen's famous phrase, "imagined ideas" as a starting point.

Having made this assumption, we consider India first. Ideational change appears to be more discernable (and even rapid) in India than in Pakistan given the unprecedented rise of far right forces in the country. It has been asserted and even accepted that post-Independence India gyrated to a certain Idea whose ingress upon its institutions is/was deep and wide. This Idea of India rested upon a Republicanism predicated upon democracy, secularism, equality and unity in diversity. This, according to Sunil Khilnani, with the passage of time led to far reaching changes in Indian society. 'Democracy as a manner of seeing and acting upon the world is changing the relation of Indians to themselves (https://www.nytimes.com). This assertion implies a modern temperament and even modernity.

However, these assertions have not gone uncontested. Perry Andersen, in his polemical tract, " The Indian Ideology", points out that the "Idea of India meant, in reality, the fusion of the idea of "nation" with the Hindu religion". Andersen goes further to impugn India's democracy and states. "India's democracy — routinely celebrated as the world's largest — is actually a sham. The much-vaunted secularism that Nehru bequeathed to India was nothing more than a cover for "Hindu confessionalism,"(Andersen: 2014). This is very important claim given that it means the Idea of India as we have come to know it, is neither deep nor wide and throws the idea of transition into question.

While the extent to which this Idea was "reified" in India is debatable in India, the rise to power of Hindu far right party- the Bhartiya Janata Party (BJP) questions and impugns the conventional Idea of India. The BJP has a certain Idea of India that it believes reflects the "essence" of India and which in the party's schema should reflect in the institutional fabric, society and polity of the country. Hindu Nationalism, according to Christopher Jaffrelot seeks to work with democracy only in terms of 'the rule of the majority' and the sidelining of religious minorities would make this automatically into the rule of Hindus (2007). Jaffrelot, delineating the peculiar nature of Hindu nationalism adds that Hindu nationalism by rejecting the state in favour of the 'nation', an idea of 'earth' or 'bhoomi' rather than territory inscribed by a legal-administrative grid is in a league of its own. In this schema, according to Jaffrelot, land becomes central to for Hindus (2011).

Now let us consider Pakistan- a nation whose self definition was that of a modern Muslim state- a synthesis of Islam and democracy (Ahmed, A, 2005). Insofar as the country is concerned, the conventional and contemporary image of the country is that of a nation in "deep existential crisis" or even a country at war with itself. This may have been the case in the first decade of the 21st century. The country was indeed in the throes of an existential crisis but it would appear that Pakistan, while "muddling along" appears to be in consolidation phase. It needs to be stated here that contra the founders of Pakistan, the gradually became or morphed into what the great political scientist, Samuel Huntington called, a 'praetorian oligarchic state"(1968). That is a state form, wherein the Weberian sense of the state co-exists with a power structure that has ingress of feudal elements complemented by an institutional structure wherein the military is a significant component of this structure. This among other things, in terms of the foreign and even domestic policy fronts implied the primacy of security and a power political paradigm wherein the foreign and security policy aspect of politics became a surrogate for the domestic. Given the foundational ideas of both India and Pakistan, this meant that each became the other's "Other" (Chaturvedi: 2003).

However, if the term of reference is Pakistan, recent developments in the country- some kind of a review of its defence, security and foreign policies which most importantly suggestion a "rapprochement" with India (Kumar & Anand:2016) and have implications for the "power structure" and the institutional manifestation of this power structure of Pakistan- its military dominated praetorian elite and its ancillary allies. More importantly, given that it is believed by many that Pakistan draws its ideational and ideological "nourishment" by being India's "Other", there are clear cut implications on/ for Pakistani nationalism. While it has been suggested by some eminence grises like Stephen Cohen that the current state of Pakistan is the result of the unresolved tensions in the ideas that prevailed at the time Pakistan was founded (Cohen: 2004). This observation has been supported by the French analyst Christopher Jaffrelot, who stated that the various contradictions that define (d) Pakistan can either be traced to the "Idea of Pakistan"- roughly speaking, a homeland for South Asia's Muslims given that Islam does not appear to have been a glue for holding Pakistan (2014). But others have questioned these explanations and asserted that weak institutions and low rates of regime legitimacy have led to the "decay" in Pakistan (Rizvi: 2000)

Despite the debate and controversies thereof regarding the ideational genesis of India and Pakistan, it may be safe to posit that what we call "core South Asia" –India and Pakistan-is in transition.

Each transition will influence the other. How India evolves and concomitantly behaves will determine how Pakistan evolves and despite India's to a large extent, will hold true for India too. In a classic game theoretic and even Prisoner's Dilemma strategies, each country's disposition and comportment will affect the other. Given the size and even importance of the region, this will have global implications. How India and Pakistan relate to each other and how the region will relate to the world at large will inevitably have global consequences- in terms of global security, world politics, and economics.

Delineation of the respective foundational premises of India and Pakistan point out to the rather adversarial nature of these. It may be then held that it is the very Ideas of Pakistan and India that lock the two nations into an adversarial zero-sum dynamic. The question now is what concrete and reified consequences have these ideas led to? Answer(s) to the questions warrant an elaboration (albeit reductive given the constraints of this essay) of the trajectories of these nations?

It could be stated with confidence that India and Pakistan embarked on very different trajectories. The paths each country trod upon determined their orientation-outward and inward. India's advantage lay primarily in its early adoption of a Constitution which left a liberal, democratic and rather plural ingress upon its polity (Khanna:2008); conversely, Pakistan struggled with in forging a consensus on its Constitution and was a late adopter (Jalal:2014). It is obvious that the early death of Pakistan's founder, Muhammad Ali Jinnah was one factor led to this constitutional morass. The attendant political vacuum was filled by the Army and allied power structures (Ibid). In India, the political class was accorded primacy (Guha:2007). The starting points of each country were then vastly different. These developments and teething issues had both domestic, international and political economy implications. Even though India, in consonance with the post-colonial mood of the times chose an autarkic, socialist, mixed economy model in terms of political economy, Pakistan's political economy was an admixture of a military industrial plus a rentier political economy model interspersed with a degree of free enterprise. On the domestic front, Pakistan's "praetorian oligarchic" power structure reached deep into society rendering it into a somewhat "deep state" (Shafi K: 2012). While India, according to its Constitution liberal democratic and plural but the degree and extent of this structure was debatable; however, even this uneven pluralism rendered India's state society relations different from Pakistan. In terms of International Relations and politics, contra international relations theory, the domestic had an impact or influence on the international. Pakistan, for example, drew its foreign and security policies impetus both from domestic compulsions especially vis-à-vis India. Given that the structure of International politics, during this time, was bipolar and the Cold War determined the focus and locus of most nations' foreign policies and international orientation, both India and Pakistan also aligned themselves on the spectrum of Cold War rivalry. While India's commitment to what came to be known as Non Alignment (aloofness and neutrality from both superpowers of the day- United States and the USSR), the country treaded a delicate path with a slant towards the former USSR. Pakistan chose the other end of the spectrum: it made use of its geopolitical position and chose to ally with the United States in a bipolar world (Fair, C: 2014). (In the alliance system devised by the United States against the USSR, the SEATO and the CENTO were the vehicles to which Pakistan attached itself).

Fast forward a few decades.

The domestic and international orientations- foreign and security policies and political economy orientations- of both India and Pakistan could be said to have been inverted. The reasons for this inversion pertain to the structure of the post Cold War international system (a drift from unipolarity to a rather loose multipolar structure), globalisation and the securitisation of the so called "Global War on terror". India, on account of systemic pressures and a self conscious choice has discarded its "socialist" and autarkic shibboleths and opted for globalisation which demands a more open economic orientation (Tendulkar & Bhavani:2005) the country has reaped enormous dividends from this –both economically and politically. Pakistan, to the contrary, seemed to be stuck in a time warp-merely muddling along with an insidious "blow back" effect (Partaw, A M:2016) of its security and defence policies on the domestic front. However, as pointed out some change in its orientation seems to be afoot. If this change becomes path dependent then it will axiomatically have an impact on its power structure. Regardless of the structural and systemic changes that both nations are undergoing, the underlying zero sum dynamic between them seems to be a constant. The question now is: will it be systemic pressures that will break this zero sum grid lock or is the name of the game ideational? If both countries are in transition, would this imply an ideational change? If so what will it mean for both India and Pakistan, South Asia and the world at large?

We will make a digression here and take recourse to modernisation theory and examine the respective "modernity/modernisation" trajectory of India and Pakistan. Modernisation was a post-colonial quest for almost all states which were under the yoke of colonialism. The reasons pertained to the quest for evolution from a "premodern" or "traditional" to a modern polity. The state form plus a governance paradigm that modern was central to this. For post-colonial India, it was defined by Nehruvian ingress which sought to nudge India to a rationalist, scientific temper; for Pakistan, modernity meant a synthesis of Islam and the state- the apogee of modernity. At the risk of sounding tautological, it may be repeated here that the depth, extent and scope of modernity and modernisation in both India and Pakistan is debatable. Having said this, while none corresponded to "pure" modernisation types, elements of modernity could be discerned in both in different permutations and combinations. It needs to be stated here that pure modern type states or nations states may not actually exist but it may be conceded that if Western modernity is held to be the yardstick of modernity then pure modern type nation states may be too western a construct; their isomorphism across the world may not be possible. As the work of Susanne and Lloyd in the introduction to their book, "Modernity of Tradition" remind us, "The myths and realities of Western experience set limits to the social scientific imagination, and modernity becomes what we imagine ourselves to be (2008). Therefore, it can perhaps be safely stated here that both countries displayed "mixed regime" type elements. (The term regime here is employed in the sense of a model here; not a governance or government form or nature).

This critical point or even assertion is significant given our hypothesis and central question that both India and Pakistan are in transition. The larger point here is that the very identity, shape and form (ideational and even material) of either country was not or even is not settled. The Idea of Pakistan is a contended one; so is the Idea of India. And this contentious is salient contemporarily. In terms of the former, the issue of contention is the shape and form of Pakistan and in a different but in some senses similar sense so is the Idea of India. India is sought to be changed to its "essence"- an alleged hoary past wherein the country was defined by a "pure and idyllic" Hindu form and shape unsullied by "outsiders". This has assumed significance given the rise to power of the far right nationalist forces in India. Implied in this flux and churn is tension. The Idea of Pakistan is also challenged by different forces and alignments. If, the question, is the very foundational ideas of both are being questioned and reviewed, what form and shape will India and Pakistan assume? And what implications will flow from this?

Here we may take recourse to the great political scientist, Samuel Huntington who, in his classic, " Political Order in Changing Societies" essentially posited that change in political systems is caused by tensions within political and social systems (1968). Huntington's assertion, if a broad sweep of political change is taken, is a truism. If the political and social system(s) in India and Pakistan are in transition, then it follows that both countries system(s) are defined by tension and if this holds, then it is safe to infer some degree or even radical change in both countries. While this analysis tells us about change and transition and the logical deduction thereof, it does not make us any wiser about the nature, shape and form of this change and transition. Pinning down the form and shape of this change may amount to a mugs game given that invariably all transitions are fluid and tricky in nature. All we can do at this stage is to speculate.

Informed speculation will take us into the domain of positing a scenario or a scenario analysis. One plausible scenario that lends itself to analytical merit is that transition(s) that are occurring in India and Pakistan might lead to, what Christoper Snedden, calls, "expansion of the subcontinent of South Asia" (2015). What is alluded to here is that the concept of sovereignty and territorial nationalism-the bedrock and pedestal of nation states- might give away to a more expansive entity along the lines of the European Union. Here sovereignty might either be pooled and a supra-state or a federalist Union created that abridges and truncates sovereignty. Obiter Dictum, in this schema, the conflict in and over Kashmir- a residual legacy of the partition of the subcontinent and an issue emerging from the detritus of sovereignty, sovereign prerogatives and jealousies superimposed by zero sum territorial nationalism-would also collapse and get resolved in the vortex of this larger Union.

The other plausible scenario is that the churn and flux defined transition(s) and the tensions thereof might intensify the zero sum adversarial dynamic between India and Pakistan. This intensified rivalry might lead to war- perhaps of a limited variety given the existence of nuclear weapons in the arsenal of both states. What the outcome of this war would be remains in the domain what was called as the "unknown unknown" by the American strategist Donald Rumsfeld.

As the aphorism, "all war is bad politics" goes and given that wars do not lead to comprehensive settlements, or conflict resolution, it is clear that the former scenario is a better and more salubrious one for South Asia than the latter. But the problem is that this scenario while being the most rational one is, in fact too rational. Politics and nationalism are the stuff of emotions and emotions can be unwieldy and resistant to salubrious change. Therefore, the more expansive Union form or supra state form for the subcontinent would call for a more rational and more refined sensibility amongst the states, peoples and stakeholders of South Asia. In this sense, this scenario lies in the mists of the future. As such, nothing definitive can be foretold about the future of South Asia with precision.

What can be stated with a degree of certainty is that South Asia or the major component states of South Asia –India and Pakistan- are in transition. And given that tension, fluidity and churn is inherent in all transitions, the post-colonial form and shape of will be different from the past or even the present. This will, given the size of South Asia and the linkages with the world-trade, political and economic- will have implications on the world at large too. Whether this change will be salubrious or insalubrious will be contingent on the form that

South Asia and its major constituent states, India and Pakistan will take. We rest the case on hope and fervently wish for a politics, statecraft and leadership that guide these transitions and re-insert South Asia into the sinews of history in an idiom that is as glorious and great as the essence of South Asia.

References

1. Andersen, B, "Imagined Communities: Reflections on the Origins and Spread of Nationalism", Verso, 1983.
2. Akbar Ahmad, "Jinnah, Pakistan and Islamic Identity: The Search for Saladin", Routledge, 1997.
3. Andersen, P, "The Indian Ideology" ,Verso Books, London, 2013.
4. Beland, D and Cox, R, "Ideas and Politics in Social Science Research Ideas and Politics" 2010 in http://www.walkerinstitute.sc.edu/sites/walkerinstitute.sc.edu/files/00%20Introduction%20Final.pdf
5. Cohen, S, "The Idea of Pakistan" 2nd Edition, Oxford University Press, 2004.
6. Chaturvedi, S, "Process of Othering in the case of India and Pakistan" Tijdschrift voor economische en sociale geografie , 125-227, Vol. 93, Issue 2, 2002 in http://onlinelibrary.wiley.com/doi/10.1111/1467-9663.00191/abstract
7. Fair, C, "Fighting to the End: The Pakistan Army's Way of War" , Oxford University Press, 2014.
8. Guha, R, "India After Gandhi: The History of the World's largest Democracy", Harper Perennial, 2007.
9. Huntington, S, "Political Order in Changing Societies", 1968.
10. Jaffrelot, C, "The Pakistan Paradox: Instability and Resilience" Hurst Publications, United Kingdom, 2014.
11. Jaffrelot, C, "Hindu Nationalism: A Reader" Princeton University Press, 2007.
12. Jaffrelot, C, "Religion, Caste and Politics in India" Primus Books, 2010; Reviewed by Rowena Robinson Economic and Political Weekly, 45 (1), January 1, 2011.
13. Jalal, A, "The Struggle for Pakistan: A Muslim Homeland and Global Politics", The Belknap Press of Harvard University Press, Cambridge Mass, 2014.
14. Kumar, H and Anand, D, "India-Pakistan Meeting Raises Hopes for Improved Relations in http://www.nytimes.com/2016/04/27/world/asia/india-pakistan-foreign-secretaries-meet.html?rref=collection%2Ftimestopic%2FPakistan &action=click&contentCollection=world&region=stream&module=stream_unit&version=latest&contentPlacement=9&pgtype=collection&_r=0

15. Khanna, H R, " Making of India's Constitution", Eastern Book Company, 2008.
16. Khilnani, S, "The Idea of India", The New York Times in https://www.nytimes.com/books/first/k/khilnani-india.html, 1997.
17. Rudolph, L, "The Modernity of Tradition: The Democratic incarnation of Caste in India", The American Political Science Review, Vol. 59, no.4, December 1965.
18. Rudolph, L and Rudolph and S, " Explaining Indian Democacy, 1956-200: A fifty year perspective": The Realm of Institutions: State Formation and Institutional Change, Oxford University Press, 2008.
19. Rizvi, H, "The Military and Politics in Pakistan: 1947-1997", Sang-e-Meel Publications, 2000.
20. Partaw, A M, "Blowback from Pakistan's Harboring of Extremist Groups" in http://www.foreignpolicyjournal.com/2016/01/29/blowback-from-pakistans-harboring-of-extremist-groups/
21. Shafi, K, " If and Only If...", 2012 in http://tribune.com.pk/story/433564/if-only-if/
22. Snedden, C, "Understanding Kashmir and Kashmiris" Hurst and Company, London, 2015.
23. Tendulkar, S and Bhavani, T, "Understanding The Post-1991 Indian Economic Policy Reforms", 2005 in file:///C:/Users/Dell/Downloads/india-final-draft_c9e.pdf

11

Social Media: A New Tool of Political Campaign in South Asia

—*Bishnu Pokharel*

Abstract

Due to the tremendous development on Information Communication Technology (ICT), world has been connected as a single village. After the evolution of social media the interaction between worlds communities have rapidly increased. It has become important tool in many social transformations. Social media users are using this as a platform for different purpose and aims. Use of social media has spread everywhere; 'home to hospital', 'police stations to parliaments', 'schools to stationeries', 'societies to share markets', 'bus stand to bank' and so on. Due to common uses of social media, traditional types of political campaigns have been replaced by the campaign led through social media. South Asian region has seen rapid increase in utilisation of social media during the course of elections and political campaigns. Now, political parties are bound to go with people through social media and it is becoming a common culture of South Asian politics.

Key Words: *Social Media, Politics, Campaign, South Asia, Facebook, Twitter, Election, Online, Information Communication Technology (ICT), Internet.*

Introduction

World is dynamic and it is changing every moment. Change is the natural law so that dynamic nature of human society was in the past; it is here in the present and it will be exist in the future. With the passage of time everything is developing and society is moving forward. The movement of progress and development of human society has never stopped; if it stops, human society might be collapsed. Media, the medium of communication has also developed by this process of progress and discovery.

We can see enormous and incredible changes and developments in media. It was started with 'sign language' and now turned into 'cloud computing' and 'virtualisation of voices and visuals'. Some decades ago it was totally like 'unimaginable', there was no sense that one would share out own information worldwide via cloud base virtual feed like Facebook, Twitter and YouTube. However, in this era, the impact of self content creating and distributing forum known as 'social media' is undeniable in our society. There may be different perspectives and perceptions regarding social media but nobody can neglect its wider impact in all affairs of society. Definitely, it has impacted political affairs of South Asia as other type of media does. Considering social media as a field of study, this paper will throw light on role of social media in South Asian political campaigns with special reference to electoral campaigns.

Social Media and Politics

Society and politics are highly interdependent; we cannot isolate politics from society and vice-versa. In this twenty-first century society is deeply connected with social media; basically in urban area, social media is extremely popular among middle class and youths. Because of its strong connectivity with middle class and youth, within short period of time it has been placed as a popular culture in all over the world. As a result, social media couldn't be far from political issues and political activism. Politicians always prefer admired technique to get connected with society and they have chosen social media to face public as it is well-liked by huge chunk of population. That is why the mobilisation of social media and campaigns through social media has gained its popularity in political spare.

After 2000 many political campaigns became successful because of the active application of social media on it. Many political forces and social mobilisation groups used social media as a tool of transformations. In *'Social Media: The New Power of Political Influence'* Auvinen (2014) quotes Clay Shirky (2011), 'What do demonstration on city streets in the Philippines in 2001, the election of Barak Obama as President of the United State in 2008, revocation of the results in Spain in 2001, the so-called 'Arab Spring' in the Middle East in early 2001, and the 'Occupy Wall Street' movements that started in New York, also in 2001, all have in common?' (P. 4).

Writer further claims, 'They have all used social media to help organise such protests and mobilise their responsible agents. Yet these were much more than just about arranging a party: they all greatly exploited social media to establish communication network and move towards their objectives' (Avinen, 2014, p. 4). Like other part of the world South Asia also witnessed such mass mobilisation and political campaigns done through social media.

Impact in South Asia

South Asia is known as developing society in every sense, like infrastructures, technologies and knowledge. But we have seen rapid growth in information communication technology development than other type of development. Social media activism and interactions are depending upon ICT development. If ICT develops more, social media can blooms in faster way; if this sector couldn't develop social media also can't be flourished. The development of internet and social media has changed the traditional notions and perceptions in society. Media culture and mode of production and consumption of media content has been transformed from elitist vertical model to non-elitist horizontal model due to the social media (McDougall, 2012). In vertical model information use to come from tradition medias where common people do not have choice except believing it, but in horizontal model common people may reply, react as well as create and distribute own contents.

South Asian media culture also transformed from traditional vertical model to new horizontal model in recent years. Almost all countries of South Asia are witnessing currently the mobilisation of social media (any of existing) in political issues and this trend has been established in each and every country.

Indian politics always use to be burning and hyper during the election time. We can see political discussions, arguments, comment and critics everywhere from 'street to stage' and from 'farm-field to business-land'. But in recent elections time these discussions, arguments, comment and critics had taken place more in virtual world rather than actual land. And, those discussions have played vital role to change voters mind and shape of politics. During 'Lok Sabha Election 2014' social media have played vital role in election campaigns.

'The campaign has always been aggressive, the media obsessed and drama aplenty. Yet it has not been the year of the sound-byte, but one of a sound-byte 'seen to be driven' by hashtags. In an era of instant judgments, which television honchos are often criticized for orchestrating - this time the pressure seems to have doubled. The social media has changed not just the ecology of news production by taking the lead; it has also added a 'googly' to the playing field in politics' (Pandalai, 2013). Due to huge impact of social media for the first time, leading parties of India have appointed 'social media management team' for that (2014) election campaign.

According to the news report in various media some researchers have predicted that 160 of the Lok Sabha seats in the 2014 polls had affected by social media. After election the leading party Bharatiya Janta Party (BJP) leaders have given statement that social media campaign was one of the most important factors in its victory. They told that social media affected 30 to 40 per cent of the overall seats in that election and this number could go up to 60 per cent in next election, which will be in 2019 (Ali, 2014).

In election time BJP and its alliance succeed to show in social media that Narendra Modi is only hope for the progress of country. Corporate sector have also played key role to making him a heroic leader of Indian society form *'Chayawala'* to Prime Minister. They also used all type of media in any possible way and gave support for social media campaigns (Hasan, 2014).

Another social media war and great mobilisation has happened in Delhi assembly election in February 2015. In this election BJP and newly emerged Aam Admi Party (AAP) both have done huge campaign through social media and influenced voter by it. The social media role is crucial behind the AAP victory in Delhi election (Philipose, 2015, p. 10).

Both elections have shown that, the powerful and important role of social media in Indian politics, which can change entire scenario of Indian society. But these are not first movement which has acquired its popularity by social media. This type of political use of the social media in India was started from Anna Hazare-led India against Corruption (IAC) movement of 2011 (Philipose, 2015, p. 10).

Social media mobilisation in political issues and politics is spared all over the South Asia. In every country social media users are increasing and they are using this platform for political changes. Afghan youth are playing vital role to establish democratic process in their society through social media. In 2014 election, the campaign through social media led by urban youth them and many education institutes are also communicated and tried to aware people through social media (Larson and Noah, 2014, pp. 10-11).

Due to the social media movement inside country and outside country Sri Lankan war crime issue became international and many human rights organisation raised question about this issue. All human rights violence and war crime picture and photograph became viral through social media at first and then it became concern of matter for international community. For that matter many Sri Lankan have involved from inside and outside the country. Tamil Diasporas are using social media very actively to raise question about war crime and human right violence in country (Jegannathan, 2013).

Nepali social media users are also very active in political issues and they are participating in political debates in social forum (FNJ, 2012). In second constitutional assembly election in 2013 some Nepali social media users formed a political party, which name was *'Bibeksil Nepali'* and that party has participated in elections too. But they couldn't get any seat in assembly election (Ghimire, 2013).

In 2013 election, Pakistani political party as well as voters also used social media. Political parties have done campaign through social media in this election. They had not done same type of campaign in 2008 election (Khattak, 2013).

Recent election in 2013, Bhutanese political parties also have used social media and they mobilised people through informing social media (BBS, 2013). They made their fan page in Facebook and own handle in Twitter in election time.

In Bangladesh many youth are involving in creating new political idea through social media and they are creating virtual feed as protest platform (Azam and Forkan, 2013). Which has made many youth 'celebrity Facebookers' and 'microblogers' and they are shaping the fresh idea of politics.

Political parties of Maldives have used social media for election campaign in 2014 election. Many international observers of election reported that social media has been used in extensive way during election. The Chairman of Commonwealth Observer Group, Bruce Golding (2014) explained, 'they have also made extensive use of social media, television, radio, newspapers and online media' after the observation of election.

In recent years social media users are increasing in South Asia and its impact is vast in public spare. That is why political groups are more interested in bring into play of social media as a new tool for setting political agenda as well as campaigns.

Conclusion

Social media has become essential medium of sharing information. Now, everybody is making use social media for getting new information and most importantly people are using it as opinion forum. It has become part of our daily living. Because of its huge users social media turn into a biggest database of the world.

Political parties and politician always want to choose popular way to address mass. In current scenario social media is being used as the most popular way to concentration on people and many politicians are taking advantage. Now, everybody wants to use social media for their benefits, 'grass root people to government', 'opposition leaders to ruling party leaders'. South Asia cannot be exception of this change in global phenomena; as a result social media is acquiring great importance in an eye of political parties and government. Not only government and political parties, every individual are following social media and opining political views.

Social media platform has given opportunity to common people to convey their voices to mass, not only that it has given way to get connected even with state authorities. But in the meantime many destructive political groups are also availing same platform in order to make their activities accessible to public. For example, Islamic State (IS)'s activity and brutal killing videos on social media.

There is no single thing exists in the universe which does not have bad part so is the case with social media. That is why every individual and institution should be alerted while getting in to it.

References

1. Ali, I. (2014, June 6). *Social Media Played Big Role in India's Election.* Retrieved March 6, 2015 from http://www.voanews.com/content/social-media-emerges-as-a-key-tool-in-indias-election/1931238.html
2. Auvinen, A. (2012). *Social Media - The New Power of Political Influence.* Suomen Toivo-Thank Tank. Version 1.o, 4-4.
3. Azam, A. and Forkan, D. (2013). *Social Media is Politicizing the Youth of Bangladesh.* Academia.edu, Australia.
4. Bhutan Broadcast Service (BBS. (2013, May 15). *Social Media to Play Vital Role in 2013 Elections.* Retrieved March 13, 2015 from http://www.bbs.bt/news/?p=27337
5. Federation of Nepali Journalists (FNJ) (2012). *Social Media Survey Report.* Kathmandu.
6. Ghimire, S. (2013, November 2). *Rise of a New Force: Nepal Gears for Round II Constituent Assembly Elections.* Retrieved December 28, 2015 from http://www.huffingtonpost.com/subhash-ghimire/rise-of-a-new-force-nepal_b_4171659.html?ir=India&adsSiteOverride=in
7. Golding, B. (2014, March 24). *Maldives Parliamentary Elections 2014: Interim Statement.* The Commonwealth Observer Group.
8. Hasan, Z. (2014). *Manufacturing Dissent: The Media and the 2014 Indian Election.* Retrieved March 6, 2015 from http://www.sacw.net/article8681.html
9. Jegannathan, J (2013). *Social Media Sri Lanka's New War Zone. IPCS ISSUE BRIEF # 226.*

10. Khattak, I. (2013, June 7). T*echnology impacts Pakistani election.* Retrieved March 13, 2015 from http://centralasiaonline.com/en_GB/articles/caii/features/pakistan/main/2013/05/07/feature-01

11. Larson, A. and Noah, C. (2014). *Youth Mobilisation and Political Constraints in Afghanistan.* United States Institute of Peace, Special Report.

12. McDougall, J. (2012). *Media Studies, The Basics.* Routledge Tylir & Francis Group, London and New York.

13. Pandalai, S. (2013, May 1). *Social media overhyped in Indian politics.* Retrieved March 6, 2015 from http://www.atimes.com/atimes/South_Asia/SOU-01-010513.html

14. Philipose, P. (2015). *Can an Election Be Tweeted to Victory? AAP, Arvind and a City State Called Delhi.* Economic & Political Weekly, Vol. 1 No.8.

Marginalisation in Kashmir and South Asia

12

Minority within a Minority: The Case of Hindu Women in Bangladesh

— *Shafinur Nahar*

The concept of 'minority' emerged in the liberal democracy and its socio-political set up. The term "minority" often described the people who have less power, who are oppressed, or who are a subordinate segment within a political unit.[1] A person's religious affiliation, age, race, disabilities, sexual orientation, or gender can define or classify him/her as minority. Minority group is very small group in the society but small does not mean always that it has to be small in number but inferior in the sense of deprivation of rights compared to the majority group. There can be people who can belong to both a minority group and the majority group at the same time. Women are considered a minority group based on their gender and because they have been oppressed and controlled, and women of colour are often considered a minority within a minority.

Religious minorities are those persons who have different faith from the majority population who are in power. It is now accepted in many multicultural societies all over the world that the people have the right to choose and the right to practice their own religion. Women are considered minority in a broader sense because of the unequal treatment compared to male members of society and deprived of basic human rights. When women belong to a religious minority group it can be defined as religious minority women group due to their different practice of religious faith to the majority group. In our part of the world, i.e. South Asia, if we take up a case study of women from minority religious communities in Bangladesh, the position of minority women is more vulnerable than majority women. They are under a 'double curse' situation i.e. first as members of a religious minority, especially one viewed with hostility and anger by the majority and secondly, by virtue of being women. This double cursed status is first at 'official' or state level, secondly at the public level and thirdly at the individual level. These hurdles make life really difficult for minority women at many levels, e.g. economic, political, and social, etc.

The Bengal (east and west) was a Hindu majority area before 1947s. The effect of 1947 partition broke the trust and the peace forever between two communities- Hindus and Muslims, which fastened the migration and exodus from both sides. People lost their home, land, family and women and children were the terrible victim of those riots. Talbot and Singh described the violence of riots in East Bengal (now Bangladesh). With respect to the Noakhali riots, one British officer spoke of a 'determined and organised' Muslim effort to drive out all the Hindus, who accounted for around a fifth of the total population."[2]

The 1950 and 1964's communal riots in Noakhali, Barisal and Khulna, exodus of Bengali Hindus during 1971 war, demolition of historic Babri mosque in 1992, Gujarat riot in 2002, the ethnic cleansing of Rohingya Muslims in Myanmar etc. have fueled a widespread anti-minority, especially anti-Hindu feeling in the country. Other critical role is played by Indian presence. As India is the neighbouring country of Bangladesh and 80 per cent of India's population is Hindu, so if anything like communal riot takes place in India, its effect also would leave a huge impact on the internal situation of the Hindu minority people in Bangladesh.

Since 1971, the Hindus have been the main target of persecution by the majority group. For different political gains, they are being used as Ping-Pong ball in the country. They are used as vote bank for particular political party during the election and when the vote game is over, they are being eliminated from the country. The trend of eliminating the minorities has gained a new dimension ever since the B.N.P. and its allied Islamic parties came to the power with an absolute majority in the parliament in October, 2000. After that election, the condition of Hindus in several places became worst such as the temples and Hindu god's idols were vandalised, some Hindu families were attacked and burnt by unknown thugs. Apparently, the Hindu women have just become the main victims of the part of the unfair aim of ethnic cleansing. They are being abused by rape for the solely biological purpose of the perpetrator. So some rapes are just animal-minded persecution. When the women from particular minority group were abused and raped continuously in a period of time by majority group, it cannot be taken as single incident rather systematic which must be very alarming to the humanity. After 2000, there are a number of cases where it has been found that women belonging to Hindu minority community became victims of rape and sexual abuse. Women have been raped as part of the strategy to terrorize and humiliate these communities[3], to grab the Hindu land and property, and to convert them into as part of Islamisation. Whenever there is any threat against the religious minority group, religious minority women are at more risk in Bangladesh. This reached to the peak in the most notorious ways in 2001, when the Bangladesh Nationalist Party (BNP) came into power on 1st October 2001. As a matter of fact, 14-year-old Purnima was gang raped at Ullapara, district: Sirajganj, eight days after the general elections. She describes as:

> "Nearly 30 people came to our house. I recognised many of them as my neighbours. They beat my mother almost senseless. I begged them to stop. They dragged me outside. I resisted but they hit me with sticks. I shouted to my sister to save me but they beat her too. I cannot tell you what happened next."[4]

Purnima's family found her unconscious three hours later in a field a mile from the village. Four young men, all supporters of the government and its coalition partner, the fundamentalist Jamaati-e-Islami party, were arrested but have not been charged.[5] When her family went to the local police station to lodge a complaint, the police refused to accept it. Finding no alternative, they obtained a certificate from the civil surgeon and lodged a case with the magistrate's court. Under Section 164, the magistrate recorded Purnima's statement in which she mentioned names of 15 perpetrators. When the magistrate asked the police to arrest the culprits, only five of them were arrested. Afterwards, the victim's family was threatened to withdraw the case. The local MP and other ruling party leaders filed a petition with the home ministry seeking reinvestigations into Purnima's rape case. The real perpetrators managed to be freed on bail.

Purnima Case is more concerned but in this style matters are still happening even till the date. Exactly similar one occurred just in November 2011, where the rapist forced to withdraw the case before the eyes of the authorities. A huge number of incidents happen that the rapists often escape. In a civilised country, for a rape case, the presumption of innocence is not applicable for a rape accused person. The accused has the burden of proving himself innocence. But in Bangladesh, the law applies differently. If the minority woman is poor and week, justice is often denied. It is very much appalling fact that 99 per cent case of the communal perpetrators have gone scot-free, whether through the lacuna of law, or by the aid and assistance of the ruling political party.[6]

The war criminals' tribunal is also one of the factors which led the violence against Hindu minority group as well as Hindu women. The ruling party came to the power promising that they will ensure justice for victims of crimes took place during the liberation war of 1971. Most of the listed war criminals that have been accused and convicted for such crimes by the war crime tribunal are several Islamic Party leaders. Consequently, the execution of some war criminals resulted in violence against minority people all across Bangladesh. But the surprising fact is that in some instances, the Awami League activists who are known to be the savior of minority people were found to be the perpetrators of violence against minority.[7] There are so many examples of how Hindu minority women are denied justice during the period of Awami League Government. For example, there is a case of Hindu girl gang raped in Satkhira district. The case is derived from Odhikar's Fact Finding Report.[8] On February 26, 2013, Gita Rani (18) a student of 12th grade and belonging to Hindu community went to a village fair and she was raped by a group of 7-8 miscreants. Her family and relatives tried to file a FIR against the scoundrels but the police denied six times to take any case. Finally, the Officer-in-Charge recorded the statement when Gita herself appeared with her family members on March 6, 2013 at the police station. The police recorded FIR with the accused people's false name. A case was filed under section 7/9(3)/30 of the Prevention of Repression against Women and Children Act, 2000 (amended 2003). Besides putting false names; for the purpose of filing the case, the Officer-in-Charge took a bribe from Gita's uncle. It is to be noted that filing FIR is a right of the victim and is provided without any cost as per law in any police station. The case of Gita Rani is just an example of how vulnerable minority women are and how they are exposed to sexual abuse. The more disappointment is the fact that it is difficult for victims to put the criminals on trial as the administration with their corrupt practices let criminals go away encouraging them to carry out such crimes over and over again.

Hindu minority women face severe consequences resulting from the oppression and attacks on them. Most often the violence leaves them in a state of fear, psychological trauma and helplessness. They are threatened, killed, raped, and propaganda is spread against them. Consequently they leave the homeland and migrated to other country. Having found no shelter, they were forced to flee to the neighbouring West Bengal, India or other parts of the country. Government and many non-government organisations in some cases stretch their helping hand to the sufferers but that can hardly repair their loss of lives and security compensated in the form of money.[9] Forced migration and deprivation of right of getting justice create an identity crisis for Hindu women. These dreadful situations make them re-think whether or not to stay where they lived for ages. In the face of all these attacks and violence some still stay bearing the tortures of the attackers who are patronised and indemnified by political parties.

Bangladeshi media plays a very strange role during the violence against the minority Hindu women. Media attention on recent minority issues is abundant. A number of national and international newspapers reported on minority issues. Despite this fact, there is still debate about the role of media on the very issue which has been largely politicised. The process of politicisation often resulted in contradictory reporting that confuses general people about the extent to which minorities are affected, which groups are perpetrating violence etc. Quality and ethics of media reporting on the issue is still questionable. Sometimes it is seen that some events go unreported with purpose. Two major attacks on Hindu community in Hathajari and Chittagong carried out in February 2012 can be cited as examples. These events remained much under the radar. The reason why media does not want to publicize certain events is to a large extent political. Much media of Bangladesh decided not to embarrass the so-called progressive secular government by publishing these stories of minority persecution. During the immediate aftermath, government leadership, in the face of utter failure to control the situation in a timely manner, found it convenient to blame the opposition political parties. Eight months have passed, but no real efforts have been made to investigate and punish the perpetrators in Hathajari.[10]

Moreover, different newspapers provide contradictory information on the same event. Moreover, when rumors against minorities are provoked, media do not play its due role by providing true and uniformed information. In an interview with The Daily Star, Salimullah Khan, professor of General Education Department, ULAB says that "The fact that people are buying the rumors and reacting to them indicates that the media has failed largely to play its role." (The Star, 17 January, 2014)

In many cases it has been seen that media reports accused a particular group behind all attacks and atrocities. After investigating those very events, it has been found that those reports exaggerated the role of a particular group in the attack while another group is found guilty. This malpractice of media around minority issues is so unfortunate that people of Bangladesh and minorities themselves being confused about the facts and figures have been losing trust over the media.

State has its machineries, the law enforcement agencies, which are remunerated to protect people's lives and properties. But in the recent spree of killing and violence all across Bangladesh after February 28, 2013 till election period, their role has been utterly inappropriate. It is reported in different media pieces that law enforcement agencies remain unmoving while the situation badly demanded them to be on the spot. No actions when actions were needed.

In last few years, Bangladesh has witnessed a dramatic escalation in anti-minority violence and a growing climate of religious intolerance. It has been observed that there are reductions of violence against minorities while the Awami League (AL) was elected in 2008. But from the past three years, religiously motivated violence targeting Hindu women have increased due to the several issues for example verdict of war criminals. Minority Hindu women have suffered extremely bearing the effect of religious violence. It is a manifesto of Islamic extremists' by doing sexual violence and forced conversions of Hindu girls and this intention comes from the idea of creating a Hindu free Bangladesh. The religious intolerance leads the violence against Hindus in Bangladesh. The minority Hindu women are always objects of political tool. India's negative role to its minority Muslim citizens has a great impact on the Hindu women in Bangladesh. The majority of Muslims in Bangladesh have the feeling that Muslims in India suffer at the hands of the majority and Muslim women suffer during communal riots. This has an impact in Bangladesh. There is a need to increase the consciousness among the ignorant majority Muslims that violating the honour of Hindu women is not an honour for Bangladesh. Media is considered as the fourth pillar of a nation. So media should act neutral and should not hide the news of violence against Hindu women done by sections of population. They should bring out the news to discourage further violence. The political parties in Bangladesh should stop playing with the sentiment of majority Muslims against Hindus and stop using Hindus as weapon. They should be more democratic to keep the rights of Hindu women. Besides, draconian laws like Vested Property Act should be removed to grab Hindu land holdings by the majority Muslim community.

In order to identify reasons of declining minority population from 29.7 per cent in 1947 to only 9.7 per cent in 2011, a special commission as well as a national minority commission should be formed. There must be a strong political commitment from political parties and from the highest level of the government to protect minorities from recurrent violence. Hindu minority women must not be used as an instrument of politics to play blame game and gain benefits. The enforcement of law with impartial outlook could make a difference and establish rule of law in the country. Media can play a responsible role towards the Hindu minority women. They serve the purpose of majority group. However, if there is an independent media (even a small one) that represents minority rights, and then there can be some protection of such Women's rights- but sadly, such media are missing.

The 9th parliament has amended the constitution retrieving provisions of 1972 constitution where secularisation of the state is a major policy basis. But mere restoration of secularism does not seem to ensure equal status and equal right of the Hindu, Buddhist, Christian and other ethnic minorities. At least, recent violence against them all across Bangladesh made it a constitutional rhetoric. So what we need to have is a concrete policy on minority affairs articulating their rights, promotion plan, and stern penalty for any sort of violence against them.

Some steps can be taken by the government or by the state to protect the Hindu minority women. There should be a separate ministry on minority issues should be established to ensure a more substantive approach towards issues relating to the minorities and to facilitate the formulation of overall policy and planning, coordination, evaluation and review of the regulatory framework and development programmes for the benefit of the minority communities. Local government/ administration should immediately intervene when Hindu minority women need help or security and take necessary initiatives. Any discriminatory law, act, or provision such as Vested Property Act against minority community should be repealed. Finally, government must compensate the affected families all over the country adequately and ensure security for them. Political leaders and parties should not use the religious sentiment against the minority group for serving their own purpose.

There must be a strong political commitment from political parties and from the highest level of the government to protect minorities from recurrent violence. Hindu minority women must not be used as an instrument of politics to play blame games and gain benefits. The enforcement of law with impartial outlook could make a difference and establish rule of law in the country. Further, protection of minorities in South Asia should be considered as a sort of new social contract among governments and civil society organisations. The countries in South Asian region have inherited divided communities along with divided borders. There are social and cultural commonalities and present day information revolution has made countries unable to block any sort of bad news from any part of the region. It is essential that countries in South Asia can use SAARC platform to fight the curse of communalism. Further we need to make use of South Asia Free Media Forum to fight all such problems which have vitiated peace and harmony in the region. Media houses of one country should be permitted to work in another and report freely on all internal matters and the same should not be considered as interference in internal affairs of a country.

References

1. Myers, 2007, p. 42.
2. Talbot and Singh, The Partition of India, Cambridge University Press, 2009, p. 67.
3. Ananta Yusuf, Communal Terror Continues, The Star, 17 January, 2014.
4. http://www.theguardian.com/uk/2003/jul/21/bangladesh.
5. http://www.theguardian.com/uk/2003/jul/21/bangladesh.
6. Shahriar Kabir, for Conference on "Election and Human Rights in Bangladesh, at 1 UN Plaza, 30 Sept 06.
7. AL men attacked Hindus: discussion, New Age, 10 January, 2014.
8. Odhikar Report 2014, "Gang rape of a girl in Satkhira District: Allegation against police for putting false information in the FIR and taking bribe."
9. Financial Times, 13 January, 2014.
10. The Daily Star, 5 October, 2012.

13

Backward *Bangladesh*: Ethnography of a Kashmiri Village

— Mohammad Zakaria

From a newspaper report suddenly I came to know that Kashmir has a village named after Bangladesh- the country of my origin. That report (Rasool, 2015) was too short to meet my quest for knowing the village and it provoked me as a Bangladeshi to investigate further the mystery of the village. Interestingly what I discovered by several visits to the small village is completely a different Kashmir. Doubtlessly, the village is too small to be a representation of social facts of the Kashmir Valley. However, there is a situation for an ethnographer to study and draw some insights having relevance for policy planners of the state. Bangladesh in popular Kashmir imagination represents poverty, economic backwardness and migration. All this carries some truth but the fact is that Bangladesh is now no longer a basket case. Its economic and developmental image is far better.

In this paper, following the topographic of the village, I present an overview of the population and different aspects of contemporary life of the village under study. How do the people express their love and heart is another aspect to understand a society and its value system. In this study all these aspects have been touched including the class structure of the village that is compared with the larger Kashmiri society. And finally the internal and external aspects of the society are brought into the discussion.

Basically, during my two years stay in Kashmir, I have developed some understanding about the overall Kashmiri society. The impact of religion in the daily life (especially the Sufi trends), hospitality, and simplicity are very common in the society. Moreover, as of now, the religious and sectarian identities are very sharp in the society. While studying the *Bangladesh* village, I have tried to crosscheck those facts, whether present or not, in the village reported to me indirectly. This study is conducted through a deductive approach.

Journey to Bangladesh in Kashmir

Bangladesh village is officially situated in Aaloosa *Tehseel* of Bandipora district. It, along with seven more settlements, constitutes Kehnoosa *panchayet*. But, *Bangladesh* is more proximate to Watlab of

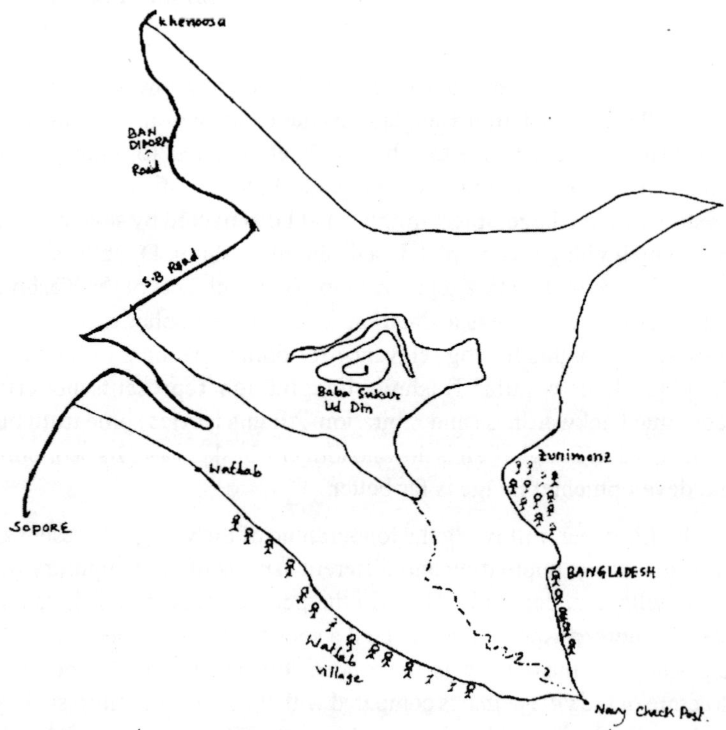

Map of the area drawn by the author, with the help of Google map

Sopore than Bandipora. From Bandipora town very few people know about the village. In order to go to the village one has to stop at Kehnoosa, the midst of Bandipora-Sopore road. There anybody can direct you the way. Turn left, walk through the muddy road for at least an hour you will reach to *Bangladesh* where people live on fishing. People ask curiously, 'why are you going there?' The left side of that road is Wullar Lake, and on the right side, it has mighty mountains. The famous Sufi shrine Baba Shukur-Ud-Din is situated on the top of the next mountain from the village which is known to each and every dweller. There are four villages – *Kehnoosa Ghat*, *Khud Mulla*, *Zurimonz* and *Bangladesh* respectively – each of them lay on the bank of the lake while the last two are very adjacent. After *Bangladesh* at the corner of Wullar there is a Navy Check post and next from that the Watlab area of Sopore starts, which is clearly manifested to be far ahead. Apple orchards, good school buildings, macadamized roads, big and beautiful homes are seen in Watlab while these were unseen in *Bangladesh*. The actual road that goes through Bangladesh village remains most of the time under water.

The village was founded in 1971, co-incidentally with the birth of my nation i.e. Bangladesh. Octogenarian Habibullah Bhat, the oldest person of the village informed, 'in 1971, some five-six houses of Zurimonz village were burnt down to ashes. They built new houses in a new place nearby. As in the same year, the then 'East-Pakistan' became free (*azad*) and named Bangladesh, so did the newly built *Mahalla'*. The local primary school teacher, who possesses masters degree in Political Science from Kashmir University, added that in last four decades the houses of the village increased to almost fifty. However, officially it was functioning as a part of Zurimonz till 2010 when it was registered as a separate village in Bandipora District Collector's (DC) office'.

Apparently, the story says, the broader political transformation of the eastern corner of the South Asian region – the creation of a new country – had set a historic effect over this small fishermen community. They had named their new built houses after the country although, after four decades, that naming of the village gives very less sense to the people. An old village man Ghulam Mohammad Bhat stated "that they were living in Zurimonz. Now the new village is called Bangladesh. And he is not aware that there is another country with the same name. But, the kids and youths of the village, even the women know the country Bangladesh through cricket. However, in their village there is no place to play cricket". In Kashmir what is observed is that anybody wearing old and dirty cloths is also someone who can be equated with a Bangladeshi. After the creation of Bangladesh International Red Cross will provide aid to the new country and many other developed countries would supply different day-to-day livelihood items to people of Bangladesh and hence any second hand and worn out clothing is known as "Bangladeshi Mall" in Kashmir.

A Demographic Overview

The village consists of around 50 houses. The school teacher of the village Mohammad Moqbool, informed that he conducted the 2011 census where the population of the village was 330 and now it must be around 350. The only government Primary School of the village has 40 student's one male and one female teacher. While visiting the school I observed that, the school has no building of its own. Two rooms of a family house, where the family lives have been rented for rupees 200 per month. But, since 2010, the rent has not been paid. However, the school is still functioning with those two rooms. There is no place to build a structure for the school because government cannot buy land. Somebody has to provide land which is not available. The 33-year old village *panch* Mohammad Hassan Bhat observed, 'a forest land in the hill side is supposedly to be given for the school, but, that needs many official settlements'. In fifth class of the school, there are seven female students and two boys as seen during the visit. Nevertheless, the children have hopes. Bilkis Farook, a student of the class comments was asked what she wants to be, 'I want to be a doctor' was her direct response.The village is largely illiterate. Only around 5-10 per cent of the people are literate while the average literacy rate in the state is 67.16 per cent (Economic Survey, 2013-14: 10). The highest educated women from the village is 9th class pass-out. During the visit a beautiful girl named Shayesta Ramjan was asked what she does. She answered, 'I left my school three years ago when I was in class VII. Now I work for the family livelihood. I climb the mountains to get firewood and grass for cows. I prepare cow dung as cooking fuel. I make handicrafts for some additional earning although our village does not have any industry of handicrafts. We don't get handicraft works from the government'. During one visit, a group of women and teenage girls were seen singing traditional song, *wanwoon*. All of them were illiterate or at best studied up to class VII. A marriage ceremony was going on. Food items, *wazwan* was being prepared. An old lady Mrs. Bhat told, 'we earn from the Wullar Lake and we burn all of that in marriages. Our marriage arrangements are no lesser than any other Kashmiri marriage. Marriage is the biggest festival for us'. From among males, there were three boys who passed BA till date. All of them are unemployed. From this village two young boys went to Saudi Arabia, they have sent good remittance for their family. Out of the nine students of the class interviewed six told they have television in their homes. Indeed, that is their primary medium of entertainment. The main food item of the people is rice. But, they have no land to cultivate. Only 5-10 families have land outside village. They buy rice from government shops. Under the Food Security Act, monthly a person can buy five kg(s) in rupees three/kg if the person is in bellow poverty line (BPL). In case of above poverty line (APL) the rice price is 10 rupees/kg. As of now maximum villagers are receiving rice in BPL category. However, under the revised policy, many of them are listed as APL on which they are not contented.

Religion-wise the village is predominantly Muslim populated. The first day when I met an old man, Ghulam Mohammad Bhat who is the father of the village *Panch*, he asked, 'are you a Muslim?' I said 'yes', he and his wife happily agreed to talk to me. A shopkeeper Faruk Ahmed Dar told, there are three shops owned by three persons in the village. They are the only people involved in small business, rest live on fishing or water nut collecting. They catch fish, consume fish and sell them at the *Mandi* in Sopore. Faruk told, 'we are Kashmiris and like other Kashmiris we also like meat but we do not eat much meat because fish is easily available to us'.

Concluding Observations

The above mentioned features of the village indicate few distinctive characteristics. Firstly, fishing as the major occupation of the people gives the village homogeneity. And that makes them quite distinctive from the general Kashmiris. This is indeed, true for the Zurimonz village as well. Religion-wise also it is an absolute homogeneous Muslim village. They have good sense of their Muslimhood. But, *Shia* and *Sunni* compartmentalisation and sensitisation seemed absent there. It gives another impression that, Kashmir as a whole does not have the sensitive sectarian-identity fraction except few pockets of the valley. Homogeneous nature of the village can be a reason of this fact. Second reason can be the absence of middle class. They are strong followers of the religious shrine. Everyone of the village is respectful to the nearby shrine, Baba Sukur-ud-din. Every new born baby being taken to the shrine as a matter of observing the ritual.

They watch cricket and almost all people support Pakistani team like other Kashmiris. Their support to Pakistan cricket team comes from the religious sympathy as, they say, that they are '*Muslim Bhai*' so we support them. Although, they do not mix politics with cricket but religion has been mixed with it. They support Pakistan in cricket, but they have no sense of '*Azadi*'(freedom) India or Pakistani have also found that much of anti-India anger gets expression in and through cricket as well. The fire crackers go up in air if Pakistani team wins against Indian team. Even the naming of the village tells that they were conscious of the larger regional politics. But, their basic consciousness is livelihood. As fishermen and water nut collectors each of them have licence. But, in Wullar Lake there are some other people who do the same business without licence which they consider as big threat for their livelihood. They are very vocal for that. They elect their *panch*. A school going kid, willingly told, my mother voted last time. She voted to party 'X'. Regarding the question of '*Azadi*' a shopkeeper told, 'here such spirit (*jajbah*) is absent. What will we get by giving blood?' Another person informed, 'from Zurimonz village two youth joined armed resistance but from *Bangladesh* village no youth has ever joined militancy even in its hay time of 1990s.The fact is that issues like self-determination or any type of protest politics or social movements basically function among the middle class. The people who fight for livelihood in remote areas, slogans of freedom hardly make sense to them.

Secondly, in terms of education, health, employment, infrastructure, livelihood it is a backward, marginalised village as newspaper report depicts it the 'most neglected and secluded place in north Kashmir' (Rasool, 2015). Few families seem to be financially well off. From the usual definition of poverty, some families are above poverty line (APL) while some bellow poverty line (BPL). But, those families who get rice under the category of APL too remain poor in many aspects if we look into the UNDP's multi-dimensional Poverty aspects. According to UNDP a family which does not have access to proper education, health facilities, environment friendly cooking fuel, proper sanitation, pure drinking water, electricity, concrete (*pakka*) floor and assets like land are considered to be multi-dimensionally poor (UNDP report 2010). In the village under study, it has been seen that every family has *Pakka* house but at least 10 families do not have a toilet. They have access to electricity for 6-7 hours a day. Almost 100 per cent of the village people use firewood and cow dung as cooking fuel. Boat and house is only asset available to them. Their access to education is absolutely poor and so is the health service. For 1100 people from two villages (Zurimonz and Bangladesh) there is one primary healthcare centre. The basic necessary healthcare facilities are inadequate there as the staff Sister Naseema informed. In severe cases like delivery or accident they give first aid and then they refer the patients to the district hospital which is far away from the place.

Further, the economic gap between BPL and APL could not create any social elite in the village. No particular family shown upward social mobility which has left the society stagnant. Understandably, education, political power, economic upliftment is catalysts for change in a society but the absence of all that has left the village far away. Interestingly, poverty in the village made all people equal. It is amazing that while neighbouring villages are advancing on almost all indicators of human development this village named as 'Bangladesh' has remained neglected even at the dawn of twenty-first century. As an observer my impression about the village under study is that all agencies and institutions need to put their act together to see how such villages can be brought on the developmental path. There must be many such villages in Kashmir valley where the reach of the government is extremely limited. In all these secluded and isolated villages some fast track developmental mechanisms are to be put in place so that little children whom I found as good as any other can have equal opportunities for advancement.

The government also needs to put in place some reservation policy both in public and private sector for the children of such villages so that they don't drop-out from schools. It is equally important that basic infrastructure like roads, school buildings etc are build up to give a fillip to the economy of such villages. The NGO sector which is otherwise very active in Kashmir due to political and social turmoil also needs to enter into rural arena so as to provide basic necessities of life to people. I earnestly hope that civil society organisations and philanthropic institutions also step in such rural areas for creating basic infrastructure for people so that people are economically empowered to boldly face the challenges of daily life. The village, while retaining its cultural moorings and heritage, is in need of a planning so that youth and particularly educated (with small number) do not migrate. Poverty does force people out. As a Bangladeshi I understand that there are around 15 million Bangladeshis living in India. Bangladesh-India migration corridor is the largest in the world. The World Bank estimates that more money is remitted to Bangladesh from India - 4.5 billion dollars than from any other country. Even in Indian Assam where feelings run high just 2,442 illegal Bangladeshi immigrants were deported between 1985 and 2012 according to a report by the state government. We in Bangladesh are trying to learn lessons from it and others also have to learn. By way of conclusion as a researcher I feel that a Bangladeshi Grameen Bank type of initiative is needed to create employment avenues in rural Kashmir. Mohammad Yunus- the founder of the bank should visit Kashmir and develop some collaborative mechanism with the government in Jammu and Kashmir so that average Kashmir can see the other side of Bangladesh. It augurs well for future that many Kashmiri young prefer medical colleges in Bangladesh as their academic destination and see my country from inside.

References

1. Contentious Politics; Mobilisation: An International Quarterly; *www.mobilisation.org*
2. Human Development Report 2014; UNDP.
3. Rasool, M T (August 11, 2015); Kashmir's Bangladesh faces discrimination; Rising Kashmir, p. 10.
4. State Economic Survey, Jammu and Kashmir; 2013-14.

14

War and Violence against Women

— Kabita Kharka

Each war represents a failure of our species to live in harmony, a waste of precious human capital, a further scourge on the environment, and a crime against all humanity. All wars claim lives of the innocent, sacrifices of the helpless, and take a toll upon the women. According to liberal feminists, women should have the same right to participate in all areas of society and political life, which includes the participation in war and combat. Although, women have also been party to many battles fought through ancient times, they have mostly been victimised in wars. The theory of van Creveld, that the constructed gender images motivate men to fight war, that women are and always have been "one of the principal objectives for which war is waged" If women do not feel protected "they may go over to the other side", was challenged by many feminist scholars.

Rape is an outcome of war as well as an expression of misogyny of the other community. Women are victims of war in every conflict. Rape has been used as a tool to humiliate and destroy the inferior group. Abduction of women in wars dates back in history as early as 750 BC when incidents like rape of Sabine women occurred, in which the first generation of Roman men acquired wives for themselves from the neighbouring Sabine families, abducting their women overnight.

Some of the infamous incidents in history based upon brutal rape and torture of women are well remembered even today. Starting from the "rape of Nanking" – rape of the women in the town of Nanking by the Japanese army, "comfort women" – women who were forced into sexual slavery, by the Japanese imperial army. Almost 200,000 women mostly from their colonies such as Korea, Burma, China, Holland, Indonesia, Philippines were raped during the Second World War. There is no particular number as to how many women and girls were raped in the genocide under the command of dictators like Stalin in USSR, under Hitler in Germany, under general Mao in China. It is estimated that the two world wars claimed the lives of 30 million people approximately.

In the liberation war of 1971, some 250,000 - 400,000 girls and women were raped, resulting in 25,000 pregnancies. The Guinness Book of Records lists the Bengali atrocities as one of the largest five genocides in the twentieth century.

In the Rwandan genocide in 1994 at least 250,000 women were raped. Women were also impaled from vagina to mouth with spears, and pregnant women were frequently eviscerated. Before being raped and killed, many women and girls had their breasts cut off and/or were forced to commit incest with a family member, Genital organs were often mutilated with sharp objects or boiling water. Almost 50000 women survived rape and sexual torture in the Rwandan genocide. Other women and girls became sex slaves to Hutu militia members, and were taken to refugee camps in Eastern Zaire after the genocide.

In 1991 ethnic cleansing in Bosnia more than 50,000 women raped. In the course of ethnic cleansing, the Bosnian Serbs also established numerous detention camps, where non-Serbs were confined in barbaric conditions. In addition to being overcrowded and underfed, the inmates were frequently tortured and often murdered. Tens of thousands of rapes took place, ordered and authorised by Serb officials, and in many cases with the explicit purpose of impregnating the victims. Foca's women's prisons have come to be known at the war crimes tribunal as the "rape camps" or "rape factories" of the Balkan conflict. All of the above mentioned cases includes systematic rape involving detention of the victims in rape camps with more than 50 assaults per day. The rapes in Bosnia–Herzegovina and Croatia were a simultaneous expression of misogyny and genocide (Catherine MacKinnon,1994).

Several ongoing conflicts that gained international attention for their notorious war crimes such as civil wars in DRC, Liberia, Sierra Leone, and Somalia demonstrate that sexual violence is not an outcome of war, but that women's bodies are an important site of war, which makes sexual violence an integral part of wartime strategy.

The victims suffer from many problems after the incident. Sexually transmitted diseases particularly the risk of HIV infection unwanted pregnancies as well as increased reproductive health problems, Gynaecological problems such as dysmenorrhoea[1] or menorrhagia[2] are also commonly reported. In 2004, it was estimated that 500,000 individuals in Rwanda are living with HIV/AIDS.

Often the victim's families and husband refuse to take them back forcing them to live in refugee camps or slums. They also lack basic health facilities and minimum requirements for livelihood and survival additionally they will have to take care of the newborn babies of war, taking care of their basic necessitates and sustaining life have been their major struggle in the aftermath of the genocide. In case of East Pakistan the victim has chosen to go to brothels for earning minimum livelihood and in Rwanda many women have been working as sex workers after their bodies have lost the dignity.

The trauma of rape and torture affects the victim psychologically as well; many victims are living with lifelong diseases such as mental disorders, post traumatic stress disorder (PTSD), bipolar attitudes, mood swings, sadism, and suicidal tendencies.

Despite the fact that there are numerous conventions and international instruments formulated for the protection of women in war, prohibiting the violation of women's rights in war, however it has not been effective in preventing atrocities committed upon women even to this day. Rape is not only an outcome of war but also a tool to commit genocide upon an inferior community. Genocide and the acts through which genocide is committed are defined in the Convention on the Prevention and Punishment of the Crime of Genocide, the first major human rights instrument adopted by the United Nations.

In 1971, Hamoodur Rahman Commission was formed by Pakistan. The Committee was conferred to investigate causes of the defeat of

Pakistan, erstwhile West Pakistan during the 1971 war. In 1973, The International Crimes Tribunals Act (ICT), was enacted by the sovereign parliament of East Pakistan to investigate and prosecute suspects for the genocide committed in 1971 by the Pakistan Army and their local collaborators, On 30 July 2009, the Minister of Law, Justice and Parliamentary Affairs of East Pakistan stated that no citizen of Pakistan would be tried under the International Crimes Tribunals Act of 1973.

In the early 1990s, the United Nations Security Council created two ad hoc international tribunals to prosecute international crimes, including mass sexual violence, committed in Yugoslavia and Rwanda (ICTR and ICTY).

In 1993, International Criminal Tribunal for Yugoslavia was established; it was the first international criminal tribunal since World War II. The ICTY made history in including rape as a serious violation of human rights and a war crime from the outset.

In 1994, The International Criminal Tribunal for Rwanda was established; ICTR took prosecuting rape as a method of war one step further. The UN Commission of Experts on Rwanda said in their report that they found rape to be "committed with the intent to destroy, in whole or in part" the Tutsi population, thus acknowledging rape as part of genocide.

The International Criminal Court (ICC) was established in 2002 and is given jurisdiction by the United Nation's Security Council. The ICC represents a shift in international thinking of human security and also establishes a permanent legal system for dealing with international war crimes, now also including rape. However, the ICC has not replaced national courts.

Rape is prohibited by the law of armed conflict but is neither specifically enumerated as a "grave breach" nor as a violation of the laws and customs of war. Rape has recently been defined as a crime against humanity in the statutes of the International Criminal Court as well as the International Criminal Tribunals for Rwanda and Yugoslavia.

The Convention on the Elimination of all Forms of Discrimination Against Women (CEDAW) adopted by UN General Assembly in 1979 calls for equality of the sexes in political, social, cultural, civil, and other fields. CEDAW is also described as the international bill of rights for women.

In 1993, UN Commission on Human Rights resolution calls rape a crime of war. UN Security Council Resolution 1325 adopted in 2000 mandates the protection of, and respect for, the rights of women and girls, calls on all parties in armed conflict to take specific measures to protect women and girls from gender-based violence, particularly rape and sexual violence.

Law on the Suppression of Violence against Women and Children in 2000, for the first time expanded the definition of rape considerably and the sexual assault and sexual harassment have been made punishable offences.

International War Crimes Tribunal in 2001 rules that rape in war is a crime against humanity. In Tokyo War Crimes Trial, rape was first identified as a war crime, also led to successful prosecution of some commanders. International Criminal Court established in 2002 codifies accountability for gender-based crimes against women during military conflict by defining sexual and gender violence of all kinds as war crimes. In the last decade, there were successful prosecutions of rape as a war crime and rape was considered as an act of genocide.

Article 27 of the Fourth Geneva convention did prohibit rape in war, provides that, "Women shall be especially protected against any attack on their honour, in particular against rape, enforced prostitution, or any form of indecent assault". Yet Article 27 was largely ignored and rape was not an acknowledged war crime despite multiple instances of widespread rape throughout the twentieth century.

Additionally, although the Fourth Geneva Convention outlawed rape in Article 27, Article 147 of the "grave breaches" of human rights violations does not mention rape. This omission implies that rape was not taken seriously. Enforcement and implementation of the convention was also a problem.

The articles of the convention did not seem to have any real power. In 1972, for example, when the United Nations Economic and Social Council became concerned about "escalating levels of brutality directed against women in war, " they appealed to those involved in combat to "respect international law". Their appeals had no effect. Hence, Article 27 remained ineffective and unenforced.

Thus, the international community should join hands to formulate instruments that have international jurisdiction. All countries in the world shall be party to it so that in the future there are no atrocities being committed towards women in the name of war. Those women shall be separated from war crimes and shall not simply become "spoils of war".

Notes

1. Very painful periods accompanied by severe cramps and hormonal imbalance.
2. Menstrual periods, with abnormally heavy or prolonged bleeding.

15

United Nations Security Council Resolution 1325 Plus 15: High time to heed the unheard voices

— Subarna Dhar

The title of my paper may sound somewhat sentimental. Why do I make the assertion that it is high time to make unheard voices heard? The reason is simple that women are kept away from any sort of peace initiatives. This is also true of South Asia where many top level positions have been occupied by women. The region where Gandhian philosophy of 'non-violence' originated, yet, most of the states of the region have gone through or even going through different kinds of conflicts and violence both latently and manifestly. Yes, it is South Asia, a political construction of a region comprised of post-colonial independent states which are troubled with both inter-state and intra-state conflict since their emergence as sovereign independent entities. Both the nature and grounds are distinctive in regard of every specific conflict. But, what is identical in all these conflict scenarios is the gender specific experience of women, their continuous struggle for peace and being unheard in peace process. Here, the issue of women engagement in peace process can be discussed referring to the notions like, 'peace for women', 'peace without women', 'women for peace' or 'no peace without women'.

The first notion 'peace for women' is based on the practice 'men fights for the cause of women and children'. In such practice women are considered as the 'Second Sex' under the patriarchal social construction. Conflict situation keeps on boosting the gendered attitudes towards women. They become the worst victims of conflict from pre-conflict to post-conflict period. Transition to peace from conflict becomes very essential for the women to lead the life with minimum human rights and dignity. The second concept, 'peace without women' is also driven by the hegemonic masculine nature of men. They consider women should be out of the peace process. Women are considered as the symbol of 'nation's respect' and as some 'objects' to be protected or disrespected for securing national pride. So, the common weapon of conflict is to exploit women of the other groups to humiliate their pride. In both, first and second notions, male members of the societies emerge as the sole agents of ensuring protection for women and children. They determine and control the peace mechanism though women go through various distinctive exploitation and violence. Women voices and their distinctive needs remain unnoticed as well as unacknowledged in almost every peace initiatives in the region. The third concept, 'woman for peace' has been one of the motivating tools for the women and peace activists and theorists all over the world. They consider women deserve the innate nature of making the world peaceful. They demand to engage women in formal peace process to utilise their natural capacity to end conflict. It has been a matter of argument from the very beginning of movement towards engaging women in peace building. In the harsh reality of war and conflict all over the world women ensured their access to some extent by questioning the patriarchal norms and attitudes.

The picture in South Asia is no different and here also women groups have emerged as strong voice against all kind of conflicts and violence. Most of their initiatives even transcend the state driven peace projects which revolve only around making of agreements and accords. Such agreement oriented peace projects fail to address the main causes of conflicts. On the other hand, the indigenous, justice oriented peace initiatives by women and other non-state actors focus to resolve conflict by uprooting the reasons of conflict. In all the conflicting countries in South Asia women have showed their urge for peace and stability either by being part to civil society groups, or, by forming distinctive platform for mothers, daughters, widows, half-widows, etc.

Women in conflict situations in the region have come out as the protector of their community, society, race and nation and bearer of peace. Women in Afghanistan, Bangladesh, India, Nepal, Pakistan and Sri Lanka have proved their stand against any sort of violence and conflict in terms of writings, cultural practices, unofficial diplomacy (both nationally and internationally), direct participation in movements for peace as well as joining fight for their cause.

There are some examples where peace initiatives have been taken by women in the region even at individual levels. Indira Goswami, had worked immensely to bring both ULFA and Government of India at negotiation table for peaceful settlement of the conflict in Assam. Her endeavour put light on the degree of consciousness and desire for peace even at individual level. Whereas, Indira Goswami is not the sole example rather we see extensive initiatives were taken by Painter Salima Hashmi to increase people to people contact between India and Pakistan.[1]

At some cases, they have even made ethnic and religious dividing lines (which are the most prominent factors in South Asia) blur for the cause of peace and stability. In Sri Lankan women's movement for peace had been questioned at some extent mentioning it suffered from lack of uniformity because of ethnic divisions.[2] But, there also women have joined in a common platform to safeguard gender and human rights issues. Women in Northeast of India are considered as torchbearer of peace for decades. Their contribution to peace building and innovative protest against gender specific violence makes the state authority to take them into consideration in formal peace process. Women of Nagaland has created a stunning example of overcoming all patriarchal domination and attained their righteous space in formal peace negotiations.[3] Their presences transcended the notion of ceremonial presence in peace mechanism rather became an influential factor in decision making. Women in Nepal have been a dominant factor in the peace movements. Their struggle was not ended with the establishment of 'negative peace' rather it has been an incessant process that aims at the attainment of 'positive peace'.

In Afghanistan women have been involved in peace building in their own traditional way for decades. Even now they are in constant movement to secure their space in formal peace process.

Similarly, in Bangladesh, women have raised their voice for democracy, peace and stability at an extensive rate. Commitment for peace by the indigenous women in CHT reached to such a stage that the state authority found it as a threat to their game of assimilation and oppression through keeping conflict alive. The result is abduction of women activist Kalpana Chakma by military forces.[4]

The irony is almost all these women's initiatives remain unacknowledged in the formal peace process. They were not made part of the formal decision-making process in spite of extensive influential activities for peace restoration. Moreover, gender specific issues don't get included in peace accords or agreements and post-conflict reconstruction projects. Moreover, till 1990s there was lack of any particular recognition towards the needs and rights of women's engagement in formal peace process. Women lag behind in the formal decision-making process not only in South Asia but in most of the peace processes all over the world. Such tradition motivated the women and peace activists to concentrate on breaking the practice of keeping women away of peace process. They emphasised on the need of including women in decision-making process here, the fourth concept 'no peace without women' comes in.

'No peace without women' is the notion, backed by the facts like, women face very distinctive kinds of violence and exploitation at the time of conflict, transition from conflict to peace is more needed for the women to lead dignified life and intervention of women is the grave need for conflict resolution and post-conflict reconstruction. The constant struggle of women and peace activists resulted in the adoption of the United Nations Security Council Resolution 1325(2000) in which, notion of 'No peace without Women' gets formally recognised.[5] It is the first Security Council resolution through which , UN had recognised women as constructive agents and acknowledged their right to participate as decision-makers at all level of peacekeeping, peacemaking, peace-building and conflict resolution. It also identifies the particularity of the measures to be taken to protect the rights of women and girls in armed conflict. The resolution brings a paradigm shift by recommending the inclusion of gender perspective on a range of activities including peace negotiations, peace operation trainings, design of internally displaced persons (IDP) camps, and reconstruction programming. It is an instrument where the recommendation to include women as a stakeholder in different level of decision-making has been made to different international, national and regional actors including UN Secretary General, member states and other actors in conflict resolution. So far, adoption of Security Council Resolution is an epoch making event to draw international attention on the need of women and girls from armed conflict situations and engagement of women in peace process. It is a political framework that recommends actions to be taken by state governments and international institutions. It encourages the member states to adopt National Action Plans (NAP) to ensure the implementations of thc rcsolution.

In addition, the Resolution provides a platform on which members of civil society can demand that their government should be accountable and upholds international commitments. In the words of women activist Dorothé Appels of Dutch Centres for International Cooperation, "the Resolution came with the collaboration between governments and civil society, in that sense it is a very unique resolution and the content of the Resolution is also very practical. So it really is a tool that women organisations, women activists, women movements all over the world can use."[6]

The Security Council Resolution (SCR) has built momentum around the world for the increased actions on addressing gender inequalities and the protection of the rights of girls and women in conflict and post-conflict situations. Bandana Rana, human rights activist from Nepal argues, "SCR 1325 is an essential tool kit that provides the platform to the government and civil society to adopt the national action plan with a view to ensuring the participation of women in peace process and safeguarding the rights of women and girls children in conflict and post-conflict reconstruction."[7] The resolution has come up with some great commitments towards engaging women in peace process. It has crossed fifteen years of its journey by October 2015. It has also been followed by few other companion Security Council Resolutions to broaden the jurisdiction as well as to strengthen its implementation mechanism. But, how far it has succeeded to change the position of women in peace process at global level is a matter of further inquiry. Particularly in South Asia, the issues of engaging women in peace process remain confined within first two notions like 'peace for women' and 'peace without women'. Implementation of the UNSCR 1325 is frustrating in the region as a whole.

The reason behind the less progress in implementing need to be analysed from two different perspectives- firstly, the challenges within the resolution itself and secondly, the challenges that emerges due to social, economic, political, and cultural set up of the region. The Resolution deserves universal attitude which fails to address the particularity of region like South Asia. It recommends complying with other human rights instruments like CEDAW, The Geneva Convention, The Refugee Convention, and the Convention on Child Rights etc. But, the region as a whole fails in ensuring implementations of almost all these at expected level though there have been some improvements.[8] Furthermore, it talks of participation of women in peace process as matter of equal rights of representation but women in South Asia don't enjoy the equal rights in terms of representation in social, economic and political decision making. There are some examples of women being engaged in peace process but those are considered as ceremonial presence not as influential in decision-making process. On the other hand, almost all the peace processes in South Asia keep on revolving within accord making that involves high profile officials and some selected representatives from conflicting groups. Most of the time conflict ends officially within the state representatives where substantive parties to the conflict remain ignorant. In such situation to be part of peace process women lack in terms of literacy and political consciousness. Even when women are part of struggle then also their male counterparts don't show much interest to involve them in peace negotiations. The SCR 1325 insists upon the inclusion of gender perspectives in training up peacekeeping forces. But South Asia being dominated by hegemonic masculine state structures and social norms and values women are considered as bearer of honour and dignity of family, community, society and nation. Here, peacekeeping indicates deployment of military forces in conflict driven places and peacekeeping forces and insurgent groups becomes rival to one another. In such rivalry women become the victims of sexual exploitations from both the part to humiliate social respects and dignity. And surprisingly, both the conflicting parties show reluctance to recognise the exploitation of women during conflict. The resolution on women, peace and security insists upon the inclusion of gender perspectives in post-conflict reconstructions but in this region, women issues are not specifically included even in peace accords.

Furthermore, this region is distinctive in terms of ethnic diversity and religious extremity. Here, women face the lack of unified voices only for women's cause and religious extremity comes in as a weapon to make the women away from peace initiatives. The 'Peace Bus' initiatives by women from India and Pakistan was stigmatized as 'Hinduisation' in Pakistan as the women from India were received by Pakistani women with candles. The initiatives failed to go further facing such criticisms. In most of the cases, women allow the male counter-parts to speak for them and decide their fate. Another reason behind such silence is not having access to the instruments like the UNSCR 1325 in their own language so they remain in dark about the global initiatives for protecting their rights. Moreover, the resolution is not binding on the member states and the states in South Asia show a little political will to take proper initiatives to comply with the provisions of the resolution. In such a case Afghanistan and Nepal can be considered as exceptions to the scenario in regard of adopting NAP on the resolution. But in both cases, the initiative is more time driven and with due influence of international community rather than being moved by political will. In brief, only two among eight states of the region NAP on women, peace and security. Moreover, mere adoption of NAP to implement the resolution will not bring any substantive change in the attitude rather it will increase the volume of documentation. Another important aspect of the political practice in South Asia is to uphold the kinship-based representations in different forums starting from government's head to grassroots level. It creates the scenario where women are represented at some extent but that does not bring any substantive change in the practice of non-inclusiveness. The UNSCR 1325 talks of state and non-state initiatives for engaging women in peace process but in this region, non-state actors have been very vocal demanding inclusion of women of peace process. State authorities have always been reluctant to engage women groups in peace process.

Nevertheless, the engagement of non-state actors on the issues cannot contribute much to change the practice of non-inclusion of women as they do not have much hold on state authorities. In addition, the peace process in South Asia does not represent any substantive peace-building mechanism or conflict transformation rather it rotates within the conflict resolution or producing accords after accords. The accords, a few of which sees the light of proper implementations fails to address the root causes of conflict. The resolution of women, peace and security also calls for the recognition of indigenous peace processes of conflict situations however no country in the region takes consideration into the indigenous peace initiatives by the people.

However, women in the region are engaged with peace struggle even before the adoption the resolution on women, peace and security. Still when the world celebrates 15 years of the UNSCR this part of the world experiences Irom Sharmila's 15 years long non-violent protest through hunger strike against The Arms Forces Special Power Act (AFSPA) in Manipur, India. It is coloured as 'suicide attempt' by the state authority. Happily she ended her fast recently. The peace-building that starts with the practice of upholding motherhood, sisterhood, daughterhood remains under the veils with the direct, naked intervention of the hegemonic masculine authorities. It is high time for the region to comply with the resolution and make women part to negotiations and decision-making process. Without involvement of women in peace process no substantive peace can be attained.

References

1. Singh, R. (2007). "Transcending Borders: Role of Women in Building Peace between India – Pakistan." Chapter 3, In *Women Building Peace Between India and Pakistan*, edited by Mulay, S. and Krik, J. pp. 23-36. New York: ANTHEM Press.
2. Thiruppathy, S. and Silva, N. D. (2008). "Women in Sri Lankan Peace Politics." In *Women in Peace Politics,* edited by Banerjee, P. Vol. 3, pp. 133-135. New Delhi: SAGE Publications India Pvt. Ltd.
3. Manchanda, R. (2011). "Northeast India." In *Peacemaking in Asia and the Pacific: Women's Participation, Perspectives and Priorities*, edited by Buchanan, C. Switzerland: Centre for Humanitarian Dialogue.
4. Naher, A. and Tripura, P. (2010). "Violence Against Indigenous Women." In *Between Ashes and Hope: Chittagong Hill Tracts in the Blind Spot of*

Bangladesh Nationalism, edited by Mohaiemen, N. Dhaka: Drishtipat writers' Collective (DWC).

5. UNSCR1325 (2000). http://womenpeacesecurity.org/media/pdf-scr1325.pdf.
6. https://www.youtube.com/watch?v=hVOLDdfOeLI .
7. https://www.youtube.com/watch?v=WvcO_lBRiJg.
8. McGrath, J. and Taylor, S. (2007). "Canada and United Nations Security Council Resolution 1325 (2000) On Women, Peace and Security." Chapter 2, In *Women Building Peace between India and Pakistan*, edited by Mulay, S. and Krik, J. 8-22, New York: ANTHEM Press.

16

Pakhtoons in Kashmir: Historical Context

— *Farah Qayoom*

Yet after a hundred years and more of close contact, the Pathan remains to the world, and even to himself, something of an enigma. Many have spoken and written of him and his country, but the surface has been scarcely scratched. There is need for deeper ploughing.

– **Olaf Caroe**

For centuries the mirrors of Central Asia have echoed with the sound of gunfire as warring tribes in and around Afghanistan have fought a never-ending battle for power and influence. These tribes have challenged allegiance, betrayed each other and feuded over land, gold and women.

Located within South Asia and Central Asia, Afghanistan is a land-locked country.To the North, Turkmen, Uzbeks and Tajiks adjoin people of similar origin living in the newly formed Central Asian republics of Turkmenistan, Uzbekistan, and Tajikistan. In the mountains of central Afghanistan live the Hazaras of predominantly Muslim Shiite faith, who in terms of religion have more in common with the Shiite Iranians than with the Sunni Muslims living throughout Afghanistan. To the North-east bordering Pakistan are the Nuristanis who before their conversion to Islam in the nineteenth century were regarded as infidels. To the South, Balochis border Pakistan's province of Balochistan; to the East, the largest group, the Pashtuns called Pathans by British colonials, who used the Indianised versions of their name and have common links with the tribes living in Pakistan's North West Frontier Province and northern Balochistan.[1] Each of these ethnic groups is distinctly unique in its different cultural characteristics such as family, beliefs and languages. The history of ethnic groups in Afghanistan is one of permanent conflict, over resources, food, women, and water. Indeed it is said about them that if there was anything worth having, it was a fight.[2]

Since the dawn of civilisation Afghanistan's history is one steeped in conflict, distress and social unrest. The Pakhtoons make up nearly half of its population. Afghanistan has two official languages, Pashtu and Dari. The Pakhtoons speak Afghanistan's principal language of Pashtu while the Hazaras speak Dari.

It is characteristic of the history of Afghanistan, that while in scattered oasis and river valleys a rich sedentary culture thrived, the surrounding steppes sheltered restless and semi-nomadic tribes who at regular intervals abandoned their traditional occupations in favour of organising predatory raids on neighbouring populations. "In fact it would almost be said that the location of nomadic steppes in the northern and north-eastern periphery of the oasis regions of Central Asia determined to a large extent the entire course of its history. The steppes of Central Asia were not only the springboards of many marauding movements, but they were also starting points of innumerable waves of migrations."[3]

Afghan population has thus been moulded by a high degree of spatial mobility. The country was criss-crossed by important caravan routes on the Silk Route until the early nineteenth century, and it has always been dominated by nomadism and other forms of moving from place to place (including peripathetic groups). Large caravan cities such as Kandahar, Herat and Kabul also had Greek, Armenian or Jewish communities which served as bases in transcontinental ethno-religious trade networks until well into the twentieth century. Even today, hundreds of thousands of nomads inhabit the country and migrate seasonally.[4]

Considering that, at any rate for the last 800 years or so, Afghanistan had been in a constant state of turmoil, civil war and invasions, and that the hardier tribes inhabiting the wilder parts possessed little else than their flocks and herds, which restricted areas of cultivable land, it is not surprising that these tribes considered it a necessity of life to plunder richer neighbours and extort all they could from passing traders and even invading armies. This can also be seen in the light of the fact that Pashtuns today constitute one of the world's largest populations of displaced persons.[5]

For Pakhtuns, geographical dislocation does not necessarily cause cultural dislocation. Although Pakhtuns too look at their land as sacred and associate it with their forefathers, they trace their original ancestry to one Afghana whom they believe to be a close advisor to Solomon and the builder of his temple in Jerusalem. Descendents of Afghana migrated from the land of Israel to central Afghanistan and later moved into their present territory several centuries ago. Though Pakhtuns believe that they have occupied their present lands for some time now, an important part of their history concerns those times when they have moved elsewhere, for instance, when Pakhtuns under Ahmad Shah Durrani conquered the Hindu kingdoms of India in the eighteenth century. In all of these myths and historical events, migration and movement emerge as part of the Pakhtun mythology just as cross-border movements in response to political pressures from neighbouring governments continue to be thought of as necessary actions taken to preserve cultural values which might otherwise be jeopardized.

A long history of migration involving Pashtun ethnic communities has enriched and complicated regional societies across Asia and the Indian Ocean, especially in the modern period after the mid-eighteenth century, as these regions were influenced and transformed by Postcolonial dynamics (Nicholas, 2010, 1). Arguably the Pashtun communities of today's northern Pakistan and Eastern Afghanistan have had their history repeatedly transformed, incrementally and cumulatively, across centuries by migration and constant movement.

For centuries, the Pashtuns have travelled within the Indian sub-continent and in the greater Indian Ocean arenas.[6] After 1775 and throughout the nineteenth century, Pashtuns camping in northern India from both urban and rural settings began moving increasingly in British Imperial spheres. The Pashtun history of migration and diaspora represents one specific, but representative strand of the 'Great Diversity' of South Asian migrations experienced over centuries by multiple peoples of differing regions, religions, ethnicities and languages.

Further highlighting an economic dimension of the migration of Pakhtoons into the Indian subcontinent, Robert Nicholas writes that regionally, for centuries, agrarian districts with little irrigation and limited rainfall in eastern Afghanistan, the northern and western Punjab and the North West Frontier Provinces produced surplus workers looking outside the village economy for subsistence and opportunity. Markovits and his colleagues have proposed that ecological differences in Indian regions ranging between dry, semi- dry and wet zones as well as opposing pastoral and agrarian political economies produced some 'highly routinised productive processes', thereby providing scope for skilful and mobile peasantry and groups of merchants and artisans including in the 'dry zone' of Afghanistan, Iran and Central Asia. Particularly in North India and arguably in the Pashtun homelands, this interaction was manifested through a regular pattern of circulation of manpower including military manpower, goods, capital, expertise, ideas, techniques etc. from the dry areas to the wet zones.

The Pathans or Pakhtoons also came to the Indian sub-continent as immigrants (mainly as soldiers and traders) in the middle of the fifteenth century when the first Afghan Empire was established in India. The Pathan dynasties of India were first introduced by Lodhi and Sur Dynasties. They were soon followed by other tribes who were generally endowed with estates by rulers from time to time. Trade and commerce also made these people to migrate from their native land to the plains of Hindustan and Pakistan. Pathans are thus spread all over the Indian sub-continent in states like Hyderabad, Uttar Pradesh, Orissa etc. and not only confined to Jammu and Kashmir.

After the 'imposition of direct rule by the British crown in 1858, Pashtuns from the Peshawar valley were also recruited for positions in Colonial plantations and trade networks that linked South Asia, Africa, and various Indian Ocean archipelagos and Southeast Asia. Some Pashtuns pursued trading, which included the selling of livestock across Northern India. Others became shopkeepers and small financiers.

Pakhtoons in Kashmir

While most of the available literature on the history of Kashmir does not discuss Kashmir Pakhtoons as a separate ethnic group, nor does it throw any light on the fact as to how these people arrived in Kashmir valley. However, we find a mention about these people in Walter R Lawrence's 'Valley of Kashmir', Parvez Dewan's 'Jammu, Kashmir and Ladakh'. 'The People of India' (Jammu and Kashmir chapter) talks about Pashtuns as people of Afghan origin residing in Kashmir.

As already pointed out, it is because of the socio-economic constraints coupled with political turmoil, that these people always yearned for greener pastures with suitable political and social environment offering better and remunerative opportunities in order to lead a peaceful and settled life. In fact, it is a common saying in Afghanistan that anyone who crosses over the Khyber Pass to the Indus Basin never returns. The migration of Afghans to the plains of Indian subcontinent across the Khyber Pass has been an obvious outcome of the inhospitable conditions, wars, and tribal feuds. It has been gradual and continuous.

Because of the disintegration of the Mughal Empire which was established in Kashmir in 1586 A.D. by Akbar, Kashmir passed into the hands of the Afghans in 1752 A.D.-1818 A.D. The province, as such remained under their control upto 1818, when the Afghans got ousted by the rising Sikh power.

During the Afghan period, some 32 Afghan Subahdars came to rule Kashmir. They were accompanied by a large administrative outfit including their personal servants, soldiers and fortune seekers.

In the same period not only Kashmiri Muslims but also Kashmiri Pandits were appointed to senior government positions in Kabul. Many of the Muslims stayed on, never to return to Kashmir. During the same period, a substantial Kashmiri Muslim diaspora formed in now what is called the North West Frontier Province of Pakistan. Similarly, some of the Afghans also migrated to Kashmir from Afghanistan or North West Frontier (Dewan, 2008, 390). Kashmir valley had started receiving earlier batches of Afghans during Ahmad Shah Durrani's rule in about

1753 A.D. In subsequent years, other groups too came as and when inter-tribal feuds in their home took place, forcing some to leave their native land. "Much later it was Maharaja Gulab Singh, the new Dogra ruler of Kashmir who offered them employment opportunities especially for the purpose of guarding the frontiers of the kingdom and in return granted them land Jagirs and settled them in colonies of their choice."[7]

Over a period of time, various batches of immigrant Afghans settled in upper reaches of the valley with a view to occupy the virgin lands with abundance of water. The Afghans are stated to have entered Kashmir via Baramulla, where they camped for some time. Some batches moved to the west of Baramulla and settled in Uri. Others moved upwards in the north-west to the South-east of Kashmir in search of suitable greener pastures and arable land. This is how they came to Ganderbal, Pattan, Mattan and other places in the valley (Indu and Ashok Aima in People of India: Jammu and Kashmir, p. 51).

In Bhiru (Beerwah) many villages are held by Swatis and Bonairwala. In 1911 there were 52,263 Pakhtoons in the state. Of these 30,338 claimed to be Khans. Several Muslim Rajputs of Mirpur told the census authorities that they were Pashtuns. The proportion of Pushtoons in post-1947 Jammu and Kashmir might not be the same. Almost the entire Pashtun elite of Srinagar migrated to Pakistan after the partition of India (Dewan, 2008, 390). The Pakhtoons who stayed back were granted permanent state subject status by the Government of Jammu and Kashmir in 1954.

The prominent Afghan clans of present day Kashmir are:

Yusufzai, Khankhail, Afridi, Swati, Malik, Durrani, Kuki Khel, Kant, Khatki, Khyberi, Niazi, and Sado-zai (Dewan, 2008, 390).

Walter Lawrence adds, 'the most interesting colony is that of Kuku Khayl Afridis of Dranghaihamma who retain most of all the old Pathan customs and still for the most part speak Pashtu.......another colony of Pathans is that of the Machipurias but by intermarriage with Kashmiri women the Machipurias have lost most of their characteristics of the Pathan...the Machipuria Pathans belong to the Yusufzai section'.

Migratory Route of the Pakhtoons

Different goups of Afghans are stated to have entered the valley of Kashmir through Baramulla, where they halted for quite a period of time. Thereafter, they moved in the North-West, North-East and North-South directions in the valley, obviously in search of greener pastures and arable land.[8] They finally settled in the districts mentioned below. Some of them have even moved to Jammu Province and settled there.

In the valley of Kashmir, Pakhtoons are concentrated mainly in Districts of Anantnag, Baramulla, Kupwara and Ganderbal.

"Pakhtoon settlements are listed below on the basis of their concentration in various villages:

District Kupwara: Deed-Koot; Machal Lolab; Manigah Gilas Daji; Nagri Malpora; Safe Wali Hai Hama; Warpora

District Baramulla: Kaliban; Sheeri

District Ganderbal: Gutlibagh; Mammar; Upper Serch; Gagangeer Maniarram (Wangat) ; Watlar; Wurpush; Yarmuqam

District Anantnag: Akingam (Acchabal); Alam Gadol; Chack Isher Dass – Mattan; Daddu Madhama; Cheerpora; Gopalpora; Kular Aurah Salar; Stari Maidan"[9]

Further the research revealed that in addition to the above, Pakhtoon settlements are also found in:

District Shopian: Saddhu Chakk

District Pulwama: Machhama, Tral

District Anantnag: Wantrag, Batkoot (Srichen), Nagabal (Seer), Andoo (Shangus), Pingwani (Acchabal), Gadweel (Kokarnag)

District Ganderbal: Wayil Wuddar, Bela Wussan.

Following is the approximiate number of households in the various districts:-

District Anantnag

(a) Wantrag : 200 Households

(b) Stree Maidan: 150 Households

(c) Akingam (Acchabal): 50 Households

(d) Alam Gadol: 20 Households
(e) Batkoot (Srichen):10-15 Households
(f) Chack Isher Dass (Mattan): 300 Households
(g) Daddu Madhama: 250 Households
(h) Cheerpora: 20 Households
(i) Gopalpora: 10-20 Households
(j) Nagabal (Seer) 5-6 Households
(k) Pingwani(Achabal) : 8 Households
(l) Kular Aurah Salar: 10 Households
(m) Gadweel: 6 Households
(n) Anra: 80 Households
(o) Andoo Shangus: 50 Households
(p) Stari Maidan: 20 Houscholds

District Baramulla

(a) Kaliban: 40 Households
(b) Sheeri: 4-5 Households
(c) Uri-Boniyar (Bela Salamabad): 2 Households

District Kupwara

(a) Deed-Koot: 8 Households
(b) Machal Lolab: 100 Households
(c) Manigah Gilas Daji: 5-6 Households
(d) Nagri Malpora: 16 Households
(e) Safe Wali Hai Hama;
(f) Warpora:
(g) Hatmulla: 3-4 Households

District Ganderbal

(a) Gutlibagh (Chanahaar, Banjar Basti, Khyber, Malakand, Aastan Mohalla): 600 households
(b) Mammar: 50 Households
(c) Upper Serch: 15 Households

(d) Maniarram (Wangat): 3 Households
(e) Watlar: 100 Households
(f) Wurpush (Nadar Bagh): 100 Households
(g) Yarmuqam Wuddar: 100 Households
(h) Wayil Wuddar (Baba Wayil, Wuddar): 1000 Households
(i) Bela Wussan: 15 Households
(j) Dursuma: 30 Households
(k) Gagangeer: 5 Households

District Shopian

(a) Saddhu Chakk: 30 Households

District Pulwama

(a) Machhama:
(b) Tral (Shikaargah): 5 households

Oral Histories

As revealed by the field study, there have been varied causes for the migration of Pakhtoons into Kashmir and those vary from family to family. One of the most important causes is the conflict in area the Pashtuns call Ellaqai Ghair and Yaghistan. Since historical records explaining the migration of Pakhtoons into Kashmir are scanty, the causes of dispersal have been transmitted by the word of mouth from older generations to the subsequent ones.

(a) Narrative of Wadood Khan (85 Years, Gutli Bagh):
As per Wadood Khan, a Pakhtoon living in Gutli Bagh in his 80s it was Shareefullah his grandfather (along with two of his sons Syed Omer and Syed Faqir) who came to Kashmir from Allayi towards the end of nineteenth century. The reason he attributes to the migration is poverty and lawlessness in the areas called Ellaquai Ghair and Yaghistan. He adds that the British Raj failed to accommodate the Pakhtoons which further added to their mobile nature. Shareefullah first came to Kupwara, and when he did not like it there he finally came

and settled in Gutli Bagh which was a huge unpopulated stretch of land. After settling here he went back to Allayi to bring his six brothers.

As per Wadood Khan, Shareefullah was the first amongst Pakhtoons to have come to Kashmir valley.[10]

(b) Narrative of Haji Ali Gowhar Khan (75 Years, Gutli Bagh):

After the death of her husband Noor Jehan, Gowhar's Grandmother came to Kashmir from Allayi to escape levirate along with her five children. He adds that in Yagistaan there was a custom that a widow had to get married to her brother-in-law. Noor Jehan came on foot via Baramulla.

(c) Narrative of Shareef Khan (65 Years, Gutli Bagh):

Sharef khan asserts that his great grandfather Shah Zamaan had come from Allayi about 150 years back. He asserts that some Pakhtoons came as Tradesmen during Maharaja Gulab Singh's time. Others came to escape the oppression of the Britishers as Pakhtoons had participated in the freedom struggle. The State subject status was given to Pakhtoons after 150 years. And, as per him, the absence of state subject is the major reason that Pakhtoon population has not been accounted for in the records of Kashmir history.

(d) Narrative of Mallika Khatoon (90 years, Bela Wussan, Ganderbal):

Her father, Sherdil Khan had migrated from Allayi to Chak Issar Dass Anantnag District in Valley). He used to sell caps in Srinagar. After partition he settled in Kashmir.

(e) Narrative of Pukhtanah (98 Years, Gutli Bagh):

Her father was imprisoned before partition when he had come to visit his niece who was married in Kashmir. That time Maharaja Hari Singh ruled Kashmir. Her father was released when Hari Singh's son was born in 1931. He returned to Allayi and got Pukhtanah married to Mateen Khan (his niece's son) in 1933. They came via Baramulla. Since then she has not seen her father. She says that partition created all the barriers.

She has visited her village in Pakistan twice in 1986 and 1992, but her father had passed away by then.

(f) Narrative of Bashir Ahmed Khan: (65 years, Chak Ishar Dass):

He attributes two important reasons to the migration of Pashtuns to Kashmir; Normlessness in their homeland for which the principal cause as per him was the custom of Badal (Revenge) which is an important feature of Pashtunwali or the Pakhtoon way of life. As per this custom, the burden of revenge was carried on from generation to generation. And since inter-tribal feuds were a regular feature of the society there, it became necessary for families caught in the practice of Badal to escape to nearby places. The second reason which he attributes to the in migrations of their ancestors into Kashmir was that during those times Kashmir was a peaceful place as a result of which the peripatetic Pakhtoons found it congenial to settle here.

Further he adds that the vast stretch of land in what is now known as Chak Ishar Dass (Anantnag District of Valley) belonged to one Kashmiri Pandit Lala Ishar Dass who was a businessman in North Western Frontier Province.

(g) Narrative of Ghulam Mohammad Khan (70 Years, Mammar, Ganderbal):

His grandfather Sarbuland Khan had migrated from Swat. He used to work as a carpenter. Those days employment opportunities there were scarce and it was difficult for people who lived from hand to mouth to make both ends meet. His grandfather along with many fellow artisans came to Kashmir for work. Subsequently got their families along and settled here.

(h) Narrative of Haji Mohammad Arsallah Khan (64 Years, Kaliban Baramulla):

His grandfather Sher Dil Khan originally from North Western Frontier Province (Subah Sarhad) worked as a labourer in

Gulmarg in 1920's. After sometime they settled in Kaliban (Baramulla District in Valley).

(i) Sallay Rahman Khan, Son of Juma Khan[11] (66 Years, Khyber, Gutli Bagh)

His grandfather Habibullah Khan migrated to Kashmir in 1890 for fruit trade from a place in Allayi called Upper Deer. as the weather was good in Kashmir he kept on coming here during the summer months and went back to his native village in winter. This was his routine till 1947 when the subcontinent got partitioned in 1947. As the partition stopped the free movement of people between India and Pakistan, Habibullah along with his wife and seven children settled in Gutli Bagh.

(j) Narrative of Ghulam Hassan Khan (50 Years, Gujjar Dajji Nagri Kupwara):

His great grandfather had migrated from Swat because of conflict with his relatives and settled in Nagri (Kupwara District in Valley).

(k) Narrative of Nawab Gul (75 Years Yarmuqam Wuddar, Ganderbal):

His grandfather Anayatullah Khan migrated from Swat. The reason for migration was conflict with the members of the other tribe which had turned into a war and had led to the death of one of his brothers.

(l) Sonaullah Khan (65 Years, Gutli Bagh):

As per him the clan to which he belongs is Yousufzai (Madaikhail). He asserts that most of the Pakhtoon migration to Kashmir has originated from 'No Man's Land' i.e, the territory between British India and Afghanistan. Since the area round Durrand Line remained as a system which was not governed by any formal legal structure, normlessness was the order of the day there.

He comes from a family of landlords. His father Haji Zakir, who was 12 years old that time came along with four of his siblings came from Rashang in Zila Battagram. The reason for migration was that after the death of Zakir's father, their family had no elder male to protect their estate. The paternal cousins of Haji Zakir had an eye over the property (a common practice of cousin rivalry among the Pakhtoons called Tarboorwali). One of Zakir's aunts who was married in the rival family came to know of the plot that they were hatching to murder Zakir and his siblings. She fled her home in the dead of the night and persuaded Zakir and his siblings to run away. They came to Kashmir, settled first at Yarmuqaam (in district Ganderbal) and later on came to Gutli Bagh.

(m) Mohammad Akbar Madhakhail: (57 Years, Gutli Bagh)

His grandfather Khitaab Khan alongwith his family came from a place called Tandol in Ellaquai Ghair or Yagistaan. He says that they came to escape Badal from a tribe whose one member was killed by their people. Sikandar Badal

Akbar's father Ahmad Tawaab married his mother Gulandaan here in Gutli Bagh in 1930's. He was a driver in British Army posted in North Western Frontier Province. After partition, he gave up his job in the Pakistan Army and in 1948 he came back to his village in Gutli Bagh.

(n) Dr. Akbar Madhakhail (60 Years, Gutli Bagh)

Habibullah Khan his great grand father Allayi (Yagistan) along with his father Abdul Qadoos Khan migrated because he was fed up of the inter tribal feuds. Normlessness as a result of lack of a stable governmental machinery as per him was a major cause for the out-migration of many Pakhtoon groups into Kashmir.

He says that the first Pakhtoon to have arrived in Gutli Bagh was named Shareefullah Khan.[12] As per him it the Madhakhail Pakhtoons have migrated from three villages of Allayi i.e., Jhangdi, Sonaullah Khan and Tandol.

He claims that all Mandhakhail Pakhtoon are descendants of Madhay Baba who was a great saint and his shrine is still in Village Madhaybaba in Jalla town of Mardhaan divison on Pakistan.

(o) Ghulam Haider Khan (69 Years, Dursum, Ganderbal)

His father Omer Khan had eloped with his wife Mahay Tabaan from Allayi (Bafa Mansera) in 1929. Mahay Taaban was betrothed to one of her cousins. Omer Khan eloped with her when the day of the marriage came near. He brought her to Kashmir as it was comparatively easier to travel here through Muzaffarabad. Haider Khan was born to them in 1947.

Thus, the causes for the dispersion of Pakhtoons in to Kashmir valley have been many and varied. The chief cause being the anomic conditions due to intermittent tribal feuds in the regions they call as Yaghistan and Ellaquai Ghair. Trade, family feuds and the search for greener pastures because of the push factors like poverty, unemployment etc. have also been some of the causes as per the oral tradition of the ancestors of the Pakhtoons of Kashmir.

Bibliography

- Hutter, Manfred (2009). 'Afghanistan und seine 'vergessenen' Hindus". Zeitschrift für Religionswissenschaft, Vol. 17: 149-164.
- Indu Bala Dhâr. Social Economy of the Pashtuns of Gutli Bagh (unpublished PhD thesis) Centre for Central Asian Studies, University of Kashmir.
- Parvez Dewan'., Jammu, Kashmir and Ladakh (Kashmir), Manas Publications, New Delhi.
- Walter R Lawrence. The Valley of Kashmir, Chinar Publishing House, Srinagar.
- Martin McCauley. Afghanistan and Central Asia: A Modern History, Pearson Education, Great Britain, 2002.
- Markovits, Claude, Jacques Pouchepaddass, Sanjay Subrahmanyam. Society and Circulation, Mobile People and Itinerant Cultures in South Asia, 1750-1950, Permanent Back, New Delhi, 2003.
- Meredith L Runion. The History of Afghanistan, Greenwood Press, United States of America.
- Robert Nicholas. A History of Pashtun Migration 1775-2006, Oxford University Press, Pakistan.
- K.S. Singh (edited). Jammu and Kashmir- People of India, Volume XXV, Anthropological Survey of India, Manohar 2003, New Delhi.
- Victoria Schofield. Afghan Frontier: Feuding and Fighting in Central Asia, Taurisparkle Paperbacks, p. 9.

- Olaf Caroe. The Pathans 500 B.C-A.D 1957, Macmillan and Co Limited, New York, 1965.
- R. Vaidya Nath. 1967. *Formation of Soviet Central Asian Republics*. New Delhi: Peoples Publishing House.
- Siddique Abubakar, The Pashtuns: the Unresolved Key to the Future of Pakistan and Afghanistan, Random House India, Haryana, 2014, p. 16.
- Schetter Conrad, Translocal Lives: Patterns of Migration in Afghanistan, Crossroads Asia: Working Paper Series, p. 2 (Schetter, Conrad (2012): Translocal Lives. Patterns of Migration in Afghanistan. In: *Crossroads Asia* Working Paper Series, No. 2.)
- George B, Scott, Afghan and Pathan: A Sketch, The Mitre Press, London, p. 29.

Notes

1. Victoria Schofield. Afghan Frontier: Feuding and fighting in Central Asia, Taurisparkle Paperbacks. p. 9.
2. Martin McCauley. Afghanistan and Central Asia: A Modern History, Pearson Education, Great Britain, 2002, p. 2.
3. R. Vaidya Nath. 1967. *Formation of Soviet Central Asian Republics*. New Delhi: Peoples Publishing House. p. 2.
4. Conrad Schetter. Translocal Lives: patterns of Migration in Afghanistan.
5. Abubakar Siddique. The Pashtuns: the Unresolved Key to the Future of Pakistan and Afghanistan, Random House India, Haryana, 2014, p. 16.
6. Robert Nicholas. A History of Pashtun Migration 1775-2006, Oxford University Press, Pakistan.
7. Walter R. Lawrence. 1895. *The Valley of Kashmir*. London. Cambridge Publications. p. 353.
8. *Ibid*. p. 48.
9. Indu Bala Dhar.1989. *Social Economy of Pakhtoons of Kashmir Valley* (Unpublished Thesis). Centre for Central Asian Studies. pp. 51-56.
10. This fact was later substantiated by narratives of other Pakhtoons.
11. I was fortunate to have interviewed Juma Khan, a Pakhtoon who claimed to be 105 years of age in the first phase of data collection including the Pilot study. Khan died while I was in the phase of collecting oral histories. So I chose to interview his eldest son (Sallay Rahman) with whom he lived.
12. (Wadood Khan's Father).

Politics and Governance in Jammu and Kashmir

17

Conflict Situation and Multiple Identity Politics in J&K

— Rekha Chowdhary

Jammu and Kashmir is highly diverse society that reflects a multi-layered identity politics. Its diversity ranging from religious to cultural-regional markers operates in such a manner that it generates a picture of complexity. Though a Muslim-majority state, it is only in the region of Kashmir that Muslims have a predominant presence. While Jammu is a Hindu-dominant region, Ladakh has larger number of Buddhists. However, it is only Kashmir region which has a homogenous demographic character, both Jammu and Ladakh represent a mixed society. The Muslims form a substantial minority in both these regions. One of the two districts of Ladakh and four of the ten districts of Jammu are Muslim majority districts.

However, the demographic complexity of the state does not exhaust with the religious plurality, the regional identity introduces further intricacy in it. Thus, rather than being identified as Hindus or Muslims or Buddhists, people here are identified as those belonging to Kashmir or Jammu or Ladakh. It is the regional identification that differentiates the Kashmiri Pundit from the Hindus of Jammu; the Kashmiri Muslims from Jammu Muslims; and Ladakhi Muslims from both Kashmiri and Jammu Muslims.

Beyond these, there are other identity markers that overlap with the religious and regional markers. The caste identity, for instance is very crucial not only for the Hindus but also Muslims, especially of Jammu region. The dominant 'Rajput' identity, cuts across the religious lines and provides a very strong sense of belonging to a large number of Hindus and Muslims of Jammu region. The tribal identity similarly operates in a crucial manner not only for the Ladakhis, but all-Muslim group of Gujjars who distinguish themselves from other Muslims on the basis of this identity. Competing with them are Hindu-Muslim combine of Paharis who have been demanding the Scheduled Tribe status on the line of Gujjars.

In a diverse society like Jammu and Kashmir where each identity marker is internally differentiated and overlaps with other identity markers, the identity politics assumes a complex character. This complexity is provided firstly by the fact that there is no clear cut context of 'majority' or 'minority'. Each of the identities while asserting its collective numerical strength also simultaneously voices its victimisation as a minority. Thus, the Kashmiri identity politics while asserting the numerical dominance within the state, bemoans the marginalisation of 'Kashmiris' and 'Muslims' in the larger context of Indian state. Those asserting the regional identity of Jammu claim that this region is larger in territorial terms in comparison to Kashmir but complain about its political marginalisation vis-à-vis Kashmir region. Gujjars claim to be the third largest demographic grouping after 'Muslims' and 'Hindus' but again lament their backwardness vis-à-vis other people of the state.

The multiple identities that operate within the state engage with each other in a variety of ways. While some identities operate parallel to each other, there are others which cut across each other – claiming to represent the same political constituency. These later identities are located in a mutually exclusive and contradictory relationship with each other.

Conflict Situation and Multiple Identity Politics

The conflict situation in which the state of Jammu and Kashmir is involved for more than six decades now, has both external as well as internal dimensions. (Bose, 1996) The contestation between India and Pakistan over their respective claims leading to a number of wars and prolonged hostility between the two countries forms the external dimension of conflict. The internal dimension of conflict, however, is defined by Kashmir's relationship with India, specifically the context of political alienation in Kashmir and the consequent political situation. Seen from this perspective, the internal context of conflict has evolved around the Kashmiri identity politics. However, this identity politics does not exhaust the whole range of political claims and assertions. Political divergence is the reality of the state and provides a complexity both to the nature of conflict as well as its resolution. (Chowdhary, 2010)

The conflict is specifically located in the identity politics of Kashmir. However, the implications of conflict reach far beyond the valley of Kashmir. The political uncertainty and instability that has been caused by Kashmir-specificity of conflict has its spillover effect on the rest of the state. It also generates its own kinds of political dynamism that goes a long way in redefining the very context of conflict. To begin with there remains a huge gap between claims and representation. Despite its specificity, the claims within the Kashmiri identity politics are made on behalf of 'all the people of the state'. Apart from the question of legitimacy of representation of those who are not located within this politics, there is the other situation of contestation both of these claims as well as representations. It is this context of internal contestations that takes the conflict to a third level – the intra-state level (besides the oft cited 'external' and 'internal' levels).

What is involved in the third level of conflict is the issue of political divergence in the context of its specificity. Apart from the Kashmiri identity politics, there are host of other identity assertions which have provided a sense of vibrancy to the internal politics of the state. While some of these identities operate parallel to the Kashmiri identity politics, there are others which are located in a mutually exclusive and contradictory relationship to it.

The very Kashmir-specific context of conflict itself has generated a number of political demands and assertions. These assertions either aim at contesting the claims made from the Kashmir-specificity and laying down counter-claims or alternatively seek to broaden the very contours of conflict so as to incorporate the interests of those unrepresented in the Kashmiri identity politics.

Identity Politics and Conflict Situation

The interplay of the competing identity politics, especially during the last two decades, has made it amply clear that the conflict resolution is not a simple process of involving a formula or delivering a package. It is also not a process that ends with a dialogue between the state and the disgruntled elements in one part of the state. It is also a long-term process of building a consensus among the stakeholders. However, before any consensus can be evolved, it may be important to delineate the basic issues emerging out of the multiple identity politics vis-à-vis the conflict situation.

The first issues relates to the question of claims and representation. Not only there is multiplicity of claims within the state but there is also a competitive context of claims. The political leaders in Kashmir tend to make claims for 'all the people of Jammu and Kashmir'. Whether referring to the demand for self-determination or Azadi, or even the demand for 'Autonomy', these leaders seek to represent all the regions and all the people of the state. However, due to the specificity of the movement politics to Kashmir, there remains a gap between the claim and representation. The claim is contested not merely by the very limited influence of the separatist politics in areas beyond Kashmir but by the explicit claims being made by various organisations. Thus, the BJP has been making claims on behalf of people of Jammu demanding 'full integration of the state with India' and abrogation of Article 370 of Indian constitution; various Hindu Rightist organisations including the RSS, Shiv Sena and Jammu Mukti Morcha, similarly seeking to represent the people of Jammu make demands for separation of Jammu from Kashmir; LBA making claims on behalf of people of Ladakh demands the UT status, and the Panun Kashmir makes demand for 'Homeland' for Kashmiri Pundits. Interestingly, each of these demands is equally exclusive in nature and seeks to make claims on behalf of a community that is supposedly 'homogenised'. Thus, it is not only the 'homogenised' representation of J&K that is reflected in the separatist demand, but also homogenised representation of Jammu and Ladakh. The internal differentiations and divergences within are equally ignored.

These differentiations and divergences, however, act as the limits on the politics of representation. All these claims therefore remain internally contested.

The second issue relates to the very nature of conflict. Despite the general perception that there is a singular context of conflict, there are multiple layers at which the conflict actually manifests itself. These layers are linked with each other in such a manner that none of the layers can be treated in an autonomous manner without having some impact on the other layers. While the Kashmir-specific nature of conflict remains central, there are other aspects of conflict which either go beyond Kashmir or are generated in response to the issues raised by the Kashmir-specificity of conflict. There is for instance, the whole context of border-related problems that range from the day-to-day hardships for the people living near the border to the issue of displacement of various kinds.[1] Then there is the unsettled problem of refugees. The division of the state in 1947 created a situation in which there were large number of refugees who came to settle in various parts of Jammu region. Mainly belonging to two categories – those who came from Pakistan administered Kashmir and those who came from Pakistan, these refugees have lot of grievances. In the case of the first category of refugees who were the permanent residents of the undivided Jammu and Kashmir, their problems are linked with the unresolved status of the state. With official claim being made that the area under Pakistan's control as part of India, these displaced people have not been treated at par with similarly displaced refugees in other parts of India. Due to the unsettled nature of conflict, their problems of rehabilitation and resettlement also continue to remain unresolved. In the case of the second category of displaced, the basic issue remains linked with their citizenship status. Despite being settled in Jammu since 1947, these people have not been granted the status of Permanent Residents of the state and hence they are deprived of various rights emanating from this status.

It is the complexity underlying the context of conflict that has made it very much intractable. Such a complexity to begin with, is provided by the way the external and internal dimensions have been fused with each other and thereafter add to this are the internal intricacies. These internal intricacies introduce a third dimension to the conflict situation which is defined by the inter-regional relations. Identifying this third dimension of conflict, Balraj Puri, with reference to Jammu's relationship of Kashmir has been arguing that without resolving the tension between Jammu and Kashmir, it may not be possible to resolve the context of conflict. (Puri, 1966, 1983)

Multiple Identity Politics and the Response of the State

The State's response vis-à-vis the identity politics in J&K has been changing over the period. It is in the last few years of the peace process, that there has developed a bit more nuanced approach to acknowledge and respond to the complexity underlying the identity politics. For quite some time, the complexity remained either unacknowledged or unaddressed, adding to the gravity of problems within the state. Many of the issues that became politically sensitive resulted from the failure of the political regimes, both at the level of the Centre as well as at the level of the states, to respond to the plurality, political diversity and divergence within the state. Much of the popular alienation that manifested through the armed militancy, separatist politics and popular upsurge in Kashmir in 1989 was in fact, a reflection of the deep-rooted sense of disenchantment with the Indian state. This sense of alienation was reflected in the Kashmiri identity politics in the period following the dismissal and detention of Sheikh Abdullah in 1953. Refusal of the state to acknowledge this sense of alienation for a prolonged period resulted in a political psyche of Kashmir that manifests not only a sense of political isolation vis-à-vis the nationalist politics but also a deep-seated distrust of the Indian state. The separatist politics that has been operating in Kashmir during last two decades, is based on these feelings.

However, it is not only the political sensitivities of Kashmir that have remained unaddressed but also the other kinds of sensitivities. More importantly, what has remained unaddressed is the fact of political divergence and multiple identity politics. As a result of the lop-sided response of the State, these multiple identities have tended to be not only mutually exclusive but also at odds with each other. The inter-regional context of conflict actually emanates from the lack of sensitivity towards the political divergence within. Right from the very beginning, the response of the governments, whether the Central or the State, towards the political issues within J&K, has been to see these as emanating from one homogenised political unit and thereby responding to these in that manner only. As a consequence, there emerged one or the other source of discontent. The political arrangements made in response to Kashmiri identity politics in the pre-1953 period, for instance, did not take into account the political response of the dominant elite in Jammu. The sharpening of regional identity politics of Jammu and its leaning towards the Rightist organisations was a result of the acute feeling of neglect in the 'negotiated' relationship that had evolved between the Centre and the state in the form of Article 370 of Indian constitution. That explains the aggressive opposition to this arrangement in Jammu, as reflected in the 1952 Praja Parishad agitation. Similarly, the post-1953 political arrangement, that emanated from a response of the Indian state to constitutionally 'integrate' the state of J&K with India, did not take into account the political aspirations of Kashmir region. Though satisfying to the dominant political elite of Jammu, these arrangements generated a very strong sense of discontent in Kashmir region. One can give similar examples about the later period. The 1975 Indira-Sheikh Accord aimed at addressing the alienation of people of Kashmir, again assumed 'Kashmiris' to be the major stakeholders in the politics of Kashmir, without considering the implication of a new arrangement on the people of Jammu and Ladakh. That the ruling Congress that had made a way for the newly revived National Conference under the leadership of Sheikh Abdullah to take on power, had a base in Jammu and represented the political voice of the region, was totally undermined and the new political arrangement was seen as 'Kashmir-centric' by the vocal elite of Jammu region. The later political developments, especially those linked with the political ambitions of the Indian National Congress as the ruling party in the Centre in the decade of eighties, alienated the people of Kashmir.

The lopsided response of the state towards the divergent political aspirations within the state continued through the decade of nineties. The most illustrious case in the context of the slackness on the part of the Centre (as well as the State government) in dealing with the multiple identity politics of the state is that of the issue of state and regional autonomy. The appointment of the State Autonomy Committee and the Regional Autonomy Committee by the NC-led state government in 1997 was first initiative of its kind to address the conflicting regional response to the issue of autonomy by acknowledging the divergence around this issue on the regional basis. The State Autonomy Committee which was to address the issue of 'restoration' of the 'pristine' form of the Centre-State relations as these were available in the pre-1953 period, was aimed to address the sense of alienation of the people of Kashmir. Meanwhile, the Regional Autonomy Committee was appointed to address the regional discontent arising from the feeling of 'political neglect' arising out of 'Kashmir-Centric' political arrangements. The presumption underlying the appointment of these two committees was that by addressing the demand for regional autonomy along with the State autonomy, the grievance of people of both the regions would be addressed. However, this could not be possible due to the tactless approach both of the Central and State governments. While the Central government totally dismissed the recommendations of the State Autonomy Committee, the state government botched up the very basis of demand of regional autonomy. Subsequent to the submission of the report of the State Autonomy Committee, the state Legislature passed a resolution endorsing the demand of restoration of pre-1953 constitutional position of the state. The resolution that was sent to the Centre was not put for debate in any forum. On the contrary, when placed before the cabinet, it was summarily dismissed, generating a further sense of despondency in Kashmir. As regards the regional autonomy, the state government after dismissing and replacing the chairperson of the committee endorsed a report that questioned the very existence of Jammu and Ladakh as regions.

It was during the initiation of comprehensive peace process that was initiated by Atal Bihari Vajpayee that greater sensitivity developed around the multiple stakeholders in the state and divergent political aspirations and responses. Hence, the idea of extending the definition of conflict from external and internal to the intra-state level was mooted in various conferences and processes of dialogue. Of these, the Round Table Conferences (RTCs) that were held under the leadership are the most important ones. The five working groups that were constituted through these RTCs came up with elaborate report that took into consideration the political aspirations not only at the state, regional and sub-regional levels but also those of the marginal and backward groups including the internally displaced people of various kinds and the tribal Gujjars. More recently, the interlocutors appointed by the Government of India have also shown sensitivity towards the multiple identity issues and have recommended the resolution of the conflict by taking into consideration the complexity arising out of the political divergence within the state. However, the reports of these groups remain mostly on papers.

Towards the Political Future: Need for consensus building

The complexity that has been generated by the multiple identity politics of the state has made the conflict-resolution a challenging task. More particularly, it is the context of mutually exclusive and conflicting claims that makes it difficult to make progress in the peace process. Politically divergent positions have already led many to think of simplified solutions like the division of the state. This idea has been floated in different forms, off and on, from different quarters at different times. Of the early formulations that have been proposed to deal with the intricacies of the state include the 'Dixon' formula or the 'Chenab-based' division. As per this formulation, the division of the state around the river Chenab is suggested. Since this divide is regional-cum-religious divide (in the sense that it not only divides Kashmir region from Jammu but also places the Muslim-dominated districts of Jammu along with Kashmir), it has met with fierce criticism on the ground that it is purely communal in nature. However, despite its dangerous communal implications, it has continued to attract many academicians, intellectuals and organisations. The Kashmir Study Group, a think tank based in USA, came up with a report in late nineties which suggested the division of the state on regional/religious lines and adoption of different approaches to deal with each part of the state. Later on, General Musharraf also suggested the 'regional' solution to Kashmir problem, defining J&K on the basis of five regions, two on the sides of Pakistan and three on Indian side (Jammu, Kashmir and Ladakh). The idea of division of the state has also been floated by the Hindu Rightist groups as well. The RSS actually passed a formal resolution about the division of the state. Nearer home, the demand for separation of Jammu from Kashmir and its reorganisation as a separate state; the separation of

Ladakh and its recognition as a Union Territory; and the demand for 'Homeland' for Kashmiri Pundits (carved out of few districts in Kashmir) has been made by organisations like Jammu Mukti Morcha/ Jammu State Morcha; Ladakh Buddhist Association and the Panun Kashmir respectively.

This simplified resolution of complex nature of conflict has been rejected by many on the grounds of its being communal in nature. The religious carving of new units or reorganisation of the state on religious principles, does not cater to context of identity politics of the state. The identity politics of the state is not simply based on the factor of religion and religious identities not only overlap with other kinds of identities but are also internally differentiated. Hence, the religious basis of division of the state, cannot succeed beyond a point. At the most it can generate communalised politics, but not actually resolve the conflict.

The only way the conflict situation in the context of multiple identities and divergent political positions can be resolved, is through the process of consensus building. Though consensus may seem to be a far-reaching idea in the State, however, it can be stated that during the last two decades, some minimum consensus has been evolved within the state. Most of the stakeholders within the state are insistent on maintaining the integrity of the state and sustaining its plural character. This in itself is a very good starting point for building further consensus on more intricate issues. There is also a consensus that the communal and divisive politics is no solution to the problems in the state.

It is on the basis of these minimums, that a process of consensus building has to be attained. However, this process has to be a very intricate one, not merely involving multi-layered dialogues and negotiations but also generating a sense of partnership among the various kinds of stakeholders. Beginning therefore has to be made through a really inclusive process of dialogue, giving a sense of ownership to all the stakeholders.

References

1. Bose, Sumantra, 1996. *The Challenge in Kashmir: Democracy, Self Determination and a Just Peace*, New Delhi: Sage Publications.

2. Chowdhary, Rekha, 2010. *Identity Politics in Jammu and Kashmir*, New Delhi: Vitasta.
3. Chowdhary, Rekha, 2010 A. 'The Second Uprising', *Economic and Political Weekly*, Vol. XLV. No. 39, (September 25), 10-13.
4. Chowdhary, Rekha, 2002. 'Kashmir: Lone's Liberal Legacy', *Economic and Political Weekly*, 37, no.25, (June 22-28): 2398-2400.
5. Puri, Balraj, 1993. *Towards Insurgency*, Delhi: Orient Longman.
6. Puri, Balraj. *Jammu: A Clue to Kashmir Tangle*, (Delhi, 1966).
7. Puri, Balraj. *Simmering Volcano: Jammu's Relation with Kashmir* (Delhi: Sterling, 1983).
8. State Autonomy Committee Report, 1999, Jammu.
9. Schofield, Victoria, 2003. *Kashmir in Conflict: India, Pakistan and the Unending War*, London: I B Tauris.

Notes

1. With the border remaining very volatile even during the peace time, the life of the people in the villages near the border has been quite difficult. Apart from Intermittent shelling and bombing and mining they have been faced with the problem of often losing the control over their agricultural land.

18

Jammu and Kashmir: A Test case in India's Asymmetrical Federal Governance

— ***Rekha Saxena***

Founding fathers of our constitution espoused asymmetrical constitutional arrangements in case of Jammu and Kashmir to deal with its unique circumstances. Article 370 of the Indian Constitution grants special autonomous status to the state of Jammu and Kashmir. But still it happens to be the most volatile state in the Union of India. The state is terribly beleaguerd due to the growing separatist and secessionist tendencies. Jammu and Kashmir has become an acid test for Indian experiment with asymmetrical federalism.

This chapter attempts to decode the problem and panacea of the Kashmir tangle in Indian federal system. I have divided this paper into four main sections. The first section provides an account of the theoretical debate on asymmetrical fedealism. The second section discusses the historical roots of the Kashmir problem. The third section examines the political history of Kashmir. The fourth section debates Article 370 as an epitome of the constitutional asymmetry in Indian constitution and finally, in the conclusion, I recommend a federal solution for Kashmir.

Asymmetrical Federalism: Secession v. National Unity

The political culture of open political bargaining to arrive at a political decision is an important feature of a federal form of government. These political bargaining's many a times results in an asymmetry in legislative, administrative and financial powers of different constituents units of a federation.The federations with this kind of asymmetry are called asymmetric federations.In these federations, some, if not all states/sub-units have differential relationship with the federal government. India is also an example of a asymmetric federation where the flexible type of union grants special status to some constituent states. Klaus von Beyme has made an astute observation about asymmetrical federalism which is very relevant here. According to him, older federalism in the age of classical modernism relied on a rational model of symmetric states with liberal multicultural rights, whereas postmodern federalism of multinational states has become more tolerant of interstate asymmetries in constitutional engineering.[12] The Canadian, Indian, Malaysian, Belgian, Spanish and Russian federations are examples of the asymmetrical constitutional arrangements in the allocation of powers to constituent units.

Charles Tarlton had coined the term asymmetrical federalism in 1965 in an article published in *The Journal of Politics* entitled 'Symmetry and Asymmetry as Elements of Federalism: A Theoretical Speculation.' He takes a dismissive view of this variation of federal governance, as he believes that more symmetrical the division of power will be in a federation, the more harmonious and unified it will be, and vice versa. For him, the concept of 'asymmetry' expressed the extent to which constituent states had differences in the conditions and concerns common to the federal system as a whole. According to him ideal asymmetrical federation would be one composed of political units corresponding to discongruities of interest, character and make up existing within the whole society.Tarlton pointed out in this article that "when we turn our attentiveness away from set constitutional-legal relationships, then it is clear that cultural, economic, social and political factors in amalgamation have in all federations produced asymmetrical variations in the power and status of different federative units, and these exert influence on degree of harmony or disunity within federations."[3]

According to Michael Burgess asymmetrical federalism, "has in practice become Janus-faced, being perceived by some as a positive instrument designed to buttress and sustain federal values and structures while simultaneously inducing fears and anxieties in others who construe it very much as a dangerous threat to the stability and integrity of the state."[4]

The literature on the concept and theory of asymmetrical federalism is full with a divided debate whether asymmetry in federal governance leads to seccession or is favourable for national unity.The literature on federal systems traditionally assumed symmetry to be the norm within federations because in three of the classical federations, the United States (1789), Switzerland (1848), and Australia (1901), the states and cantons were assigned basically symmetrical constitutional status and authority.[5] Initially scholars were against the idea of asymmetry in federation and supported symmetrical division of powers between the constituent federative units. They had a belief that a asymmetrical division of power can intensify secessionist tendencies and foster social and political disintegration.These misapprehensions also finds resonance in contemporary debates in India on asymmetric federal provisions wherein granting more autonomy to J&K is seen by some as an en route to secession. However, the recent literature on the subject shows that instead of being inherently secessionist in potential, asymmetrical federalism, is a way forward in controlling secession by constitutional process.The experience of multinational federations around the world evinces that some degree of constitutional asymmetry is of great consequence for establishing enduring federations in the contemporary world today. Federations like India, Belgium, Canada can be seen as a flawless example of the same.

Ronald Watts' theoretical distinction between political and constitutional asymmetry is of interest here. He argues that the former exists in every federation with regard to the geographical and demographic size of the units whereas the latter "refers specifically to differences in the status or legislative and executive powers assigned by the constitution to the different regional units."[6] Indian union has accommodated the diverse needs and aspirations of the different federative units through the mechanisms of both constitutional and political asymmetry. Article 370 of Indian Constitution was one such constitutional provision provided to accommodate the Kashmiri sentimentalism.

Article 370 guaranteed the much needed space to Kashmiri people in matters of governance. Article 370 does not promote secessionist and separatist tendencies but in lieu of that it is just a step forward in decentralisation and devolution of power. There is no relation between the anti-India secessionist sentiments in the valley and the State's desire for increased autonomy in the Union of India as envisioned in this Article. The Secessionist and separatists are microscopic minority in Kashmir where the majority of population favours the continuation of Kashmir's accession to India but with a increased autonomy within the Union of India.The demand for increased autonomy is not a new thing, it has remained since the days of accession, the pulse of the people of the State.

Historical Roots of the Kashmir Problem

The case of J&K is an unique one, so it must be distinctively dealt with. The history of the federative units that come into federations has great impact on the federal division of power. The roots of Asymmetrical constitutional arrangements for Kashmir can be traced in its historical roots. Jammu and Kashmir came into existence as a separate political entity in the year 1846 by the Treaty of Amritsar concluded between the Britisher and Dogra ruler Gulab Singh. This treaty was a commercial deal because East India Company transferred the Kashmir along with its people to Gulab Singh for 75 lakh Nanakshahee Rupees. The treaty fulfilled British strategic interests at the cost of the interests of Kashmiri populace. Inking of this treaty was a beginning of Hindu Dogra dynasty rule over the large majority of Muslims subjects in Kashmir. Gulab Singh ruled Kashmir until his death and was succeeded by his son Ranbir Singh in 1857, who in turn was succeeded by his son Pratab Singh in 1885. Pratap Singh was without a male heir therefore after him his nephew, son of his brother Amar Singh, Hari Singh, occupied the throne in 1925. The movement for more autonomy and self-governance is as old as the state itself but under Hari Singh the seeds of a political movement for self-determination aggrandized in Kashmir due to his misrule and persecution of Muslims. Dogra rulers had a obsession that since Maharaja Gulab Singh paid for his rights on Kashmir, Kashmir; its land, wealth and people were there personal property. Although, the difference in the religion of the ruler and ruled had a defining impact on the politics of Kashmir but the Problem of Kashmir was more a economic and political problem than a religious one.

Kashmir's vast majority of Muslim subject started mobilising against the Maharaja and got a messiah in Sheikh Abdullah. Who emerged as the leader of the simple, uneducated and underprivileged subjects. In him they saw a person who dared to present their grievances before the Monarch. The discontent against the autocratic rule of Maharaja kept growing deeper and Kashmir witnessed many uprisings in 1930s. In October 1932, Sheikh Abdullah in collaboration with Mir Waiz Yousuf Shah and Chaudhry Ghulam Abbas founded the All Jammu and Kashmir Muslim Conference. The Muslim conference mobilised the masses and lead the struggle against the unpopular Maharaja's rule. The struggle of the people was against the Dogra rulers feudal dispensation. Sheikh Abdullah launched a civil disobedience movement in 1933 which also led to the first democratic election in the state in 1934. The movement in Kashmir was for the political and economic emancipation of Kashmiri masses. This Movement was not to divide people on religious ground or launched for religious motives, from beginning this struggle against the autocratic monarch has progressive and secular character. The conversion of Muslim Conference into National Conference on 11 June 1939 is a testimonial of the secular character of the movement lead by Sheikh Abdullah.

In 1944, Sheikh submitted the 'Naya Kashmir' memorandum to Hari Singh on his return after attending the Imperial War Council meeting in Britain. This brief document outlined the plan of the transition of the Jammu and Kashmir state from an absolute monarchy to a constitutional democracy wherein the Maharajah remained the Head of the State as the Constitutional Monarch of Britain. Subsequently, 'Naya Kashmir,' was adopted as a manifesto of the National Conference. This Manifesto also underlined the need for communal unity and social harmony.

In May 1946, Abdullah launched the Quit Kashmir movement demanding the sovereignty for the people of Kashmir. The movement aimed to abolish the old age feudal order. They wanted to abolish Monarchy and wanted land to be given to tiller. They also demanded withdrawal of British paramountacy and abrogation of the Treaty of

Amritsar. The slogan of the movement was abrogate the treaty of Kashmir and vacate Kashmir. Quit Kashmir movement is very pertinent in understanding the Kashmir problem because it was for the first time during this movement that the Kashmiris'demand for autonomy and the right to self-determination was vigorously made. Quit Kashmir Movement also reflected the resentment of the masses against the unpopular Hari Singh's rule. The historical roots of Kashmir problem can be traced back to this kind of alienation, disillusionment and resentment against the monarch.

However, the history of hasty accession, inclusion of plebiscite in the Instrument of Accession, reference of Kashmir to UN are other chapters in history of Kashmir further aggravated the Kashmir problem.

Since J&K was acceded to India in 'unique circumstances', the state poses a 'Unique Problem'. It is noteworthy that J&K is the only unresolved dispute resulted from the accession exercise after the British colonial rule withdrew from Indian subcontinent in 1947. With the lapse of paramountcy over the princely states, with effect from 15 August 1947, the Indian Independence Act 1947 recognised the right of states to accede to either dominion, India or Pakistan. As sovereign entities their decision to join either of two dominion was to be voluntary. They were free to decide as they were under no constrain to accept any future constitution except by voluntary acceptance or agreement. They were entitled to accept or decline provisions of the constitution that either Dominion would ratify for itself.

The Maharaja of Kashmir, Hari Singh refused to acede either to India or to Pakistan. Maharaja wanted to retain the Independent status. He wanted a standstill agreement with both the countries. Identical telegrams were sent by the Prime Minister of Kashmir to Dominions of India and Pakistan, on August I2, 1947. Subsequently, Pakistan agreed and he succeded in concluding the standstill agreement with Pakistan but Government of India wanted a representative of Kashmir to visit Delhi to negotiate the agreement. The representative of Kashmir did not visit Delhi and no standstill agreement was concluded between the State and the Dominion of India. However, contrary to the standstill agreement Pakistan applied economic and other sanctions to put pressure on Kashmir with a view to securing its accession by force.

Pakistan being impatient launched a tribal invasion of Jammu & Kashmir on 22 October 1947. In a state of panic to defend the state, Maharaja was left with no other alternative and decided to accede to the Dominion of India and signed instrument of accession on October 26, 1947. Unlike other Princely States, the accession of J & K State was limited only to the areas of Defence, External Affairs and Communication. The state of Jammu and Kashmir did not accept any provisions of the Indian Constitution other than those agreed in the Instrument of Accession and retained its autonomy till the Delhi Agreement of 1952.

The accession offered by the Maharaja was an unconditional offer but to contain the emotions of the Muslim majority population of J&K, the then Governor General Mountbaten promised to refer the question of accession to the people of Kashmir once the situation became normal. The question of Plebiscite cropped up due to the Mountbatten's letter in reply to Hari Singh's letter of 26 October, Mountbatten wrote on 27 October: "In the special circumstances mentioned by Your Highness my Government have decided to accept the accession of Kashmir state to the dominion of India. Consistently with their policy that in the case of any State, where the issue of accession has been the subject of dispute, the question of accession should be decided in accordance with the wishes of the people of the State, it is my Government's wish that as soon as law and order have been restored in Kashmir and her soil cleared of the invader, the question of the State's accession should be settled by a reference to the people."[7]

Government of India promised to refer the question of accession to people to contain the Kashmiri masses and please Kashmir's tallest leader Sheikh Abdullah. Sheikh wanted a greater autonomy for his state within the Union of India and consequently negotiated the terms of Kashmir's membership with the Union. Nehru government promised Sheikh Abdullah that it would respect the Kashmiris'desire for autonomy and the right to self-determination. Article 370 was the product of the negotiations between the Union Government headed by Jawaharlal Nehru and the Kashmir government headed by the Sheikh. The Indian Constituent Assembly adopted Article 370 of the Constitution on 17th October 1949, ensuring a special status and internal autonomy for Jammu and Kashmir.

Electoral Politics in Jammu and Kashmir (J & K)

The electoral politics in Kashmir has been full of challenges. The subsequent elections that followed the accession of Kashmir were alleged of blatant rigging. The history of the uncontested seats in assembly elections can be seen as a testimonial of the allegations of rigged elections. In the first election, held in August-September 1951, the National Conference, under the dominating leadership of Sheikh Abdullah won all the 75 seats. Election was alleged to be rigged as opposition parties were not allowed to file nominations and only 2 of the total 75 assembly seats were contested in true sense and on other 73 seats NC leaders won unopposed. The next assembly election was held in February- March 1957.The National Conference won 68 out of 75 seats in the elections. Opposition parties again claimed that election was rigged. In this election again half of the seats were uncontested. In the 1962 Assembly election, the National Conferencc got 70 out of 75 seats with 66.96 per cent vote share. But ironically again half of the seats were uncontested.

In 1967, the INC came to power with 61 out of 75 seats and 53.02 per cent vote share, in this assembly election twenty-two of the seats were uncontested. These high numbers of uncontested seats were result of the disqualifications of the nominations of opposition party candidate on weak grounds with amusing arbitrariness of the ruling party. Free and fair election in Kashmir was a distant dream for Kashmiri masses. National as well as regional Political parties failed democracy in Kashmir for there narrow interest. The party in power misused election machinery to keep a grip on power. Ruling parties concentrated on returning to power in lieu of nurturing the democratic spirit.

Congress returned to power in 1974 Assembly election as INC won 58 out of 75 seats and 55.44 per cent vote share. An interesting fact is that in all the three assembly elections, rest of the other parties did not even cross the double digit in terms of seats. In 1977 assembly elections, Jammu and Kashmir National Conference came to power as they secured 47 seats and 46.73 per cent vote share. Janta Party and INC were in opposition with 13 seats and 23.72 per cent vote share and 11 seats and 16.89 per cent vote share respectively. Jammu and Kashmir National Conference continued in power in 1983 assembly elections as well as they got 46 seats and 47.29 per cent vote share. INC was the main opposition party with 26 seats and 30.32 per cent vote share. Assembly elections of 1974, 1983 and 1987 are also alleged to be rigged. The election held on 23 March 1987, in Jammu and Kashmir is considered a watershed moment in the political history of the state. Contesting in the elections were the National Conference (NC) and Congress (I) in coalition, and the Muslim United Front (MUF) a coalition of Islamic parties. The NC-Congress (I) Coalition contested all the 76 seats and the MUF, 43 seats. MUF mobilised the Kashmiri Muslim identity and seeing the response of the public during its campaign meetings and rallies many predicted of its strong presence in Kashmir politics after the result of the election. But the election results come as shocker, The NC-Congress alliance won 66 seats and the MUF got only four seats, even though it had polled 31 per cent votes. The election is said to be rigged and the repression of the popular will led to the Insurgency in the state in the years that followed. The only exception in this dismaying political history of Kashmir elections was the election held in 1977 after lifting of the emergency which is believed to be free and fair one. Behera argues, "The blatant rigging of the 1987 elections and abandonment of constitutional process proved to be last straw persuading the young protagonist that "the bullet will deliver where the ballot had failed."[8] She further adds, "Many MUF leaders who contested or campaigned in the 1987 elections later became the chief and area commanders of various militant outfits, a prominent example being Syed Salahuddin, supreme commander of the Hizb-ul-Mujahideen, who had contested the Srinagar elections."[9]

P.S.Verma in his book, *Jammu and Kashmir at the Political Crossroads* explained, "All the periodic elections in the state have thus repeated the same old story of illegal rejection of nominations, proxy voting, booth capturing, beating and abducting rivals, disrupting public meeting etc. The entire democratic process has been strangulated and trampled time and again by the local zealots to serve their narrow political ends. These perversions in the long run have not only ridiculed the electoral process but also contributed to the spurt of fundamentalism, subversion and militant violence in the state".[10] Electoral process was stalled in the state from 1990-1996 following the insurgency and President's rule was imposed in J&K. President rule concluded in 1996 and it is supposed that the subsequent elections held after spell of President rule had been fair. In 1996 Jammu and Kashmir National Conference won 57 seats out of 87 seats and 34.78 per cent vote share. The BJP was the second largest party with 8 seats and 12.13 per cent vote share. The INC got only 7 seats and 20.00 per cent vote share. After dominating Kashmir's politics for 25 years, the National Conference was the single largest party with 28 seats in a fractured mandate in 2002 assembly elections but they were in opposition. INC and PDP formed a political alliance and came to power (PDP won 16 seats, INC 20, and JKNC 28). In the 2008 Kashmir elections, the JKNC and the INC together formed government in a fractured mandate (JKNC won 28 seats and 23.74 per cent vote share, PDP 21 seats and 15.39 per cent vote share and the NC 17 seats and 17.71 per cent vote share). In 2014assembly elections, the voter turnout was recorded at 65 per cent - thc highest in the history of the state. The results gave a fractured mandate once again (the PDP won 28 seats, BJP 25, NC 15 and INC 12). The assembly elections of 1996, 2002, 2008 and 2014 was conducted in free and fair manner.

Jammu and Kashmir Assembly Election Results

Year	*Won Seats*	*Vote Per cent*	*Party*
1962	70	66.96	National Conference
1967	61	53.02	Indian National Congress
1972	58	55.44	Indian National Congress
1977	47	46.73	Jammu and Kashmir National Conference
1983	46	47.29	Jammu and Kashmir National Conference
1987	40	32.98	Jammu and Kashmir National Conference
1996	57	34.78	Jammu and Kashmir National Conference
2002	16	09.28	PDP and INC coalition government
2008	28	23.74	NC and INC coalition government
2014	28	22.67	PDP and BJP coalition government

Source: Data taken from http://eci.nic.in/eci_main1/ElectionStatistics.aspx and collected by the author.

Governor's Rule in J&K

In India, President's rule is imposed under Article 356 of the Indian constitution and executive authority is exercised by the Governor but in the case of Jammu and Kashmir, Governor's rule is imposed under Section 92 of the J and K state constitution. Power is exercised by the

Governor. During President's rule, legislative power resets with the Parliament of India, but in case of J and K, the power of legislation rests with one person i.e. Governor. Governor's Rule was for the first time imposed on 26 March 1977 in Jammu and Kashmir when Congress withdrew support to the then government headed by National Conference founder, Shiekh Muhammad Abdullah-led coalition government. The second time it was imposed in March 1986 when 26 Congress MLAs withdrew support extended to the minority government headed by Sheikh Muhammad Abdullah's son-in-law, Ghulam Muhammad Shah.The longest spell of direct central rule in JK i.e. six years and eight months was imposed on July 19,1990 which continued till October 1996.This is because the elections could not take place due to outbreak of militancy in many parts of the state. Governor's Rule was imposed in the State for the fourth time in October 2002 as Farooq Abdullah refused to continue as a caretaker chief minister of the state in the backdrop of party's loss in the assembly elections that year. It was the shortest period of Governor's rule i.e. 15 days because PDP and Congress with the support of 12 independents formed the government on November 2. In July 2008, the Governor's Rule was imposed in the state for 178 days after the PDP withdrew support that was extended to Ghulam Nabi Azad-led Congress- PDP government. The PDP had withdrawn its support to the Azad-led government on the Amarnath land transfer issue and had resigned without even confronting a confidence vote on the floor of Assembly. The last time it was imposed was 9 January 2016 due to the death of chief minister Mufti Mohammad Sayeed.

Date	***Period***	***Governor***
26 March-9 July 1977	105 days	L K Jha
6 March -7 November 1986	246 days	Jagmohan
19 January 1990- 9 October 1996	6 years, 264 days	Jagmohan
18 October -2 November 2002	15 days	GC Saxena
11 July 2008-5 January 2009	178 days	NN Vohra
Jan 9- 04 April, 2016	93 days	NN Vohra

Source: Data collated by Author from http://www.greaterkashmir.com/news/news/what-is-governor-rule/183615.html and http://www.newindianexpress.com/nation/J-K-Sees-7th-Governors-Rule-Since-47-Sayeed- Important-Player-in-All/2016/01/10/article3221123.ece

Article 370: Epitome of the Constitutional Asymmetry in the Indian Constitution

Article 370 grants Kashmir a large degree of autonomy under the Indian Constitutional order. Union Home Minister, Gulzari Lal Nanda said in Lok Sabha on December 4, 1964 "only way to take Indian constitution to Jammu and Kashmir is through the application of Article 370. It is a tunnel. It is through this tunnel that a good deal of traffic has already passed and more will."[11] According to the constitutional expert, A.G. Noorani Article 370 embodies following six special provisions for Jammu and Kashmir.

1. It exempted the State from the provisions of the Constitution providing for the governance of the States. Jammu and Kashmir was allowed to have its own Constitution within the Indian Union.
2. Centre's legislative power over the State was restricted to three subjects - defence, external affairs and communications. The President could extend to it other provisions of the Constitution to provide a constitutional framework if they related to the matters specified in the Instrument of Accession. For this, only "consultation" with the State government was required since the State had already accepted them by the Instrument.
3. Other constitutional provisions of the Central Government could be extended to the State only with the concurrence of the State Government.
4. The concurrence was only provisional. It had to be ratified by the State's Constituent Assembly. Article 370(2) says clearly: "If the concurrence of the Government of the State... be given before the Constituent Assembly for the purpose of framing the Constitution of the State is convened, it shall be placed before such Assembly for such decision as it may take thereon."
5. The State government's authority to give the "concurrence" lasts only until the State's Constituent Assembly was "convened". *It was an "interim" power.* Once the State's

Constituent Assembly finalised the scheme and dispersed, the President's extending powers ended completely.

6. Article 370(3) empowers the President to make an Order abrogating or amending it. But for this also "the recommendation" of the State's Constituent Assembly "shall be necessary *before* the President issues such a notification".[12]

Tillin questions the conceptualisation of Article 370 as an examplar of de jure asymmetry in India's constitution. She argues that Article 370 regarding Jammu and Kashmir was included in the constitution in Part XXI under the caption "Temporary, Transitional and Special Provisions". Importantly, it was neither included in recognition to the state's "distinct", Muslim majority status to embed corresponding group rights nor intended as a challenge to India's composite and equal vision of territorial nationhood inclusive of all religions, languages, and ethnic groups.[13] Though Tillin's argument is an interesting one, Saxena finds it difficult to accept it at least in constitutional law and argues that as regards Jammu and Kashmir, whatever the intent and theory of the Indian Constitution, Article 370 has lived to date and may well be the basis of a final settlement with amendments. Saxena further contends that what actually matters in the case of Jammu and Kashmir is not what was intended by the founding fathers of our constitution but what has actually come to exist in these 65 years and is unlikely to alter in the predictable future.[14] It is actually remarkable here that Article 370 cannot be abrogated or modified through the amending provisions of Article 368 which is applicable to all other states. This is because in relation to Kashmir, Article 368 has a provison which says that no constitutional amendment "shall have effect in relation to the State of Jammu and Kashmir" unless applied by Order of the President under Article 370. That requires the concurrence of the State's government and ratification by its Constituent Assembly.

Saxena claims that autonomy to the Jammu and Kashmir under Article 370 has stood the test of time. It has survived the changes of regimes both in New Delhi and in Jammu and Kashmir. She adds that the kind of federal autonomy that the state of Jammu and Kashmir has enjoyed in the Union of India on the basis of democratic elections and federal arrangements in the state may well be the foundation on which some sort of "cosmopolitan democracy" (a la David Held 2002: 313-20) across the Line of Control (LOC) may well be built up in due course if the peace process under way for the last decade or so bears fruit.[15]

The Way Forward: A Federal Solution for J&K

Union of India will have to take tangible measures to tackle the causes of alienation, trust and development deficit in Jammu and Kashmir.A main step in this course will be to yield thedelusions related to Article 370 and recognize its necessity in accommodating the Kashmiri senstivities. The Union of India should acquire an optimistic view on the asymmetrical federal arrangement under Article 370 and endorse that it is well within the Indian constitutional scheme and is more than a temporary provision. The 1974 Kashmir Accord signed by G. Parthasarathy on behalf of Indira Gandhi and Mirza Afzal Beg on behalf of Sheikh Abdullah concluded that, "The State of Jammu & Kashmir, which is a constituent unit of the Union of India, shall in its relations with the Union, continue to be governed by Article 370 of the Constitution of India."[16] The Supreme Court of India also recognised the special provisions of Article 370 in *Khazan Chand v. State of Jammu and Kashmir* (1984) verdict and held that, "The Constitution of India, however, does not apply in its entirety to the State of Jammu and Kashmir because that State holds a special position in the constitutional set up of our country. Article 370 of the Constitution of India makes special provisions with respect to the State of Jammu and Kashmir."[17] In the Indian context, asymmetrical provisions like Articles 370 and 371 have helped in holding the nation together.

Any attempt to erode Article 370 any more should be proscribed by all the political players at the national level.The purpose of Federalism is not to impose administrative and cultural uniformity but to bring unity while simultaneously preserving diversity.

People and political parties of Kashmir should also move forward in the direction of peaceful solution of the Kashmir problem and break the ice by giving up the extreme demands of plebiscite or the restoration of Article 370 to the pre-1953 status which is not at all practical in the today's circumstances and look for greater autonomy within the framework of the Indian Constitution. Political parties of Jammu Kashmir should refrain from fuelling the secessionist tendencies by supporting excessive tendencies for their narrow political interests.

A foundation for a truly federal structure can only be laid if both the stake holders get rid of the trust deficit. India will have to go a long way in acclimatising Kashmiri sensitivities.Tangible confidence-building measures need to be taken by the Central Government to defeat the separatist and secessionist tendencies in the Kashmir valley. Free, fair and regular elections, check on the misuse of Article 356 and Governor's powers, and, defence of Article 370 against future assaults, will be the basic premises of those confidence-building measures. Sheikh Abdullah rightly said "Only that accession will endure which is acceptable to the hearts of people… People's hearts can be won only by love, justice, truthfulness and sincerity and not with subsidised rice, Army and offering largesse."[18]

D5 (Devlopment, Devolution, Democracy, Decentralisation and Dialogue) can be the possible panacea for the Kashmir problem. It will empower the people of Kashmir and ensure their participation in the political process. Development of the state will be the most important step to win back the confidence of the unemployed disillusioned youth of Kashmir. Devolution will be another significant step because devolution process puts power closer to the people and with proper devolution local factors are better conceded in decision-making. Democracy is important because the rigged elections has done the most severe damage to the political, social and economic life of Kashmir. A free and fair democratic electoral process is must to win back the confidence of the masses. Decentralisation which will guarantee autonomy to the state from New Delhi, accommodate the divergent aspirations of the people of all three regions of the state: Jammu, Kashmir valley, and Ladakh and strengthen the framework of local governance. Multilevel Dialogue is necessitated to abridge the trust deficit between the different stakeholders (Leaders of different political parties, local representatives, civil society members, and the separatists). A purposeful dialogue was must to find a "permanent and lasting solution" within the framework of the Indian Constitution. Article 370 and a new federal deal can be the basis of moving ahead from the current impasse. Many scholars have taken a completely unfounded position that the Article 370 gives the President the power to cease the operation of its provisions or amend it only with the consent of the Constituent Assembly of the State. Ordinary processes of constitutional amendment do not apply to Kashmir under Article 370. Hence only the 1954 Constitution (Application to Jammu & Kashmir) Order extending numerous provisions of the Indian Constitution to the state is valid as it was made with the approval of the J&K Constituent Assembly then in session, and all the subsequent Presidential Orders made with the consent of the state legislature and the government are illegal. It is a prepostrous argument. For even if not formally so provided, after the state's Constituent Assembly finally dispersed, the implied power of amendment was inherited by the successor governments and their legislative branches – in Srinagar and New Delhi. No Constitution is cast in stone; it would be a fundamentalist scritural position totally alien to constitutionalism and law. After an earlier confused and mistaken reasoning on this issue in *Premnath Kaul v. State of Jammu & Kashmir* (1959), the Supreme Court of India in two subsequent cases – *Sampat Prakash v. State of Jammu & Kashmir* (1969), *Mohd. Maqbool Damnoo v. State of J&K* (1972), — corrected its earlier position and sustained all the Presidential Orders later made.[19] Prime Minister Narendra Modi's pitch for 'Insaniyat (Humanity) Jamhuriat (democracy), and Kashmiriyat' might become instrumental in tackling the Kashmir problem. The Modi government has taken an important step in the direction of peaceful solution of Kashmir problem by sending All Party Delegation to Kashmir in the month of September 2016.If the all-party delegation remained infructous, the Modi government could proceed to look back and look ahead unilaterally. The UPA governments headed by PM Manmohan Singh had taken some initiatives in appointing some committees on J&K with non-governmental representatives and sent a team of interlocutors to J&K. They had made some sensible recommendations. PM Modi could make a start by acting on acceptable suggestions of the all-party team and Kashmiri leadership that came to participate in the recent exercise, plus take stock of the recommendations that are actionable in the two previous deliberations made during the two UPA governments preceeding the present NDA regime. The Kashmir question is a truly multi-partisan issue and needs a national approach and a new federal deal. In follow-up to the initiative of the all-party delegation on returning to New Delhi at a meeting held in the Parliament House, the opposition advised against any ill-conceived hasty action like scaling down security cover provided to the separatist leaders, and the government assured it will take the opposition into confidence before doing anything. The Kashmiri delegations that came to meet the all-party team in New Delhi made a plethora of points: non-implementation of the promises made by the state government as also the points in the PDP-BJP agenda for governance, election to local bodies and allowing West Pakistani refugees to participate in them, appointment of SC/ST /minority commissions in the state, review of AFSPA, regulation of the media and state government's advertisements, relief packages for Kashmiri Pandits and for Muslims also, curb on radicalisation by madarsas and mosques, investigation of funding of unrest in the state and building of new mosques, crackdown on drug smuggling and government corruption, firmer action on foreign infiltration, and terrorism, complete registration of migrants in various camps, intra-state federal autonomy to Jammu and Ladakh, youth exchange programmes between J&K and other Indian states, private sector and public sector investments in industrialisation and employment. Small incremental steps may lead to greater openings for post-conflict democratisation, federalisation and deveopment.[20]

References

1. K. Von Beyme. "Asymmetric Federalism between Globalisation and Regionalisation", *Journal of European Public Policy* 12:3, 2005, pp. 432–47.
2. Charles, D. Tarlton. "Symmetry and Asymmetry as Elements of Federalism: A Theoretical Speculation." *The Journal of Politics*, 27, 1965, pp. 861-874.
3. Michael, Burgess. *Comparative Federalism: Theory and Practice*, Routledge, New York, 2006, pp. 209.
4. Ronald, L. Watts. "A Comparative Perspective on Asymmetry in Federations." *Asymmetry Series IIGR*, Queen's University, 2005.
   http://www.queensu.ca/iigr/sites/webpublish.queensu.ca.iigrwww/files/files/WorkingPapers/asymmetricfederalism/Watts2005.pdf [Accessed 30 May 2016]
5. Ronald, L. Watts. *Comparing Federal Systems in the 1990s*, Institute of Intergovernmental Relations, Queen's University, 1996, p. 57.

6. Lord Mountbatten's letter dated 27 October, 1947 to the Kashmir Ruler signifying his acceptance of the Instrument of Accession signed by the Kashmir Maharaja.
7. N.C. Behera, *Demystifying Kashmir*, Washington, DC: Brookings, 2006, pp. 47.
8. *Ibid.*
9. P. S. Verma. *Jammu and Kashmir at the Political Crossroads*, New Delhi: Vikas Publishing House, 1994, pp. 125.
10. A.G. Norrani. *Article-370, A Constitutional History of Jammu and Kashmir*, Oxford University Press, New Delhi, 2011, p. 2.
11. *Ibid,* pp. 6-7.
12. Louis, Tillin. "United in Diversity? Asymmetry in Indian Federalism," *Publius : The Journal of Federalism,* Vol. 37, No.1, 2007. pp. 45-67.
13. Rekha Saxena. "Is India a case of Asymmetrical Federalism?", *Economic and Political Weekly*, 47, no. 2, January 14, 2012, pp. 70-75.
14. *Ibid.*
15. 1974 Indira-Sheikh accord.
16. *Khazan Chand and Ors. vs State of Jammu and Kashmir and Ors.* on 9 February, 1984 , *AIR* 1984 *SC* 762.
17. www.jknc.in
18. *Prem Nath Kaul vs. the State of Jammu & Kashmir* on 2 March, 1959,AIR 749 1959: *Sampat Prakash vs State of Jammu & Kashmir* on 6 February, 1969, *AIR* 1153; *Mohd. Maqbool Damnoo vs State of Jammu and Kashmir* on 5 January, 1972, *AIR* 963.

    Also see Rekha Saxena, "*Of more, not less, concessions*", *The Pioneer*, Monday, 26 September 2016.
19. This section is extracted from Rekha Saxena, "*Of more, not less, concessions*", *The Pioneer*, Monday, 26 September 2016.

19

Story of Kashmiri Women in Indian-Administered Kashmir: Dialectic of Resistance and Accommodation

—*Nyla Ali Khan*

Introduction

Does the use of monolithic terms such as "Kashmiri women," "Kashmiri women's experiences" account for the diversity among women and the effects of ethnicity, class, economic level, and geographic location? Is the legislation and execution of political, economic, and social policies and programmes in contemporary Kashmir addressing women's as well as men's experiences and concerns?

Inadequate attention has been paid to the gender dimension of the armed conflict in the Kashmir province of Indian-administered Jammu and Kashmir (J & K), which stymies even further the emergence of peace, political liberty, socioeconomic reconstruction, and egalitarian democratisation. As Dyan Mazura, Angela Raven-Roberts, Jane Parpart, and Sue Lautze (2005) observe,

> inattention to, and subsequent miscalculations about, women's and girl's roles and experiences during particular conflicts and in early postconflict periods systematically undermines the efforts of peacekeeping and peace-building operations, civil society, and

women's organisations to establish conditions necessary for national and regional peace, justice, and security." (2).

Although women of Indian-administered Kashmir have been greatly affected by the armed insurgency and counter-insurgency in the region, they are largely absent in decision-making bodies at the local, regional, and national levels. Although substantive ethnographic work has been done by local and diasporic scholars on the brunt borne by Kashmiri women during the armed conflict as well as on the atrocities inflicted on women by Indian paramilitary forces, the local police, and some militant organisations. Kashmiri women continue to be near absent at the formal level. As a Kashmir observer, I recognise the attention paid to gender-based violence in Kashmir by scholars, ethnographers, and NGOs, but not enough attention is given to the political, economic, and social fall-out of the armed conflict for women. I contend that not enough emphasis is laid on how Kashmiri women of different political, religious, ideological, and class orientations can become resource managers and advocates for other women in emergency and crisis situations. Although the international community made a commitment to incorporate gender perspectives in peace efforts and underscored gender mainstreaming as a global strategy for the growth of gender equality in the Beijing Declaration and the Platform for Action in 1995 (Mazurana *et al.* 2005: 12), I observe that not enough is being done toward increasing women's participation in peacekeeping and postconflict peace-building and nation-building in Kashmir.

The following questions motivated the writing of this article: Twenty-two years of armed insurgency and counter-insurgency; the devastation rendered by militaristic discourse; the consequent sequestration in the Kashmir Valley; my physical and geographical remove from Kashmir; my imperative need to emotionally reconnect with a land that has never ceased to be an integral part of my being; the linkages between personal and collective identity and between identity and action; a questionable unwillingness to recognise the separate niche of women's narratives in the larger political context of Kashmir, which is symptomatic of exclusionary patriarchy in the culture, and which did not establish women's activism as an actuality and an ideology, drove me to write this article.

The story that I narrate here is not one of statistics, insurmountable devastation, irretrievable lives, hopeless death tolls, but one of women willfully combating the modernist as well as the traditional discourses of female gender construction. Responsible feminist scholarship on Kashmir would make an enormous contribution to the plethora of work on the subject by considering the assertion of Kashmiri women's agency not in "isolationist admiration" but as historicised moments in a particular geographical location. Without a rich body of scholarship on Kashmiri women, transnational, comparative, and diasporic studies would be impossible. It would be erroneous to impose a "collective identity" on "Kashmiri women," without considering how Kashmiri women, including those in the diaspora, see themselves within the arbitrary and shifting contexts of regional, national, communal, and transnational identities. As Judith Butler (1993) explains, "the reconceptualisation of identity as an effect, that is produced and generated opens up possibilities of 'agency' that are insidiously foreclosed by positions that take identity categories as foundational and fixed" (147). Butler locates agency in possibilities created in the variability of spaces that create identity.

I suggest that plurality, heterogeneity, and dissidence adorn the architecture of Kashmir, with an emphasis, similar to Nelly Richard's in her essay "Postmodernism and Periphery," on local political projects, regionalism, peripheral social communities, traditions that survive the ravages of time, and marginalised forms of knowledge. I seek in multiplicity a powerful politics that facilitates my ability to engage in different struggles, regional, national, and transnational. For the further delineation of my purposes here, it might be beneficial to quote Chandra Talpade Mohanty, who succinctly observes in the Series Editor's Foreword to my book *Islam, Women, and Violence in Kashmir: Between India and Pakistan* (2010), "Militarisation, environmental degradation, heterosexist State practices, religious fundamentalisms, sustained migrations of peoples across the borders of nations and geo-political regions, environmental crises, and the exploitation of women's labour by capital all pose profound challenges for feminists at this time. Recovering and remembering insurgent histories, and seeking new understandings of political subjectivities and citizenship has never been so important, at a time marked by social amnesia, global consumer culture, and the world-wide mobilisation of fascist notions of 'national security'" (xii). Concurring with Mohanty's acute observation, I consider it incumbent upon responsible feminist scholarship on the Kashmir imbroglio to underscore and analyse not just the gendered violence that has bedaubed the landscape of post-1989 conflict-ridden Kashmir, but also the agentive capacities of Kashmiri women to engage in "a temporally embedded process of social engagement, informed by the past (in its habitual aspect), but also oriented toward the future (as a capacity to imagine alternative possibilities) and toward the present (as a capacity to contextualise past habits and future projects within the contingencies of the moment)" (Emirbayer and Mische, 1998: 964). I underline, at the outset, that my focus in this article is on the gendered activism of the women of the Kashmir province in the state of Indian-administered Jammu and Kashmir (J & K). The battlefield of armed insurgency and counter-insurgency has been the Valley of Kashmir, and the political, economic, and sociocultural dimensions of the conflict have rendered asunder the fabric of that province of J & K, more than the other two, Jammu and Ladakh. Also, considering my analysis of gendered violence and gendered activism in Kashmir is interwoven with my own personal and intellectual trajectory, I explore the struggles of a particular ethnic group, Kashmiri Muslim and Hindu, in the most conflict-ridden part of the State.

Complexity of the Historical and Political Context of Kashmir

In order to contextualisation my perception of the gendered aspects of Kashmir politics, I examine the historical and political roots of the Kashmir conflict. The nation-states of India and Pakistan have employed aggressive strategies in the former princely state of Jammu and Kashmir and overtly imperialist methods since the inception of independence in 1947. The partition of India legitimised the forces of masculinist nationalism and enabled virile hatred for the "other" to irreparably mutilate a shared anti-colonial legacy and cultural heritage so systematically that the wounds inflicted by the partition are yet to heal. The geographical borders, political animosities, and religious hatreds dividing the two sides were not orchestrated just by British imperial cartographers but were ignited by nationalists of the Indian National Congress and the Muslim League as well. As historian Uma Kaura

(1977) keenly observes, the partition of India was orchestrated not just be the machinations and quiet diplomacy of the British Viceroy, but by the egregious mistakes made by the leadership of the Indian National Congress as well as by the acrimony and belligerence of the Muslim League (170). Ever since the inception, in 1885, of proindependence political activity in pre-partition India, the Muslim leadership insisted on the necessity for a distinct Muslim identity (Kaura, 1977: 164). Kaura also underlines the inability of the nationalist leadership to accommodate Muslim aspirations because its primary concern was to ingratiate itself with the militant Hindu faction, which would have created ruptures within the Congress. The creation of India and Pakistan were pyrrhic victories for their denizens because the political, socioeconomic, psychological, and culture havoc wreaked by that momentous event is reflected in those pogroms, ethnic cleansing, proliferation of nuclear weapons, poverty, and riots that continue to cause seismic tremors in the Indian subcontinent. "The fundamental character of this relationship [between India and Pakistan] has been one of *strategic hostility*, unchanged and essentially unquestioned since the birth of the two as independent countries" (Chenoy and Vanaik, 2001: 125).

For India, Kashmir lends credibility to its secular nationalist image. For Pakistan, Kashmir represents the infeasibility of secular nationalism and validates the rationale of the partition, which occurred along religious lines. Once the Kashmir issue took an ideological turn, Mahatma Gandhi remarked, "Muslims all over the world are watching the experiment in Kashmir.…Kashmir is the real test of secularism in India." On 26 October 1947, Maharaja Hari Singh, monarch of the princely state of J & K, signed the "Instrument of Accession" to India, officially ceding to the government of India jurisdiction over defense, foreign affairs, and communications. The monarch made this momentous decision in order to ward of the ruthlessness of the Pakistani tribal raiders' miscalculated attack, which drove various political forces in the state to willy-nilly align themselves with India. The accession of J & K to India was accepted by the last British Viceroy and first Governor-General of India, Lord Mountbatten, with the stipulation that once the region was stabilised, a referendum would be held in which the people of the state would either ratify or interdict the accession.

In January 1948, India referred the Kashmir dispute to the United Nations (Hagerty, 2005: 19).

Subsequent to the declaration of the cease-fire between India and Pakistan on 1 January1949, the state of J & K [this reference is not just to Indian-administered J & K, but to the princely state of Jammu and Kashmir] was divided into two portions. The part of the state comprising the Punjabi-speaking areas of Poonch, Mirpur, and Muzaffarabad, along with Gilgit and Baltistan, was incorporated into Pakistan, whereas the portion of the state comprising the Kashmir Valley, Ladakh, and the large Jammu region was politically assimilated into India. Currently, a large part of J & K is administered by India and a portion by Pakistan. China annexed a section of the land in 1962, through which it has built a road that links Tibet to Xiajiang (see Rahman, 1996: 5–6). The strategic location of Indian-administered J & K underscores its importance for both India and Pakistan. The state of J & K borders on China and Afghanistan.

Although Pakistan distinctly expresses its recognition of the status of J & K as disputed territory, it dithers from doing so in areas of the state under Pakistani control. Pakistan arbitrarily maintains its de facto government in "Azad" (Purportedly Free) Kashmir. Gilgit and Hunza are strategically important to Pakistan because of the access they provide to China through the Khunjerab pass. Therefore, advocating self-determination for the entire former princely state of J & K would irreparably damage Pakistan's political and military interests.

The governments of India and Pakistan have been pursuing autocratic policies vis-à-vis Kashmir and have been accelerating the political, economic, and social impairment of the state. The unwillingness and inability of the two governments to enable the emergence of Kashmir as a bastion of democracy, secularism, and development speaks volumes about the disfigurement of the public diplomacy of the two nation-states. Josef Korbel (2002: 304) wrote with foresight that "whatever the future may have in store, the free world shares with India and Pakistan common responsibility for the fate of democracy and it awaits with trepidation the solution of the Kashmir problem. Its own security may depend on such a settlement."

Ethnic, Religious, and Religious Divisions in Indian-Administered Jammu and Kashmir

The various ethnic, linguistic, and religious groups in Indian-administered Jammu & Kashmir, Kashmiri Muslims, Kashmiri Pundits, Dogra Hindus, and Ladakhi Buddhists and Shi'ite Muslims, have been unable to construct a shared cultural and historical legacy that would enable them to fashion a cultural alterity to that of the Indian nationalist one. But due to the regional sentiments that are becoming increasingly religionised, the ideology and rhetoric of a shared cultural and historical past have been unable to garner public support and mobilisation for reconstruction and nation-building. The signifiers of nationhood in Jammu and Kashmir, flag, anthem, and constitution, have thus far not been able to move beyond a nebulous nationalist self-imagining. Regional political forces have sabotaged attempts made to construct a unitary identity. The political acts of demanding the right of self-determination and autonomy for J & K have not been able to nurture a unity amongst all socioeconomic classes, but, on the contrary, are threatening to create unbridgeable gulfs (Rahman, 1996: 148-9; Ganguly 1997: 78-9). Now more than ever, the three regions of the state of J & K are at daggers drawn about the future political configuration of the state. This doleful truth was forcefully brought home to me at the conference organise by the Government of India selected Interlocutors for Jammu and Kashmir on "Pluralism and Diversity in Jammu and Kashmir," held in Jammu, Jammu and Kashmir, July 11, 2011. At this intraregional conference, I was a member of the Kashmir delegation and I presented a paper on the restoration and revitalisation of the autonomous status of J & K.

The predominantly Hindu province of Jammu sees its unbreachable assimilation into the Indian Union as the only way to safeguard its future. However, of the original six districts of Jammu, the three predominantly Muslim ones, Poonch, Rajouri, and Doda, would undoubtedly align themselves with the predominantly Muslim Kashmir Valley. In the Ladakh region of the state, predominantly Buddhist Leh, which has always been critical of the perceived discrimination against it, has zealously been demanding its political severance from the rest of the state and pushing its demand for Union Territory status within the Indian Union, whereas the predominantly Shi'ite Kargil district in the Ladakh region does not perceive a jeopardized cultural and linguistic identity and advocates retention of its political alignment with the rest of the state. The resounding slogan of self-determination resonates loudest in the Kashmir Valley. Among the Dogra Hindu populace of Jammu and the Buddhist populace of Ladakh, this slogan is perceived as exclusionary and insensitive to the diversities and divergences in the state. The political instability that has ensued in the wake of the rekindling of this slogan in 1989 is perceived as detrimental to the germination and evolvement of developmental projects, institutionalisation of political processes that would enable the devolution of powers to the grassroots cadres by the aforementioned populaces of Jammu and Ladakh. That perception, however, is not shared by the Muslims of the Kashmir Valley, who live in the toxicity of a trust deficit between the state and the Government of India.

The confluence of religious nationalism, secular nationalism, and ethnic nationalism create the complexity of the Kashmir issue. The political asphyxiation of a viable trajectory for Kashmir has further vitiated the political space, mainstream and separatist, of Kashmir. The Kashmir conundrum is a complex and multifaceted issue. There is a plethora of opinions about the political, cultural, religious, and social complexity of Kashmir. Indian- and Pakistani-administered Jammu and Kashmir is a space in which conflicting discourses have been written and read. For more than sixty years the Kashmir conflict has remained like a long pending case in a court of law between the two nuclear giants in the Indian subcontinent, India and Pakistan: "Kashmir has been an enduring and intractable problem. For decades the greatest barrier to eliminating nuclear tension in South Asia was India's unwillingness to give up its nuclear option because of its more ambitious self-perceptions.…A new dimension—the possibility of a nuclear outbreak between the two countries—has been added to an already conflict-filled situation" (Chenoy and Vanaik, 2001: 127). The Kashmir imbroglio has worsened partly out of disillusionment that was generated by perceiving the hollowness of Indian secularism, partly out of the ignominy that Kashmiris felt in being tied to a government and a polity that is getting increasingly religionised: "The self-perceptions that have led to India taking up the nuclear option have everything to do with the rising popularity of a belligerent and aggressive form of nationalism among a frustrated and increasingly insecure elite. This is embodied in the rise of Hindu communalism and of the various cultural and political forces associated with it (*Ibid.:* 127).

The insurgency in Kashmir, which surfaced in 1989, grew into a low intensity warfare made lethal by the firepower of India, accompanied by killings, assassinations, plunder, pillage, rapes, taking of hostages, counterinsurgencies, ambushes, and the duplicitous politics of Pakistan. The initial response of the Indian military and paramilitary forces to the armed insurgency in Kashmir was belligerent and repressive. The history of the past twenty-two years has degenerated into statistics and data: number of land mines, number of ambushes, number of suicide attacks, number of abductions and rapes. Although in the highly militarised sociocultural ethos of Kashmir, rape was construed as a weapon of war in the then burgeoning discourse of armed insurgency and the corollary discourse of human rights violations, "dishonored" women retained their status as familial and cultural chattels lacking control over their bodies, unable to play a proactive role in the process of conflict mitigation. Custodial disappearances, custodial deaths, and summary executions in Kashmir have been documented by several human rights activists, social scientists, and writers.

Since the onset of armed insurgency and counter-insurgency in 1989, more than 50,000 Kashmiris have been killed by Indian troops, paramilitary forces, paramilitary and militia divisions of the J & K police, and some militant groups; more than 100, 000 Kashmiri Hindus have migrated to other parts of India for fear of religious persecution, loss of lives and properties; more than 8,000 Kashmiris have been victims of custodial disappearances; and by a conservative estimate more than 5000 women have been raped (Amnesty International, 1995). According to an official statement made by the Director General of Police, J & K, of the 3,500 militants active in the state, 2,275 were foreign militants and 1,225 were local militants.

Intersectionalities of Gender and Politics in Indian-Administered Kashmir

In my work, previous and current, I attempt to foreground the radical potential of voices that are considered marginalised. In doing so, I neither attempt to neglect the adverse effects of domination or displacement, nor do I associate the authoritarian qualities of writing and pedagogy exclusively with the West. How did Kashmiri women navigate the undulating, often impenetrable terrain of formal spaces of political power created not just by elites but by insurgent movements as well, which are often striving for forms of nationalism that are similar to the exclusionary and patriarchal nationalisms of neocolonial elites? Did Kashmiri women create new forms of subjectivity that were radically different from the essentialist and dichotomous state-nationalist subject? Do these new forms of subjectivity enable the construction of resistance feminisms? Does this subject provide "a constant critique of nationalist and even insurgent agendas, of power relations that structure global economic flows, and will never be complete" (Grewal, 1997: 234)?

I briefly examine the oppositional and nonessentialist narratives of Kashmiri women that forge new niches in Kashmiri society through the pathways of multilayered identities and inclusiveness. It is pertinent to acknowledge my debt to Inderpal Grewal's theorisation of women's multiple subjectivities that allow for "a mobility in solidarity that leads to a transnational participation in understanding and opposing multiple and global oppressions operating upon them; that is, these subject positions enable oppositions in multiple locations. Multiple locations also enable valuable interventions precisely because the agendas of one group are brought along to interrogate and empower those of another group" (234). The multiple narratives of Kashmiri women, including my own, disrupt the voicelessness of women placed on the altar of cultural iconicism.

The renowned Kashmiri scholar Prem Nath Bazaz assesses the scintillating role that Kashmiri women of ancient times played in the social and cultural life of Kashmir (Bazaz [1967] 2005: 12), but these women were cushioned by their royal lineage in a monarchical regime, untormented by the lack of wherewithal that women of other socioeconomic classes were had to contend with. How did Kashmiri women, from different walks of life, express their political agency during the nationalist awakening in the 1930s; during the Quit Kashmir movement in the 1940s; during the invasion by raiders from the North West Frontier Province of Pakistan in 1947; during the period preceding and succeeding the accession of the former princely state of Jammu and Kashmir to the Indian dominion; at the onset of the militant movement in the late 1980s; and during the era of gross human rights violations by the Indian army, paramilitary forces, Pakistani-trained militants, mercenaries, and state-sponsored organisations in the 1990s and 2000s? Does the insurgent movement in Kashmir create parameters for women that are just as restrictive as those created by the politics of the nation-state? Have Kashmiri women signified a reconciliatory presence and been harbingers of peace?

Kashmiri Woman's Selfhood and Her Ability to Act in the Public Domain

One example of powerful agential roles played by Kashmiri women is the Women's Self-Defence Corps (WSDC) formed in 1947. This organisation comprised Kashmiri Muslim as well as Kashmiri Hindu women of diverse class backgrounds. Unfortunately, there is a dearth of scholarly work on this revolutionary organisation, which addresses the reconceptualisation of identities, opening up agentive possibilities. Krishna Misri writes about the formation of the National Militia and Women's Defence Corps—volunteer forces of men and women organised under the leadership Sheikh Mohammad Abdullah [first Muslim Prime Minister of Indian-administered J & K],—to ward off the hordes of tribesmen from the North West Frontier Province, backed by Pakistani army, when they crossed the border of the princely state of Jammu and Kashmir on 22 October 1947, in order to coercively annex the region. (It is ironic that those who were considered invaders in 1947 were portrayed as liberators in the late 1980s and the early 1990s). This organisation is a compelling example of the formation of a coalition across religious and class divides to further the nationalist consciousness of a society in the process of self-determining. Women's empowerment was further bolstered in 1950 when the government of J & K developed educational institutions for women on a large scale, including the first University, and a College for Women, which provided an emancipatory forum for the women of Kashmir, broadening their horizons and opportunities (Misri, 2002: 25–26). The educational methods employed in these institutions were revisionist in nature, not revolutionary.

In the second half of the twentieth century, Kashmiri women like Begum Akbar Jehan, Mehmooda Ahmad Ali Shah, Sajjida Zameer, and Krishna Misri, made a transition from keepers of home and hearth to people engaged in sociopolitical activism within the confines of nationalist discourse. Sajjida was in the forefront of the cultural movement, designed to awaken and hone a political consciousness through mass media: "The women's militia played a substantive role in repulsing the raiders. Zoon Gujjari of Nawakadal, Srinagar, Jana Begum of Amrikadal, Srinagar, and Mohuan Kaur, a refugee from Baramullah, Kashmir, [all three of whom had emerged from the grassroots level] were active participants in the women's movement. Kashmiris from all walks of life, irrespective of religion or race, actively participated in the various activities of the Cultural Front of the militia" (E-mail from Sajjida Zameer to author, 1 April 2008). Most of the members of the Women's Self-Defence Corps were wives and mothers of diverse religious, class, and educational backgrounds who shared the nationalist hopes, anxieties, ardent desire to define their future in a more participatory way with their male counterparts. But their participation in the fervent political awakening and cultural resurgence of that era did not, by any means, endorse the traditionally submissive and self-denying role of the wife and mother. I would posit that similar to nineteenth-century French feminist leaders, these women, "used the concept of motherhood figuratively to refer to women's spiritual qualities and social mission" (Allen, 2006: 104), articulating a new sensibility linked by multilayered identities in which politics and selfhood are profoundly interrelated. It is imperative to recover these women's histories to understand ways in which some aspects of Kashmiri women's lives were marked by monarchical domination and the stirrings of a nationalist awakening. I underscore this point to bring into relief the constructed and historical nature of gender. But did the socialist leaning of the WSDC create spheres of emancipation for Kashmiri women?

The WSDC's political and social activism for the empowerment of women vocalised the desire for freedom and liberation as "a historically situated desire whose motivational force cannot be assumed a priori, but needs to be reconsidered in light of other desires, aspirations, and capacities that inhere in a culturally and historically located subject" (Mahmood, 2001: 223). Although the members of the WSDC were harbingers of the political participation of women and fashioned educational opportunities for them, I would take the liberty of reminding the reader to make a more nuanced analysis of the agency and choice asserted by Kashmiri women by complicating her/his conceptualisation and measurement of women's empowerment:

> ...creating constitutional provision for political participation or equalising educational opportunities are unlikely to be automatically empowering in themselves, but they do create the vantage point of alternatives which allows a more transformatory consciousness to come into play. (Kabeer, 1999: 462)

Did the socialist leaning of the WSDC create spheres of emancipation for Kashmiri women? I observe that the interactive grassroots outreach and mobilisation tactics of the WSDC initiated an advocacy "on behalf of women which builds on claimed synergies between feminist goals and official development priorities" (Kabeer, 1999: 435). This strategy "made greater inroads into the mainstream development agenda than advocacy which argues for these goals on intrinsic grounds" (*Ibid.*: 435).

One of the most formidable challenges facing Sheikh Mohammad Abdullah's National Conference, an organisation that had rid J & K of monarchical rule, disenfranchised the feudal aristocracy and empowered peasants, and given Kashmiri nationalism a voice in the 1930s, 1940s, and 1950s, and the social activism of the WSDC was the palpable hostility between Muslims and Hindus, which was the insidious fall out of the discriminatory treatment against Kashmiri Muslim during monarchical rule if the former princely state of Jammu and Kashmir and also of the partition of India. About his tenure as Prime Minister of J & K in 1948, Sheikh admitted that, "the biggest problem for me was to create mutual confidence between the two communities and to remove all fear from their minds" (Abdullah, 1993: 41). It was in this climate of fear, paranoia, mutual suspicion, and vendetta that the WSDC undertook the arduous task of bridging the nigh impassable gulf between the two communities in the state. It is necessary to recognise the determination and perseverance of the other members of the WSDC as well in overcoming seemingly insurmountable challenges. Acknowledging Begum Akbar Jehan's role in his political and social activism during the turbulent partition of India in 1947, Sheikh Mohammad Abdullah [Akbar Jehan's spouse and Prime Minister of Indian-administered J & K from 1948 until 1953] observes,

> In the midst of this time of political confusion and emotional stresses, swarms of refugees were moving from one country to the other and sick and wounded were everywhere. I was moved to alleviate the sufferings of both the Hindus and the Muslims. When I asked my wife about it, she agreed at once to help me in relief work. She gave up the *purdah* and did commendable work in organising relief camps. For her hard work and sincere efforts, she was named "The Benevolent Mother" by the Kashmiris and was known by this name throughout the state. (Abdullah, 1968 and 1974: 35)

Considering that in the aristocratic and wealthy strata of society to which Akbar Jehan's parents belonged women's seclusion from the public realm and the donning of purdah were status markers, her relinquishment of the security, privilege, and dependence that the institution of purdah bestowed on women, which reinforced a powerful cultural ideal and was a pivotal element in the reproduction of family status, was a courageous move.

I would, however, point out the contradiction that although the activism of the WSDC was appropriated by traditional organisation politicians at a critical moment in the history of J & K, these activists were not invested with substantive political power, other than Begum Akbar Jehan, who was Sheikh Mohammad Abdullah's spouse. My attempt to retrieve the stories of the surviving members of the WSDC is a modest attempt to trace the historic lineage of the sociopolitical activism of Kashmiri women today, although the contexts are not the same.

Another example of an assertion of women's agency is the institute Markaz Behbudi Khawateen, established by Begum Akbar Jehan.

It imparts literacy, training in arts and crafts, healthcare, and social security as tools of empowerment. This organisation was established at a time when such endeavours were rarely, if ever, undertaken by Kashmiri women, elite or otherwise.

This institute effectively employs an instrumentalist form of advocacy "which combine[s] the argument for gender equality/women's empowerment with demonstrations of a broad set of desirable multiplier effects" offering "policy makers the possibility of achieving familiar and approved goals, albeit by unfamiliar means" (Kabeer, 1999: 436). The institute founded by Akbar Jehan, I observe, endeavoured to further the project of women's empowerment by deploying "collective solidarity in the public arena as well as individual assertiveness in the private" (Kabeer, 1999: 462). Akbar Jehan, by virtue of her positioning within the institutional domains which make up Kashmiri society had a decision-making authority, which formed the vantage point from which she could conceive alternatives that would shape the processes of empowerment in a particular context.

Contemporary Kashmiri Women's Activism and Attempts to Rearticulate Social Reality from the Historical Experiences of Women

Armed insurgency and counter-insurgency in the late 1980s and early 1990s scorched the landscape, blighting educational and economic opportunities. Despite their active role in political mobilisation of 1931, the Quit Kashmir movement (anti-monarchical movement) of 1946, and the fierce nationalism of 1947, terror made women revert from the public to the private realm. But there are some compelling examples of Kashmiri women working through the discourse of victimhood to construct their identities as survivors.

For example, Parveena Ahangar is a lower middle-class Kashmiri Muslim woman, who after her son was said to be arrested and killed in custody of the security forces, instead of lamenting voicelessly, formed a grass roots organisation called the Association of Parents of Disappeared Persons (APDP) in the early 1990s, comprising other bereaved mothers like her. The APDP relies on the cultural and moral authority of the mother, sanctioned by religion and mobilises women to courageously challenge the apathy and complacency of the political and bureaucratic machinery. The rhetorical strategy employed by this group is highly expedient and enunciates a well-developed political and ethical position, because Kashmiri culture accepts claims based on motherhood and the inherent maternal qualities of a woman more easily than those based on an erasure of gender difference. I see this organisation as a powerful illustration of the connection between biological motherhood and the political participation of women in bringing the nurturing and communal spirit, traditionally identified with the family, into the public sphere. Women like Parveena are fighting hard against legal discrimination, social pariahism, and economic disadvantage against bereaved mothers. The work being done by the APDP at an informal level toward the construction of a democratic society, demilitarisation, and disarmament is commendable, but not enough is being done to bring about structural changes that would lead to a simmering and eventual dousing of the violence. While the APDP has the potential of legitimising the "politics of feminisation" in Kashmir, which "is an integral part of a wider politics of democratisation and empowerment which has now decisively altered domestic and international politics alike" (Chenoy and Vanaik, 2001: 123), I observe that this organisation has not had a great degree of success in influencing branches of state government responsible for women's issues and humanitarian assistance. The state government has yet to recognise the worth of the peace-building work that this organisation has the potential to contribute to at the local and regional levels. Nor have the aspirations for state accountability, healing, and peace of the members of the APDP been translated into a powerful force that would determine the substance of conflict resolution. The demand of the bereaved mothers in the APDP for accountability and the return of their children is yet to be employed for the reinstatement of democracy and restoration of justice. This organisation, like the Northern Mothers' Front in Sri Lanka, is mobilised "around women's role as mothers and their duty and moral obligation to protect their children," so, again like the Northern Mothers' Front, the APDP has "never challenged disempowering or limiting gendered roles" (Samuel, 2001: 193).

Kashmiri Women's Vigilante Groups: Forms of Subjectivity that Reinforce Essentialist and Dichotomous State-Nationalist Subjects

There are other instances of women's mobilisation, which some Kashmir analysts might see as agential but, which I would argue, attempt to validate the "isolationist admiration" of Kashmir, which I have alluded to earlier and of which I am wary. For instance, the *Dukhtaran-e-Milat* (DM), instead of pressing for women's political empowerment and addressing the protracted crises of security and legitimacy, sanctifies the reductive portrayal of a Muslim woman as a veiled sociocultural icon who is mobilised more for who she is than for what she believes in, ignoring the diverse interpretations and the rich heterogeneity of cultural traditions and the paradoxes within them. This assertion of the salience and meaning of the identity of a "Kashmiri Muslim Woman" takes the form of trying to legitimise sociocultural practices like veiling, polygamy, punitive action against behaviour deemed "unIslamic," such as the mixing of sexes in public places, in an attempt to define the "proper" place of women. The regressive discourse propounded by this organisation creates a determinate concept of Islam. In other words, it does not allow negotiation between different value systems. This rigidity rends the consciousness of the Kashmiri subject, who is caught in the quandary of living her life in the constant epistemological tension of having to take more than one reality system into account. Also, the model of hierarchy between men and women might be institutionalised in legislations made and executed by the state or in Muslim Personal Law, but gender ideologies are neither impenetrable, nor do they remain fixed till kingdom come. Even when cultural values and religious law are incorporated into legislations, they are capricious and subject to personal discretion (Doumato, 2000: 228).

On the other end of the spectrum is the Daughters of the Vitasta, a Kashmiri Hindu women's organisation, which seeks the resolution of the Kashmir conflict in the creation of a separate homeland for internally dislocated Kashmiri Hindus within the Valley. The Daughters of the Vistasta is an exclusionary Kashmiri Hindu women's organisation, comprising middle-class, and professional women. Lower-middle class Kashmiri Hindu women are not part of the upper crust of this organisation. These organisations are glaring illustrations of those insurgent manifestations of the armed rebellion and counterinsurgency in Kashmir that are striving for exclusionary and patriarchal nationalisms. It might be useful to point out that the DM comprises educated as well as uneducated women of the lower middle-class. Its influence is restricted to the summer capital of Jammu and Kashmir, Srinagar city. The ideology and politics of this vigilante group have not seeped into grassroots cadres in rural areas. My contention is that fundamentalist ideologies of organisations like the DM and the Daughters of the Vitasta have grown in spaces created by structural inequities, repression, and a sense of injustice by the Government of India. Although the Daughters of the Vitasta would align itself with an ultra Indian-nationalist ideology, its growth is the blowback of the dislocation and displacement of the Kashmiri Hindu community subsequent to the inception of armed insurgency in 1989, and the inability of the Government of India to take substantive measures toward facilitating its return and rehabilitation in the Kashmir Valley. The Daughters of the Vitasta gives an essentialist Hindu identity a privileged place in political discourse, unambiguously defining that identity and projecting it in order to solicit support. Such political assumptions and claims are "a negation of the role of values, understanding and intellect" (Smith, 2001: 43). An astute observer must recognise that given the gender, ethnicity, and class status of the members of the DM and the Daughters of the Vitasta, they experience and recover from the effects of violence, displacement, and disenfranchisement differently. Also, both organisations espouse an identity politics that "appeals to that part of individual identity that is shared in a collective identity." But, "the question to ask about this kind of politics is, 'Which collective identity?' It is a question that is never asked in the process of political mobilisation on the basis of identity; indeed, the question is often actively suppressed, sometimes violently" (Smith, 2001: 36). Given the essentialist politics of these two organisations, I would point out that they feed on each other.

I, as a Kashmiri Muslim woman, find the agenda of the DM highly problematic. I can vividly recall the reign of terror unleashed by the DM in women's educational institutions in the late 80s and early 90s, which sought to impose a blanket dress code on women through intimidation and coercion. The resonances that the "superior truths" spouted by these organisations have for me in relation to my own cultural reality, history, and class, indubitably, make me hesitant to embrace their ideologies. The oppositional positionings of such organisations, I argue, do not enable the forging of new paths "in this combat locked within action and reaction" (Grewal, 1997: 249). These organisations do not have clear nation-building programmes, which would involve reviving civil society, resuscitating the shattered economy, providing sources of income, and building social and political structures. How will these organisations pave the way for sustainable peace, human rights and security which would diminish the potency of militarised peacekeeping, following closely on the heels of militarised interventions? It wouldn't be presumptuous to assume that members of the *Dukhatan-e-Milat* and Daughters of the Vitasta embrace intransigent and monolithic versions of Islam and Hinduism, respectively, as a viable way to find meaning in their origins, and also, perhaps, a rationale for their lack of access to the global market. Despite their audibly separatist politics, women in these vigilante groups, which are more reactionary than revolutionary, are unable to climb to the highest rung of the hierarchy. I would like to conclude my analysis of the politics of these two vigilante groups with Dan Smith's pertinent point about conservative gender politics. Dan Smith (2001) is Director of the International Peace Research Institute, Oslo. He observes that, "people who make essentialist generalisations about women's roles are usually unable not just to explain but even to acknowledge the diversity of women's experiences and abilities" (38).

This dismal fact of women not being able to rise to the highest rung of revolutionary/ separatists organisations is borne out by Anjum Zamarud Habib, who although not a vigilante herself, is one of the founding female members of the Hurriyat organisation, a conglomerate comprising separatist organisations of disparate political ideologies bound by their insistence on the right of self-determination for the people of Kashmir: "The Hurriyat Conference gave the militants a united political platform through which they could voice their grievances, but their demands did not permit them to consider a solution which lay within the existing framework of the Indian Union" (Schofield, 2002: 60). The Hurriyat organisation embraces a separatist ideology and has been critical of state repression, human rights violations, lack of civil liberties in post-1989 Kashmir. This organisation, in its current manifestation, is a house divided against itself, with some members vociferously and inflexibly advocating accession to Pakistan as the only feasible solution to the Kashmir conflict, while others consider the reunification of the two parts of Kashmir, Indian-administered and Pakistani-administered, and the subsequent independence of the entire state as the more acceptable solution.

In her poignant memoir, *Prisoner No. 100* (2011), Zamarud Habib agonisingly observes that she wasn't given access to the top tier of the organisation, nor did her male comrades try to expedite her release from Tihar jail in Delhi, Asia's largest prison complex, where she languished for five years. Her narrative highlights the micropolitical that deconstructs not just state-nationalism but an insurgent movement as well. But, I would assert, more work needs to be done to strengthen the work of women in civil intervention in the conflict, campaigns for demilitarisation, rehabilitation of dislocation Kashmiri Hindus, rehabilitation of detainees, revocation of draconian laws, and restoration of civil liberties. The essentialist politics of the vigilante groups I have explored do not allow for change that would enable "peaceful conflict resolution, reconciliation between traditional enemies, justice between different races and gender equality" (46).

Effectiveness of Women Politicians in a Militarised Kashmir

I often find myself asking if the militarisation of the political and sociocultural ethos of Kashmir, which regulated gendered violence and marginalised gendered justice, will enable female politicos in the Legislative Assembly of J & K to assert themselves as agents of transformation and progress. Unless there is a qualitative difference to policy-making and behaviour, the chances of the existence of women ministers, bureaucrats, and diplomats making a difference seem rather slim. I would, however, be doing the reader a disservice by limiting my theorisation of the Kashmir conflict and the subsequent brutalisation of its ethos to the history and experiences of non-mainstream women. The intellectual agenda of scholars working on Kashmir, particularly those located in the diaspora, is defined by the histories and perspectives of non-mainstream or non-state actors. I too have been guilty of relegating the distressing experiences of some female state actors, in the interests of maintaining "objectivity," to the background.

Therefore, before I conclude, I write about a female member of the J & K Legislative Assembly, Sakina Itoo, affiliated with the political organisation that was founded by Sheikh Mohammad Abdullah in 1939, the National Conference. Sakina's father, Abdul Salam Itoo, a National Conference worker, was assassinated in the early 1990s by a militant outfit that had pro-Pakistan leanings and espoused an ultra-conservative religious ideology. I have chosen to write about a state actor because I firmly believe that in order to address wider political, socioeconomic, and democratic issues in Kashmir requires "rethinking the relationship between state and non-state actors, between state and society, and therefore between the structures of decision-making in these two arenas" (Chenoy and Vanaik, 2001: 124). Sakina, who was then in medical school, took the plunge into mainstream politics. In the political climate of the late 1980s and early 1990s, those who had not supported accession to Pakistan in 1947 were on the wrong side, and Abdullah's organisation, the National Conference, had assertively opposed accession to the then newly formed nation-state of Pakistan. I might be critical of current centrist policies of the National Conference, but that hasn't prevented me from commending Sakina's courage for having donned her father's mantle at a precarious and perilous time on the landscape of Kashmir politics. Also, a student of history, culture, and politics would construct a much richer narrative of Kashmir by tying in the current insurgent, counter-insurgent, nationalist movements, and militarisation of Kashmir with the larger political context. The National Conference has a diminished mass base and a depreciated credibility in this day and age, but the organisation is credited with having played a significant and evolutionary role in the creation of a Kashmiri nationalist identity. Currently, Sakina is the Minister for Social Welfare in the J & K cabinet. Her, undoubtedly, intrepid decision to join mainstream politics in Kashmir at a chaotic, frenzied, and precarious time is, in my opinion, a forceful critique of insurgent nationalism. It is in the arena of domestic politics that "changes in gender composition to favour [sic] women today may have significant effects on policies and practices, and here that such rearrangements of personnel can themselves be seen as responses to the presence of real and growing social processes of a pro-democratic and pro-feminist kind" (*Ibid.*: 128). Although Sakina has risen from the grass-roots, it remains to be seen if the increase in female participation in the 2008 Legislative Assembly elections in J&K will facilitate the creation of forceful positions for Kashmiri women in decision-making bodies in the regional and national scenario, which is not yet a reality. I observe that there is a serious lack of a feminist discourse in political/activist roles taken on by women in Kashmir, where the dominant perception still is that, "politics and policy-making are linked to the powerful, strong, male realist rather than with the archetypal gentle, negotiating woman" (*Ibid.*: 132). As in other political scenarios in South Asia, Sakina's feminine traits, like reticence and a demure demeanor, have caused her to be relegated to the "soft area" of Social Welfare. Although political parties in Kashmir, either mainstream or separatists, have not relinquished paternalistic attitudes toward women, women's rights and gender issues are secondary to political power.

Women politicos in the current legislative assembly and legislative council of Jammu and Kashmir are token members, who are seen as symbols of their entire group. Today, in the politics of Indian-administered J & K, women do constitute a minority, increasing the pressures of high visibility, unease, stereotyping, inability to make substantial change, over-accommodation to the dominant male culture in order to avoid condemnation as "overly soft." Even those with access to the echelons of power are unwilling or unable to forge "broad feminist coalitions and informal networks along party lines" (Dahlerup, 2001: 104), refusing to challenge state-centered, elitist, and masculinist notions of security.

Construction of the "Kashmiri Woman" by the Discourses of Religious Nationalism, Ethnonationalism, and Secular Nationalism

The encounter with essentialist notions of identity is inevitable in the construction of the Kashmiri woman as a parchment on which the discourses of religious nationalism, secular nationalism, and ethnonationalism are inscribed, and the most ruthless acts are justified by Indian paramilitary forces the only viable way to assert an aggressive nationalism, and by militant organisations as means to claim ownership over the putatively impregnable boundaries of women's spaces. Secular as well as ethnonationalists claim that as long as the core of the culture is retained, an unchanging essential Kashmiri identity, reducing the diversity of the society to one criterion, which came to be seen as the definitive component of Kashmiri identity, particularly a Kashmiri woman's identity. Nationalist discourse creates Kashmir as a space inhabited by monochrome women "whose identity is simple and straightforward." This discourse "recognises only a limited range of the spectrum of collective identity. It gives that part of identity a privileged place in political discourse, simultaneously defining the identity, projecting it and appealing to it for support" (Smith, 2001: 39). For example, ethnonationalists assert that a Kashmiri woman who marries a non-Kashmiri loses her legal right to inherit, own, or buy immovable property in the state. This argument gives legitimacy to the supposedly "unchanging essence of individual and social identity" (Smith 34), by asserting that the Kashmiri woman is the repository of primordial culture and ethnicity which would get tainted by her stepping outside the cultural threshold. As a strategy to maintain the inviolability of the cultural sanctum sanctorium, ethnonationalists problematize the law concerning state subjects which was promulgated in Jammu and Kashmir on April 20, 1927 by Maharajah Hari Singh. This injunction was meant to protect the interests of the local landed class and the peasantry against wealthy people from outside the state who had the wherewithal to buy the locals out of hearth and home. In 1957, the new constitution of the state changed "state subject" to "permanent resident." Permanent resident status was accorded to individuals who had been living in the state for at least a decade before May 14, 1957. On March 25, 1969, the state government issued an injunction requiring all deputy commissioners to issue certificates of permanent residence to Kashmiri women with the stipulation that status was valid till marriage. After that, women who married permanent resident men would need to get their certificates reissued, and those who married outside the state would indubitably lose their permanent resident status, whereas, a male permanent resident be entitled to bestow on his non-state subject spouse the ability to own and inherit property in the state as long as she didn't leave the state for permanent residence elsewhere

(Abdullah, 1993). This essential identity becomes "normative, a pressure…to conform…, as members of one nation or another, or along" a "single dimension out of the many that make" people "who they are" (Smith, 2001: 39).

In 2002, the state High Court declared that this proviso had no legislative sanction because it violated the gender equality clause of the constitution of the state as well as of India. The High Court held that the proviso relied on Section 10 of the British law which governed pre-partition India, and that law had itself been amended (Bhagat, 2002; Puri, 2004). The bench quoted section four of the Sri Pratap Consolidation Law Act to declare that the only legislative prohibition was that the property inherited by a woman permanent resident who married a non-permanent resident could not be sold to a non-state subject. But this decision created an uproar in which the then opposition National Conference asserted that the declaration of the earlier proviso invalidating the permanent resident status of women who married outside the state as antiquated was an attempt to undermine the normative cultural identity of the state. This political discourse greatly influenced the dominant sense of Kashmiri identity, "defining the identity, projecting it, and appealing to it for support" (*Ibid.:* 39). The National Conference (NC) accused the then ruling People's Democratic Party (PDP) of having kowtowed to the federal government by withdrawing its appeal from the Supreme Court against the judgment of the state High Court. The PDP, rattled by its fear of losing electoral support in the Kashmir Valley, which is the province in which it holds most sway, overlooked the gender perspective and violations that women could potentially experience in the spheres of socioeconomic and cultural rights, and, without wasting much time, drafted a Permanent Resident Bill in the assembly reinforcing the earlier stipulation. The High Court's decision was supported by the then ruling PDP's coalition partner, the Congress, which later formed a coalition government with the NC in 2008. The issue of permanent residence was communalised by Hindu fundamentalist originations, the Bharatiya Janata Party (BJP) and the Rashtriya Samaj Sevak, to inflame regional divisiveness by condemning the opposition of the NC and the PDP to the High Court's decision as acts of Muslim secession, underscoring the religious identity of predominantly Hindu Jammu. The representatives of the NC and the PDP in the legislative assembly and legislative council vociferously opposed the decision of the High Court that declared the earlier proviso obsolete, and the representatives of the Congress and the BJP unequivocally endorsed it (Puri, 2004). The process of identity politics here became a "battle to assert the salience and meaning of a given identity" (*Ibid.*: 37) of a Kashmiri woman. The women members of the legislative assembly and legislative council acted as agents of the state as opposed to recognising identity as multidimensional, because "it is in the nature of political mobilisation that the arbitrary nature of an appeal to identity cannot be acknowledged....the political insistence that one category of identity has the highest salience and a particular meaning is accompanied by a denial that there is any real choice in the matter" (*Ibid.*: 38).

My Personal and Intellectual Trajectory: The Narrative of a Diasporic Kashmiri Muslim Women

How do I choose to remember Kashmir? The mellifluous music of life; verdant, rolling hills; sparkling snow topped mountains; gushing streams; dew sprinkled meadows in summer and snow flake blanketed meadows in winter; horses with trappings, sleigh bells, shingled roofs, and the cocooning smell of burning wood in furnaces; the aroma of pines, firs, and conifers; a fertile landscape inundated with the alluring ripeness of loquat, cherry, apple, pomegranate trees, firmly denying stagnation or any hint of barrenness; an unmistakable vitality and zeal for life in the air; the rustling of autumnal leaves that becalms the harried soul; the lustrous snows of winter that promise to expiate the most egregious sin; a palpable rapture that beckons the unsuspecting observer to plunge into the tempestuous waters of existence; the tenuous throes of infancy in the vibrant atmosphere of spring, with tenderly sprouting flower buds feeling their way into existence; the unflinching faith of the mystic in communion with the divine; a mysticism that cannot be reduced to history. It was in this Valley of languid beauty, a cornucopia of passions, mysticism, syncretism, and evanescence, best symbolised by changing autumnal hues, that I came to consciousness. (The reader wouldn't be grossly wrong in attributing this description to my colonial education). Although interrogating my own narrative produces angst, it allows me to examine the blind spots in my perception, which I have attempted to do by closely looking at women's movements launched by marginalised groups as well as at the class dimensions of the gendered activism in a highly militarised Kashmir. While struggling to develop a critical awareness of my positionality, I recognise the validity of political ideologies and activisms that were orchestrated by elite women as well as by women at the grass roots level, some of which get dismissed all too easily in some narratives of Kashmir as "unrepresentative." And yet, as I write this piece at a geographical and physical remove from my land of origin, the Valley of Kashmir, it is not halcyon days that haunt my memory, but the disintegration of that world and the subsequent dispossession and dislocation for some, which has had a profound impact on my subjectivity. There are times, however, when I am wracked by nostalgia for a past when political repression, conscripted democratic spaces, jeopardized cultural emancipation, bigotry breeding intolerance, militarisation stunting growth were not even specks on the horizon. A student of the History of Kashmir might accuse me of wearing blinkers. Perhaps, I speak from a position of privilege, which I sporadically examine in this article. The history of Kashmir, similar to histories of other conflict zones, has never been sanitised. Also, although a class/ caste hierarchy does not enjoy religious legitimacy in predominantly Muslim Kashmir, socioeconomic class and caste divisions in Kashmir are as well-entrenched as they are in other South Asian societies. There is also a rigidly entrenched gender hierarchy in Kashmir, to deconstruct which some substantive attempts have been made. The role of women in a conflict zone; the reconceptualisation of a woman's identity in a politically militarised zone; intersectionalities of class, education, ethnicity, religious identity in theorising a woman's identity; women's agential roles or lack thereof are issues that can no longer be relegated to the background.

Although I am wary of the construction of a monolithic "Kashmiri" female subject and well-aware of the repressive politics of a homogenising cultural nationalism, I do not wish to forestall the possibility of a unified subjectivity as the basis of nationalist politics. I acknowledge the political productivity of the construct of a unified subjectivity, while cautioning the reader against eliding specific, varied, and unique forms of agency deployed by Kashmiri women in times of relative calm, conflict, political turbulence, resurgence of nationalism, and internal critique not just of state-nationalism, but insurgent nationalism as well. Although every instance of the resurgence of nationalism in Kashmir has strategically employed the term "women" to further engender this category of subjects, I reiterate that there is no monolithic "Kashmiri woman."

Her mother, my maternal grandmother, Begum Akbar Jehan, supported her husband's struggle and represented Srinagar and Anantnag constituencies in Jammu and Kashmir in the Indian parliament from 1977 to 1979 and 1984 to 1989, respectively. She was also the first president of the Jammu and Kashmir Red Cross Society from 1947 to 1951. But during Grandfather's incarceration, she had been burdened with the arduous task of raising five children in a politically repressive environment that sought to undo her husband's mammoth political, cultural, legalistic attempts to restore the faith of Kashmiri society in itself.

Conclusion

New efforts and new forums are required not just in Indian-administered Kashmir but in other parts of the world as well for the germination of new ideas, broad based coalition politics that transcends organisational divides, and gives women the space and leeway to make important political decisions. In order to mitigate the conflict in Indian-administered Kashmir, "women have to re-establish their historic links with peace and the peace movement, asserting themselves as the harbingers of a genuine alternative. It is with this perspective in mind that women have to speak to those in public power and when they themselves are in public authority. This is very different from adopting, in the name of the search for equality, the existing masculinist and militaristic mentality" (Chenoy and Vanaik: 2001, 137). The most effective way to make a gender perspective viable in Kashmiri society would be for women, state as well as non-state actors, to pursue the task of not just incorporating and improving the positions of their organisations within civil society, but also by forging connections between their agendas and strategies for conflict resolution and reconstruction of society with the strategies and agendas of other sections of the populace impacted by the conflict. It is imperative that women actors in collaboration with other civil society actors focus on the rebuilding of a greatly polarised and fragmented social fabric to ensure the redressal of inadequate political participation, insistence on accountability for human rights violations through transitional justice mechanisms, reconstruction of the infrastructure and productive capacity of Kashmir, resumption of access to basic social services. It is imperative that the state government recognise the worth of the peace-building work that women's organisations can contribute at the local and regional levels. The aspirations for state accountability, healing, and peace of the members of the APDP must be translated into a powerful force that would determine the substance of conflict resolution.

Works Cited

1. Abdullah, Sheikh Mohammad. *Flames of the Chinar: An Autobiography.* Translated by Khushwant Singh. New York: Viking, 1993.
2. Abdullah, Sheikh Mohammad and Y. D. Gundevia. *The Testament of Sheikh Abdullah*. New Delhi: Abhinav Publications, 1968 and 1974.
3. Ahmed, Leila. *A Border Passage: from Cairo to America—A Woman's Journey.* New York: Penguin Books, 2000.
4. Ali, Suraiya. Vice Chairperson of Behboodi Khwateen, an Oganisation for the Upliftment of Downtrodden Women and Children. Srinagar, March 2008.
5. Ali, Tariq. "The Story of Kashmir," in *The Clash of Fundamentalisms: Crusades, Jihads and Modernity*. London: Verso, 2003: 217–52.
6. Allen, Ann Taylor. "Lost in Translation? Women's History in Transnational and Comparative Perspective." In *Comparative Women's History: New Approaches.* Edited by Anne Cova. New York: Columbia University Press, 2006.
7. Amnesty International, "India." November 2005. http://web.amnesty.org/report2004/indsummary-eng (accessed 15 December 2005).
8. __________. "India Must Prevent Torture." *Article,* 1995. Kashmiri-Canadian Council, November 2005. http://www.kashmiri-cc.ca/quarterly/kq2-4/AMNESTY2.htm (accessed January 10, 2007).
9. Bazaz, Prem Nath. *Kashmir in Crucible*. New Delhi: Pamposh Publications, 1967. Reprint, Srinagar: Gulshan Books, 2005. (Page references are to the 2005 edition.)
10. Bhagat, Pamela. "Women in Kashmir: Citizens at Last." *Boloji Media*, November 2005.

    http://www.boloji.com/wfs/wfs110.htm (accessed November 2005).
11. Butler, Judith. *Bodies that Matter: On the Discursive Limits of "Sex."* New York: Routledge, 1993.

12. Chenoy, Anuradha Mitra and Achin Vanaik. "Promoting Peace, Security and Conflict Resolution: Gender Balance in Decision Making." In *Gender, Peace and Conflict*. Edited by Inger Skjelsbæk and Dan Smith. London: Sage Publications, 2001: 122-138.
13. Dahlerup, Drude. "Women in Decisionmaking: From Critical Mass to Critical Acts in Scandinavia, in *Gender, Peace and Conflict*. Edited by Inger Skjelsbæk and Dan Smith. London: Sage Publications, 2001: 104-121.
14. Dasgupta, Jyoti Bhusan. *Jammu and Kashmir*. The Hague: Martinus Nijhoff, 1968.
15. Doumato, Eleanor Abdella. *Getting God's Ear: Women, Islam, and Healing in Saudi Arabia and the Gulf.* Second edition. New York: Columbia University Press, 2000.
16. Emirbayer, Mustafa and Ann Mische. "What is Agency?" *American Journal of Sociology* 103 (1998): 926-1023.
17. Ganguly, Sumit. *The Crisis in Kashmir: Portents of War, Hopes of Peace*. New York: Woodrow Wilson Center Press, 1997.
18. Grewal, Inderpal. "Autobiographic Subjects and Diasporic Locations: *Meatless Days and Borderlands.*" In *Scattered Hegemonies: Postmodernity and Transnational Feminist Practices,* edited by Inderpal Grewal and Caren Kaplan. Minneapolis: University of Minnesota Press, 1997: 231-254.
19. Habib, Anjum Zamarud. *Prisoner No. 100: An Account of my Nights and Days in an Indian Prison.* Translated by Sahba Hussain. New Delhi: Zubaan Books, 2011.
20. Hagerty, Devin T. *South Asia in World Politics*. Lanham, MD: Rowmanand Littlefield, 2005.
21. Kabeer, Naila. "Resources, Agency, Achievements: Reflections on the Measurement of Women's Empowerment." *Development and Change* 30 (1999): 435-464.
22. Kaura, Uma. *Muslims and Indian Nationalism: The Emergence of the Demand for India's Partition 1928–40*. Columbia: South Asia Books, 1977.
23. Khan, Nyla Ali. *Islam, Women, and Violence in Kashmir: Between India and Pakistan.* New York: Palgrave Macmillan, 2010.
24. ______, ed. *The Parchment of Kashmir: History, Society, and Polity.* New York: Palgave Macmillan, 2012.
25. Korbel, Josef. *Danger in Kashmir*. Princeton: Princeton University Press, 1954. Reprint, New York: Oxford University Press, 2002. (Page references are to the 2002 edition.)
26. Mahmood, Saba. "Feminist Theory, Embodiment, and the Docile Agent: Some Reflections on thc Egyptian Islamic Revival." *Cultural Anthropology* 16, no. 2 (2001): 202-235.

27. Mazurana, Dyan, Angela Raven-Roberts, Jane Parpart, and Sue Lautze. Introduction. *Gender, Conflict, and Peacekeeping*. Edited by Dyan Mazurana, Angela Raven-Roberts, Jane Parpart, and Sue Lautze. Lanham, Maryland: Rowman and Littlefield Publishers, 2005: 1-26.
28. Misri, Krishna. "Kashmiri Women Down the Ages: A Gender Perspective," *Himalayan and Central Asian Studies* 6, no. 3–4 (2002): 3–27.
29. Mohanty, Chandra Talpade. Series Editor's Foreword. *Islam, Women, and Violence in Kashmir: Between India and Pakistan,* by Nyla Ali Khan. New York: Palgrave Macmillan, 2010: xi-xiii.
30. Pederson, Susan. "Comparative History and Women's History: Explaining Convergence and Divergence." In *Comparative Women's History: New Approaches.* Edited by Anne Cova. New York: Columbia University Press, 2006: 117-142.
31. Puri, Balraj. "Analysis of the J & K Permanent Resident Bill." *PUCL Bulletin*, April 2004. http://www.pucl.org/Topics/Law/2004/jk-pr-bill.htm (accessed November 2005).
32. _________. *Jammu and Kashmir: Triumph and Tragedy of Indian Federalism*. Delhi: Sterling, 1981.
33. Rahman, Mushtaqur. *Divided Kashmir: Old Problems, New Opportunities for India, Pakistan, and the Kashmiri People*. Boulder: Lynne Rienner, 1996.
34. Richard, Nelly. "Postmodernism and Periphery." *Third Text* 2 (Winter 1987-88).
35. Samuel, Kumudini. "Gender Difference in Conflict Resolution: The Case of Sri Lanka." In *Gender, Peace and Conflict*. Edited by Inger Skjelsbæk and Dan Smith. London: Sage Publications, 2001: 184-204.
36. Schofield, Victoria. *Kashmir in Conflict: India, Pakistan, and the Unending War*. Second revised edition. London: I. B. Tauris, 2002.
37. Smith, Dan. "The Problem of Essentialism." In *Gender, Peace, and Conflict,* edited by Inger Skjelsbæk and Dan Smith, London: Sage Publications, 2001: 32-46.
38. Warley, Linda. "Assembling Ingredients: Subjectivity in Meatless Days." *A-B Autobiography Studies* 7, no. 1 (1992): 107-23.
39. Zameer, Sajjida, member of the 1947 Women's Militia organised by the National Conference, and Former Director of the Education Department, J & K, April 2008.

20

Jammu and Kashmir as a Modernisation Laboratory- State Development Policy from 1948

— Sehar Iqbal

Abstract

The scope and focus of development discourse and policy has been evolving since the end of the Second World War as new theories bring into it new subjects, new goals and new terrain. The following of particular developmental theories has over time been determined by their influence on state policy. One of the earliest development theories that acquired a mass following in the decolonised world from the 1950's was Modernisation. The Modernisation orthodoxy emerged alongside the nationalist ethos of the newly independent ex-colonies, as governments sought to fulfil the expectations of their populations by intervening heavily to develop the economy. The goal was an uncritical imitation of the west, underpinned by the enlightenment notion of a "modern" society characterised by democracy, industrialisation, urbanisation, collapse of the traditional social hierarchy, and a demographic transition.

In this article, I use Kashmir as a case study of modernisation. I argue that state developmental policies were based, unquestioningly, on the Modernisation model. Though much literature exists on state development policy in Jammu and Kashmir from 1948 onwards, it is focussed mostly on how the inspiration for the same came from Socialism and even Communism..But the argument I'm making is a broader one- that policy in Jammu and Kashmir since 1948 was based on the Modernisation model in its entirety- that it aimed to change not just patterns of asset distribution or infrastructure but to change all traditional structures and ways of life. I aim to prove this by studying the construction and consequences of state policy in what it defined as the main developmental areas- from agriculture to urban development to education.

My reasons for choosing Jammu and Kashmir is that current literature on Kashmir concentrates almost without exception, on the conflict and politics of the region, thus deflecting focus from other important issues like development. This article seeks to address this gap in the literature.

Second, though Kashmir is by no means the most modernised state in terms of industrial and urban growth it is a distinct Himalayan environmental and cultural unit that before 1947 was largely untouched, by external influences and had evolved its own unique society and self-reliant economy underpinned by the philosophical foundations of Sufism and Vedanta.[1] It has since been exposed to various changes due to developmental activities and is now at a critical phase of cultural and economic transformation, (Aaradhana, 1998:2) studying the characteristics and consequences of which would be valuable in drawing lessons for similar traditional societies elsewhere.

I am at answering the following questions: First of all, were the state's developmental policies based on the Modernisation model i.e. did they aim at bringing about a transition from "traditional" to "modern" in Kashmir's economy, society and polity? Second, were they based only on the Socialist/Communist paradigms or the Modernisation doctrine in its entirety? Third, did the slavish adoption of the Modernisation orthodoxy have negative impacts on the society and environment in Jammu and Kashmir?

My argument is that from 1948 with the implementation of the "Naya Kashmir" (New Kashmir) developmental agenda, the state aimed at building a new social, economic and political order on the pattern of modern societies in the West. It has continued since then, to both subscribe to Modernisation theory and to formulate and execute policy based on its recommendations. Further I emphasise the state's commitment to the Modernisation model in its entirety, leading to somewhat disastrous policy initiatives that did not suit local resources or needs.

My belief is that the greatest failing of state policy in Jammu and Kashmir since 1948 was its complete belief in Modernisation theory's structuralist logic that assumed the state had to develop in a particular direction (along the Western trajectory). This led it to reject the traditional in its entirety and it lost elements that are recognised as vital to development today – the emphasis on sustainability, participation, social cohesion and responsibility towards the environment and every member in the community.

A. Introduction

Modernisation Theory

The Modernisation discourse emerged after the Second World War, as decolonisation gave birth to new states, aspiring to emulate the development experience of their erstwhile colonial masters. Its central concern was how these foundling countries could lessen the developmental gap between themselves and the West.

Around this time Redfield modified Weber's nineteenth century proposition that the world was divided into polar opposites – traditional and modern societies- and gave it a Third World dimension through his 'Folk-Urban dichotomy' (Klaren: 1986:9). This was supplemented by Enlightenment ideas like Comte's and Spencer's theory of evolution of human society through progressive stages to culminate in modern (Western) 'scientific' society. The result was 'stage-growth' theory which proposed that the only way for the traditional Third World countries to develop was imitation of the modern societies developmental journey.

Put simply Modernisation theory was the fundamental proposition that people in traditional societies should adopt the characteristics of modern societies in order to modernise their social, political and economic institutions. (Spybey, 1992:68)

This theory was crystallised most famously in Walt Rostow's *Stages of Economic Growth*: *A Non-Communist Manifesto* in 1960, wherein he identified five stages of development experience that a traditional society needs to go through to become modern. At the start the society is at a Traditional stage; the pre-conditions for 'Take off' itself whereby society makes rapid qualitative and quantitative improvements; the society then reaches the modern stage where the innovations in economics and society begins to reach other aspects of society and finally the last stage is one where little or no growth is needed for society to maintain itself. (Rostow, 1971: 13)

Crucially, a central concern of Rostow and other Modernisation theorists is that in order to modernise, the Third World needs to replicate primarily the application of technology to the control of nature as a means of increasing per capita growth. (Knock, 2002:2)

Talcott Parsons (1951) added another dimension to the theory – the 'structuralist – functionalist approach' to social change (Klaren, 1986:14). This emphasised the effect the processes of Modernisation had on traditional (hierarchical and personalist) structures of authority and association. Accordingly, Modernisation required the transformation of these collective emotional relationships and relational structures into the impersonal, rational form that characterised 'modern' societies.

In case of traditional society these elements were both the cause and effect of underdevelopment and constituted obstacles to Modernisation (*ibid:*3).

Lerner (1958) explained how this social transformation would take place in the Third World – through diffusion. Progress for the Third World had to be introduced from the West; i.e. there would have to be a wholesale importation and assimilation of not only Western technology but also Western institutions and values into their existing society.

Emile Durkheim – nineteenth century French sociologist and philosopher had focused on the degeneration in the strong bonds of community that traditional societies would necessarily face in assimilating modern (Western) values based on rationalism and individualism. The transition to modern society would, through its attendant processes like urbanisation, weaken traditional sources of authority like the family and erode traditional bonds of community. The result of this soulless individualism according to him would be 'anomie' – a sense of alienation and isolation felt by each individual (Klaren, 1986:22).

Thus, Modernisation required the replication of the processes associated with the Western model – industrialisation, urbanisation, mobility of population, democratisation and breakdown of cultural hierarchy. The 'Compatibility approach' conceived by Lipset (1967) and others assumed not only that these could be done simultaneously but that they are mutually reinforcing i.e. there is a locomotive effect of one on all others.

To sum up, Modernisation theory saw development as a linear continuum along which Third World societies had to but also naturally aspired to progress. And with the hegemonic position it occupied in intellectual and policy-making circles for nearly three decades. Modernisation theory even acquired the status of a policy ideology (Latham, 2000:45)

Modernisation-based Policy

The post-war period saw the state acknowledged as the most powerful economic and social actor as Keynesianism and the ideal of the Welfare State reigned supreme. As such it was seen as the only institution powerful enough to bring about the large scale, all pervading change in traditional structures and their ideational foundations, that Modernisation theory demanded. Modernisation theory claimed to provide the state with a 'fool proof' way to development, i.e. to bring about industrialisation, urbanisation, modernisation of agriculture, building modern infrastructure, etc. This was to be brought about by large scale interventions to 'modernise' the existing sectors like agriculture (through removing anomalies and introducing modern production techniques) and establish new ones like industry.

Employment was a key area for change, traditional subsistence economies were characterised by the dominance of the agricultural sector and low mobility of labour from traditional occupations. Modernisation, with its stress on technological change and specialisation dictated the diversion of the bulk of employment away from agriculture and other primary activities to secondary and tertiary occupations like working in industry or education or the health sector.

But Modernisation was not just a practical project; it had a normative role too. It aimed not only at changing collective emotional relationships and relational structures into the impersonal, rational form that characterised 'modern' societies but in order to do so, had to change the normative foundations these were based in. Accordingly 'modern' education had to be imparted to the citizens to prevent them bring held back from the 'march towards progress' by 'backward' ideas. Individualism, reason and a 'scientific' world view had to be instilled into the citizenry for them to fit into the new structures and associations. Education thus became a crucial policy area for the furthering of Modernisation.

The Marxian Socialist Influence

Many Third World states were drawn to the Soviet Planned Economy model that claimed descent from Marxist ideology as the best way to ensure their successful Modernisation. The Marxist emphasis on equity in distribution further provided these states with powerful rhetoric to ensure popular support. The states thus incorporated this model into their policy.

Though the 'modern' society conceived of by Rostow and other Modernisation proponents was a Capitalist one, Marxian Socialism shared the same underlying belief that modernisation of traditional societies was essential in order to develop; the assumptions that change is a fundamental characteristic of human society and that economic change is the key to social change. They both saw capitalism as a necessary stage in the process of societal transformation and the promotion of industrialisation, technological change and urbanisation as policy essentials. Thus, the incorporation of Marxian Socialist methods and rhetoric into the Modernisation project was non-problematic.

B. Problems with Modernisation

After dominating the discourse and practice of development for nearly three decades Modernisation theory came under heavy criticism from various quarters from the 1970s. Its philosophical foundations were challenged by not only in the West but also within developing countries, the main opposition coming from post-modernism and traditionalism. And with rising social and economic inequalities in the Third World, the practical value of its recommendations was also questioned.

Normative Problems

The importance of the (modernisation) ideas that were taken as self-evident during the time, in retrospect seemed debatable if not wrongheaded (Latham, 2000:2). These criticisms resulted directly from a critical reappraisal of the meaning and objectives of development that was taking place around this time. As a development theory broadened its horizons from strictly economistic preoccupations with GDP growth and macro-economic regulation to include social, environmental and sustainability aspects; for the first time questions were asked about the purpose of development. Significant progress in theory was brought into the mainstream by the UN Human Development Report of 1994 which established as the purpose of development, the enhancement of the material and spiritual condition of the individual (United Nations Development Programme (UNDP), 1998: 16). The individual was thus firmly instituted as the subject of development. The Basic Human Needs approach (1979) was designed to measure how much of the benefits of development actually reached the individuals in whose name it was being organised, there being dissatisfaction with the 'trickle down' Modernisation hypothesis that assumed economic growth would automatically lead to improvement in people's condition. Instead research came to support the 'trickle up' mechanism that recognised that meeting the needs of people at the grass roots level would contribute positively to economic growth (Newman and Thomson, 1989: 469).

Rostow's idea that the West had reached the pinnacle of development and thus had nothing left to achieve was also discredited. Amartya Sen's famous observation that black males in certain parts of the US had a lower life expectancy than in certain 'developing' countries like India or China (Sen, 1999: 96) sealed this fact.

Simultaneously, postmodernists attacked both liberal Modernisation theories and their Socialists alternatives, as self-justifying 'meta-narratives' that had long outlived their usefulness. They criticised their totalising ambitions – like all other meta-narratives they emerged out of a particular culture but assumed grander ambitions and sought to impose themselves on others. Postmodernists aimed at deconstructing these theories and replacing them with 'multiple cultural and constructivist contingency theories' (Zapf, 2003:6) that looked at development as an ever changing and not a standardized, automatic process. These theories argued primarily that there was no uniform, self-replicating development experience that would necessarily lead to cultural convergence (with the West) and that believing otherwise would actually hamper development by ignoring the unique cultural, environmental and human resources that each country had been bestowed with.

The other side of the challenge came from the Traditionalists, like the Swadeshi Movement in India, who criticised the idea that development could be brought about by mere imitation of the West as a form of neo-imperialism, and labelled development based on this format as Westernisation. They argued that instead, the goal of development should be a society based on the cultural and environmental heritage of each country.

Some studies pointed to the components of Modernisation being mutually impeding e.g. Huntingdon's study demonstrated that democratisation and development were in direct conflict in the Third World; development in these countries being associated with oppressive authoritarian governments (Huntington, 1984: 9). This seemed to prove that Modernisation theory was inoperative.

Modernisation was also viewed as a self-fulfilling theory – based on the presumption that socio-economic change was a natural, and indeed defining feature of all societies, it projected a normalised pathway illustrating how change along the Western experience would occur for other "modernising" countries. Cultural convergence to the Western model was taken as inevitable. But it was only when the State adopted Modernisation and executed policy that ignored and subverted traditional values and structures (in favour of modernisation) that change became inevitable (Figure 1). Its central premise was thus proved dubious.

Another problem with the modernisation model was that it assumed isolation, seemingly oblivious to its surroundings globalised world where "diffusion" was marginalised by new forms of linkage between the west and the developing world. How these relationships transformed the development process in the Third World, by restructuring the crucial economic processes of production, consumption and distribution was the focus of Dependency thought that concluded that this kind of contact was responsible for "the development of underdevelopment" (Gunder Frank, 1983: 2) in the Third World. It advocated the severing of these ties with the West altogether if development was to be achieved.

Practical Problems

High Social and Environmental Costs of Modernisation in the West

Evidence from both capitalist and socialist countries in the West seemed to show that Modernisation actually destroyed the social fabric of societies and the environment, whilst creating questionable benefits for the majority of people.

Goldblatt highlighted the link between one of the main components of Modernisation, i.e. industrialisation and environmental degradation. He demonstrated that industrialisation has at least two impacts on the relationship between environment and society. (1) The transformation of nature is accelerated by industrialisation. (2) A variety of complex cultural changes take place in association with the development of industrial society. The first of these impacts has to problems like indiscriminate pollution of water, air and soil, while the latter has transformed social relationships and the relationships between people and the environment (Goldblatt, 1996:2). Melosi cites the example of the US in the nineteenth century where industrialisation led to "smoky skies, mounds of putrefying wastes, polluted waterways....an environmental crisis on a scale not encountered before in America". (Melosi, 2001:23)

Mol (1995) in his study of the Danish chemical industry gives an example of Goldblatt's predicted transformation of the relationship between people and the environment. According to him, the environment in Denmark was being degraded by industrialisation because it had been pushed to the periphery and was not at the centre of decision-making for Danish society as it used to be (Mol, 1995: 10).

With global warming and ozone depletion becoming too pressing to ignore the impact of studies linking modernisation, especially its component industrialisation with environmental damage, waste and pollution increased, prompted Schumacher (1973) amongst others, to call for deindustrialisation, in order to protect the environment for ensuring the welfare of future generations.

Similarly, Goldblatt's transformation of relationships between people produced by the advent of industrial society is traced by Hawken in the US where Modernisation has exacted a heavy cost from society in terms of "social waste-homelessness, crime, drug addiction and our forgotten infirm and elderly". (Hawken, 1997:1)

There were other problems as a direct result of modernisation itself: as the state dominated the conception and execution of development in the country, corruption gained ground. Corruption, in this sense is "private gain at the public's expense." (Friedrich in Hiedenhiemer, 1989: 10), This has a negative effect on development and as the burden of corruption falls hardest on the poor, the state is directly guilty of placing it there.

The example of this can be seen in the "Modernised Socialist" former Soviet Union where high levels of official corruption prevailed as a result of the centralisation of developmental power in the hands of the sate (Coleman, 2004:1)

2. Problems Created by the Implementation Framework in "Developing" Countries

Other problems arose in the implementation of the Modernisation model – when 'developing' countries adopted Modernisation as state policy they constructed a framework in which the state had an all-powerful role as driver and moderniser. This led the state to develop vested interests in keeping the processes and fruits of development out of the hands of its citizens. The state in this case could be seen to

> Comprise a group of self-seeking individuals and groups interacting strategically with private agents. The state becomes predatory, seeking to maximise its utility often at the expense of the welfare of its citizens. (Lal, 1988, 27)

This manifested itself, for example, in the developmentalist state's preference for large, high cost-high impact, technology intensive projects over low cost, local (often traditional) solutions; which were chosen to line the pockets of the corporate sector-government nexus, often at the expense of the local communities.

The developmental state turning against its citizen's interests was also explored by the New Political Economy (NPE) literature, developed by Bhagwati (1993) and Srinivasan (1985). It presented a model of how the political influence of a state hampers its economic policies and was based on empirical studies of government interventions in trade and industry in India. It focused particularly on one characteristic of the developmental state in India – rent seeking.

> Rents are defined as the excess returns over social opportunity costs and rent seeking is the attempt to redistribute the rights of such returns through political action. (Krueger, 1974: 35)

Simply, a rent seeking state over-regulated the economy through controls, subsidies, import quotas, etc in order to gain 'windfall' bureaucratic rents from the agents involved, leading to underdevelopment.

The Modernisation model as applied in 'developing' countries could also neglect of certain areas of the economy and society in favour of others. Lipton (1991) highlighted one such imbalance, the 'rural-urban bias. He argued that the rural sector contained the most poverty and the most low cost sources of advance but the urban sector most of the organisation and power to further its interests. Modernisation theory's stress on urbanisation as a component of 'modernising' meant that

> Even though the rural population in low income countries is larger, the political market strongly favours the urban population at the direct expense of the rural people. (Shultz in Varshney, 1995:23)

Though the agricultural sector generally contributed most to the GDP in developing countries, most of the investment was diverted to industrialisation favouring the urban sector. Thus, state intervention "urbanised the benefits and ruralised the costs of development." (Lipton, 1991: 112)

Thus, Modernisation had considerable failings in all its forms – as theory, strategy and process which over time led to a number of negative consequences for the traditional societies and economics into which it was introduced by state policy.

History of Developmentalism in Kashmir

Here the development policies pursued by the state will be analysed, focusing on land redistribution, industrialisation, education, employment creation, rural development and policies favouring urbanisation (like food subsidies favouring the urban sector). It studies the motivations behind these policies and traces their adherence to Modernisation theory, arguing that their aims at least live up to it. It also examines if state policies brought about Modernisation as process and argues that they did.

The information is derived from various official documents, principally State Development Reports, Digests of Statistics and Five Year Plans and Indian Planning Commission Reports. Studies by experts like Bhat, Misri and Prakash on the state's agricultural and industrial sectors are also used. The monetary figures are expressed in terms of lakhs and crores of Rupees. A lakh is Rs 1,00,000 and a crore is equal to Rs 10,000,000.

A. The First Developmental Agenda: 'Naya Kashmir'

Perhaps the most important in Kashmir's developmental history was the 'Naya Kashmir' developmental agenda of Sheikh Abdullah's National Conference (NC), authored before independence (in 1944) that later became part of the State Constitution and laid the foundations of state developmental policy.[2] Its strong socialist language drew constant support from the peasantry.

The NC took power in 1947, and by 1950 had carried out its promised redistributive land reforms. While Abdullah's strong ideological and political affinity with Nehru led to support for India's Soviet – inspired developmental model, the message coming out from his administration was,

> Kashmir is not going red. As in the agrarian sector there is nothing ultra or especially communistic about the lines of Kashmir's industrial development. What they are based on instead is social realism. (Banerji in Bakhshi, 2001:89)

Change was still the key aim, indeed the basis, of state development policies.

> The essence of successful planning is the rearrangement of social forces in such a way that the productive forces are released from all obstacles for giving the maximum result. (*ibid*)

Whether it claimed socialist inspiration or sought to emulate the economic structuring of capitalist models, Naya Kashmir was essentially a modernising agenda – a "political social and economic plan for the new order." (Beg in Bakshi, 2002: 124)

Kashmir was primarily a feudal, agrarian economy; agriculture was viewed as the starting point.

> Any reforms can only be brought about by shaping the economy of the country upon a complete overhaul of the present system of agronomy. (*ibid*: 143)

At the same time, however Naya Kashmir sought not only to change the social relations of production in the agrarian sector but also the method of production; seeking not only to industrialise as fast as possible but also to diversify from traditional small scale industries like handicrafts to medium and heavy industries like cement.

Again, industrialisation was envisaged as developing from the products of a 'take off' in agriculture, brought about by changing the traditional agrarian structure (primarily land reform)

> From the land must come more food to feed the people as well as the goods by the exchange of which machines can be bought to industrialise the country and mechanise agriculture itself. (Banerji in Bakshi, 2002: 227)

At the same time, Naya Kashmir aimed at a more widespread change in society and social relations – "*a social revolution in a peaceful manner.*" (Beg in Bakshi, 2002: 210) Its main aims were

> To raise the standard of living of our people, enhance the wealth of the community, and to eradicate all invidious social divisions. (*ibid*: 207)

On the political front it had been instrumental in initially demanding "*Responsible government,*" by the Maharaja, but later its demands became more radical: a complete overthrow of the monarchical system and the establishment of "*Awami Raj*" (popular rule) and democratic institutions.

Thus, the fundamental proposition of developmentalism in Kashmir, as put forward by Naya Kashmir, was that the traditional societal, economic and political structures needed to be changed on the pattern of 'modern' (Western) societies; successful replication of these 'modern' social, political and economic institutions was regarded as *synonymous* with development.

B. The Planned Economy Model: the Five Year Plans

The policies that informed the various development programmes of the state were set forth in the Directive Principles articulated in the State Constitution. These aimed at

> The development, in a planned manner (of) the productive forces of the country with a view of enriching the material and cultural life of the people. (The Constitution of J&K and Plan Documents of the J&K Government, 1956: 1)

Thus, development in Kashmir started, like the rest of India, along the Planned Economy model. Drawn up in 1950 under Sheikh Abdullah, the first five-year plan was heavily subsidized by the Indian government, with 90 per cent of the funding coming from the centre (Prakash, 2000:2).[3] Its primary aim was agrarian reform, as the backwardness of the state was attributed mainly to the common peasant suffering in the clutches of landlordism.

This was to be supplemented by,

> Economic remedies like improvements in the production technique and agricultural equipment of all kinds, better marketing facilities and consolidation of holdings. (Beg in Bakshi, 2002: 207)

Besides this, development of the industrial sector was given priority allocated Rs 35.61 lakhs[4] (Prakash, 2000:8). Building up industrial infrastructure was stressed, there even being proposals to export natural products like silk skins and hides to Czechoslovakia in exchange for machines. (Banerji in Bakshi, 2002: 233).

As part of the Plan, expenditure was also allocated to irrigation and administration. This pattern continued for the next three Five Year Plans, but because some sectors like industry, irrigation and administration did not generate sufficient returns to the amounts invested in them, the state was faced with recurring budget deficits, for example Rs 58.55 lakh in 1956-57. (J&K Review of Progress, 1961:3)

The state also invested in public works, primarily road building and supply of water and electricity, in an effort to *"modernise the infrastructure of the state"* (Prakash, 2000:5). It promoted urbanisation and the expansion of existing cities like Srinagar and Jammu, through power and food subsidies and other policies. (*ibid*: 7)

From the 1970s onwards, the state was designated in the 'General' (i.e. non-backward) category of Indian states, and the centre reversed its aid policy to 30 per cent grants and 70 per cent loans, which tied-up half of the state's expenditure in debt and interest repayments. (J&K Digest of Statistics: 1960-1990, 1991:34) Though the expenditure on and important of the industrial and administrative sectors grew more rapidly, the developmental priorities of the government remained much the same.

Thus, it is clear that the Five Year Plans were based on the Modernisation model, as they aimed at eradicating the

> Characteristics of a backward economic region the predominance of the agricultural sector, low degree of urbanisation, inadequately developed infrastructure, low industrial development and low levels of investment. (J&K State development Report, 2003:25)

2.1 Policy Implementation

The adoption of Modernisation theory as the basis of developmental policy as well as the progress of the Modernisation process can be traced in all the key development policies put in place by successive governments till present. We start by looking at agriculture.

Land Redistribution: Big Landed Estates Abolition Act

Naya Kashmir decried

> The development of agriculture shall be the foremost task of the government. (J&K Constitution, Article 1, 1956:2)

This was again reiterated in Article 15 of the J&K Constitution, which enjoined the state to develop agriculture and allied activities by bringing to the aid of the cultivator the benefits of modern research and techniques (State Planning Department Report, 2003: 1). This preoccupation with reforming agriculture led to direct intervention in the traditional system of production through the Big Landed Estates Abolition Act of 1950, which transferred land to the tiller without any compensation to the landlords. The ownership rights of some 24.7 crore acres of land were transferred to 2 lakh tiller families and debts of Rs 175 lakh were reduced for farmers (Alam, 1988: 23). It was hoped that rural inequalities, deemed the basic cause of underdevelopment,

> Would now be reduced and peasants would cultivate the land more efficiently. (Prakash, 2000:5)

Despite the socialist emphasis, giving lands to individuals without a serious attempt to cooperative ownership actually led to the strengthening of individual property rights – a capitalist outcome.

Besides redistribution, the state also invested heavily in providing better facilities and modern technologies to farmers. In the 1960s it started the Intensive Agricultural District Programme and the High Yielding Varieties Programme by which new hybrid varieties of seeds as well as subsidized fertilisers and pesticides were provided. This yielded positive results such as,

> High Yields of food and non-food crops especially paddy, wheat, maize and apples. (Prakash, 2000: 4)

Thus, the main developmental thrust of these actions was to "modernise" agriculture and increase productivity (recommendations of Modernisation theory), which by their own standards they achieved successfully (furthering Modernisation as process).

State Industrialisation Policy

State developmental policy envisaged that industrialisation was an essential component of development as it would,

> Absorb rural surplus labour in non-agricultural occupations and raise incomes and standards of living of wage workers. (Bhat and Misri, 1994:4)

Despite the major role of industrialisation in the first two five-year plans,[5] concerns began to grow that industrialisation in the state was lagging behind the rest of the country, and the state government declared in the Third Five Year Plan that it would "*establish basic industries based on our natural wealth.*" (J&K State Draft of Third Five Year Plan, 1966:13) Accordingly, it increased public sector investment in the industrial sector and

> Established a number of corporations over the years such as J&K Industries, J&K Minerals and J&K Cement. By 1975 the total output from the various units operated by these corporations stood at Rs 8.19 crore. (Prakash, 2000:8)

The state also set up other organisations like the State Industrial Development Corporation and State Financial Corporation to provide infrastructure and raw material to these industries where "private investment was not available." (J&K State Development Report, 2000:96)

The Development Committee's Report in 1975 stressed that

> To accelerate the pace of development, steps must be taken to welcome the maximum possible investment of private capital and entrepreneurship in the state. (Report of the Development Review Committee on Jammu & Kashmir, 1975:33)

The state tried to attract private investment into the industrial sector, but with geographical factors and the onset of militancy, this did not meet with much success. However, by 1998 the state's new industrial policy state that,

> In order to achieve rapid industrialisation in the state the government must adopt the strategy of developing industrial infrustructure. (J&K State Development Report, 2003: 31)

The policy included allotment of land in lease for a period of 90 years in industrial estates and a capital investment subsidy of 30 per cent (subject to a maximum of Rs 30 lakh) to be given on capital investments. This preferential treatment for industry becomes even more significant when considering that J&K is "*a land scarce state*" and "*capital is lacking*" (Prakash, 2000: 4)

Thus, it is clear that industrialisation, an essential component of Modernisation theory and process was introduced and expanded in Kashmir.

State Education Policy and State Employment Strategy

When the state became independent in 1947, only five per cent of the population was literate and there were very few educational institutions, concentrated mainly in the larger towns. (Bhat and Misri, 1994:28) The state government took immcdiate measures like free education from the primary to the university level. The aim was to increase enrolment, literacy levels and open new institutions.

In the Five Year Plans too, expenditure for education kept increasing. (J&K State Development Report, 2003: 199) These efforts paid off as the literacy rate started to rise. In 1961 it had risen to 11.03 per cent, in 1981, 32.68 per cent and in 2001, 54.46 per cent. (*ibid*: 197). The state is now ranked seventh out of the 20 big states in terms of education though it still is behind the national literacy average of 65 per cent (*India Today,* 2004:29).

However, the stress of these policies remained primarily on pushing up numbers. The education imparted, especially in schools, was too generalised and academic to equip people for satisfactory employment. Vocational education, which would have provided an answer to the problem of unemployment amongst the educated, was not provided at the secondary and higher-secondary levels. Moreover, the quality of education in government institutions was poor. (J&K State Development Report, 2003:208)

The state employment policy tried to provide the required number of jobs for educated youth in the civil administration sector, which over the years led to the creation of the largest bureaucracy in the country. (Prakash, 2000: 8) Over the years, as political pressure built up on the state to provide more white collar jobs, it kept repeating the same strategy, leading to the present situation in which 312 per cent of the state's internally derived revenues go to pay salaries and pensions while the percentage of unemployed educated youth is still more than 60 per cent of the total unemployed and rising![6] (Planning Commission, 2000-2002:89)

Educated youth who didn't find employment in civil administration or industry could not be absorbed into the largest economic sector – agriculture due to the changes brought about by the land reforms of 1950 (Bhat and Misri, 1994:131). Shrinkage in size of average land holdings and increased technology replacing labour meant that the agrarian sector could not provide jobs in spite of its growth in output. (J&K State Development Report, 2003:67)

Thus, following the recommendations of Modernisation theory, the state government not only introduced reforms that would over time move the traditional concentration of employment away from the agricultural sector, but to overcome this problem, tried to provide the required jobs in the tertiary sector. But this Modernisation process created for it severe economic problems.

Rural Development Programme

A number of development programmes were introduced from the 1950s onwards, mostly conceived of and funded by the Indian central government, aimed at socio-economic transformation of rural areas.

> It was expected that all these processes of change would lead to higher levels of living, especially for the (rural) poor and a general improvement in the quality of life. (*ibid*: 250)

These included the Intensive Agricultural Development Programme and Intensive Area Programme of 1964, both of which were part of the "Green Revolution" programme to make the country self-sufficient in food. It also introduced programmes to 'develop rural infrastructure', (*ibid:* 250) and bring about social development in villages.[7]

The social development programmes proved not very successful in reaching their objectives (Bhat and Misri, 1994:18) and

> the restructuring and revamping of old schemes and the introduction of new ones, in some cases, created more confusion than clarity in the process of rural development. (J&K State Development Report, 2003:253)

Public works like the provision of piped water to villages were attempts to better the lives of the rural population by providing them with 'modern facilities'. The various programmes introduced by the state led to

> A total of 4200 villages, covering a population of 25.86 lakhs (being) provided with piped water supply by 1985-86. (Bhat and Misri, 1994:41)

The state's road network was also expanded considerably, tripling in length in the twenty years from 1965, with special emphasis on connecting rural and border areas to the rest of the state, and continuing today. (*ibid*: 38 ; J&K State Development Report, 2003:273)

> As a consequence the remoteness of various areas and micro regions has shrunk to some extent. (Bhat and Misri, 1994:37)

In the 1970s, the government under pressure to try new approaches to development, initiated a 'single line administration' approach. (*ibid*:284) This divided each of the state's districts into 'Halqas' comprising a certain number of villages.[8]

> The twin objectives of the Single Line Administration were to secure a mechanism for developing the planning process at the district level to take full account of the resource endowments, potentialities and needs structure; and also initiate a process of equitable development of various areas within a district. (Choudhary, 1990:34)

In reality this more traditional, participatory approach to development remained crippled by the centralised planning that was the staple of state developmental policy. Village administrations were deprived of adequate administrative powers which were "still exercised by the field level bureaucracy" and "not granted adequate financial resources to discharge various functions." (J&K State Development Report, 2003:248)

Another important initiative was the Integrated Rural Development Programme (IRDP) of 1980, which aimed at providing productive assets to parts of the rural population. However, due to imperfect knowledge of markets and prices, the beneficiaries were exploited by urban middleman.[9] Bhat concludes that the implementation of the IRDP actually widened the gap between the poor and the poorest. (Bhat, 1991:34) the failure of this scheme clearly demonstrated the urban bias embedded in state policy, as the market system created by Modernisation actually worked against the rural poor by capitalising on their lack of market knowledge, even where the objective was to benefit them.

Despite the introduction of all these schemes, the predicted transformation of the rural sector along 'modern' lines (high productivity, better resource management and better standards of living) have not automatically been produced; for most schemes, the bulk of funds have gone to the administrative machinery. The official figures remain incomplete and provide no concrete idea of what benefits were provided and to whom, though it is generally known that

> The identification of the beneficiaries was not done in accordance with the guidelines and the poorest of the poor were actually left out; this trend continues even now. (J&K State Development Report, 2003:276)
>
> And,
>
> State interventions in agriculture and industry were constantly subjected to the pressures and pulls of various interest groups. As a result, policies that were conceived to benefit society at large were often implemented by a small group of the population to benefit themselves. (Prakash, 2000:4)
>
> The results of other developmental schemes are similar
>
> The implementation developmental schemes in the state has been sluggish and fallen short of targets. Studies reveal that in a number

of cases, the actual achievement has been only to the extent of one-third of the target set in the beginning. (*ibid*: 277)

Land Reform and De-agriculturalisation

State-initiated land reforms were designed to modernise the structure of the rural economy by ending landlordism, but over the long term they had undesirable effects on agrarian structures and land use.

The pattern of landholdings changed from large to small ones, as population growth meant increasing subdivision of land through inheritance by several children. In 1953, only 14 per cent of all land was under holdings less than one hectare; by 1986 this had increased to 32 per cent, and the trend continues. (Prakash, 2000:6). The result is extreme land fragmentation and parcellisation, with the average farm size now considerably below the optimum size agreed upon on the all-India level (*ibid:* 6): the average land holding in Kashmir is a mere 0.76 hectares as compared to 1.82 hectares on the all India level (J&K State Development Report, 2003: 54)

Given the current cropping pattern and farming technology, small farms are becoming unviable: parcellisation has been negatively correlated with productivity in studies by Bhat and Misri (1994), Sadhu (1989) and Bhat and Alam (1987). This continuing fall in productivity has meant that more and more farmers and their families are moving away from agriculture, converting their land for residential use as population growth puts pressure on existing housing (Greater Kashmir, 2004:5).[10]

Increased individualism bolstered by enhanced property rights along with parcellisation of land led to the break-up of traditional Kashmiri joint families working the land. This created more pressure on land for housing as villages started to spread into the surrounding countryside. This was especially true in districts like Anantnag where, in the past decade, housing has taken up most of the prime agricultural land.

De-agriculturalisation has also occurred as those who could not find skilled jobs and found agriculture unappealing started to change the use of the land they inherited, mostly converting it for shops and other commercial establishments. Ironically, they were helped in this process by the state-initiated development programmes, like the scheme in the 1980s that granted subsidised loans to unemployed youth to set up businesses. (Prakash, 2000:8)

This de-agriculturalisation of land, in a state where and is the scarcest resources, constitutes a grave threat to food security in the future. In the present political scenario, where a nascent elected government is desperate to ensure for itself continued popular support, there is no political will to reverse this illegal de-agriculturalisation and incur the ire of the masses.

Persisting Inequality

The end of feudal ownership brought about by the Big Landed Estates Abolition Act did not mean the end of inequality, even in the rural sector. Instead some, particularly revenue officials or "Patwaris", gained most from the reforms, extracting money from all the parties involved in return for beneficial decisions. In many cases the amount of land given to families was based not on their entitlement but their political affiliation. (*ibid:* 5) Political machinations thus undid much of the intended egalitarian effect of the land reforms, and inequality was merely restructured and not eradicated. As Bhat (cited in V. Balsubramanyam, 1984:92) observes,

> The post reforms period has given birth to a new class structure in rural Kashmir....of commercially oriented landowners, land speculators, bureaucrats, transport owners and bootleggers wielding both money and political power.

This persistence of inequality was compounded by the failure of rural development programmes.

> These programmes failed to generate sufficient levels of income to bring the rural poor above the poverty line on a sustainable basis. (J&K State Development Report, 2003:281)

The number of people below the poverty line continues to increase (*ibid*)

Further, economic growth in the 1950s and 60s brought it inflation, and the price of food, especially coarser varieties increased – worsening the lot of the poor (Bhat and Misri, 1994:67). This practical failure of Modernisation policy, in Kashmir as in the West was them the reliance on the "trickle down" effect of structural change (land reform) and economic growth – when this failed to occur poverty and inequality persisted.

Rent Seeking and Corruption

The Modernising state's centralised model of development was removed from the individuals it aimed at helping; the political leadership and bureaucracy developed vested interests in keeping the practice of development out of the hands of the masses, and the system of regulation, quotas and subsidies became increasingly complicated to ensure windfall gains for bureaucrats and politicians. The state in effect became 'predatory' seeking to benefit a few individuals within it against the larger social interest. (Lal, 1988:36)

> The grants of loans, import quotas and orders of supplies have come to depend on the discretion of a single individual, rather than a set of rules. (Prakash, 2000: 10)

Corruption became widespread. The burden fell heaviest on the rural poor as the level of corruption was worst in the high spending government departments like Rural Development. In some cases, individual beneficiaries of poverty-alleviation schemes, whom subsidies were supposed to be helping, actually had to pay as much as 50 per cent of the value of the subsidy as bribes and other transaction costs. (Prakash, 2000:7). By the 1970s the problem had become so acute that

> Most of the efforts at seeking official favours, without which it is not easy to carry out most of the economic activities in the state, invariably involve some amount of humiliation and corruption. (Puri, 1981:58)

Successive governments diverted development funds for personal use as well as making generous grants of subsidies and licences to their party supporters. (Punjabi, 1991:25) Prakash (2000:10) refers to this system as 'parasitic capitalism'. Existing developmental schemes suffered, and declining agricultural productivity made the state increasingly dependent upon imports from the rest of the country.

The problem of corruption as experienced by other Modernising and Modernised societies thus became embedded in what had been traditionally been a society with strong moral and ethical values rooted in Sufism and Vedanta philosophy. (Prakash, 2000:9)

Rural - Urban Bias

The developmental policies of the state, based as they were on the goal of modernisation, gave much support to its component urbanisation. Even the State Development Report of 2003 saw it as

> An integral part of the development process, bringing in its wake new opportunities and new possibilities. (*ibid:* 218)

The state put in place policies that favoured the small section of the population that lived in the cities and towns at the expense of the rural majority.

According to the Development Committee Review's Report of 1975, power and drinking water subsidies were provided primarily to the urban centres that comprise less than 20 per cent of the population. The 80 per cent that lived in villages and contributed 60 per cent of the state's income secured only a small fraction of these benefits.

The Report pointed out that

> The ultimate burden of these subsidies falls on those sections of the community living in the rural areas, who are too poor to make use of electricity and have no access to filtered water supplies. (Report of the Development Review Committee on J&K, 1975:65)

Food for the urban population was also heavily subsidised (Prakash, 2000:9)

The subsidy meant that the government had to pay low prices to farmers when buying this grain and as a result

> Food farmers are left with the depressed price offer and the law of supply clearly states that the lower the price, the less the production. (Report of the Development Review Committee on J&K, 1975:65)

In many cases, farmers were not able to invest in costly technological changes to improve long-term productivity. This added to the deterioration of agricultural productivity brought about by land fragmentation.

The 'rural urban divide over subsidies' (Bardhan, 1984:57) over the years led to the widening of disparities between rural and urban incomes. In 1975 only five per cent of rural incomes exceeded Rs 10 000 whilc thc urban incomes performed better at 17.6 per cent. (Prakash, 2000:7) There is a huge difference in literacy rates, only 48 per cent in the rural areas as compared to 72 per cent in the urban areas in 2001. (UNDP, J&K Human Development Fact Sheet: 2). As ever, 'modernising' state policy is directly responsible for this.[11]

Looking at Kashmir's present situation, the social cost of the state's Modernisation policy has been very high. Increase in poverty, persistence of inequality, breakdown of close joint family relationships, spread of corruption, rural urban bias, de-agriculturalisation and threat to food security are all either the direct results of state interventions in favour of Modernisation or the results of problems created by the Modernisation model that concentrated absolute developmental power in the hands of the state.

2.2 Environmental Impacts

The environmental effects of the modernisation model and argues that the modernisation-based state policies have, through their short term perspective, failed to take into account the heavy toll they exacted on the environment and how this will hamper development in the long run. It puts forward evidence that state development policy has directly led to deforestation, eutrophication affecting lakes and other water bodies, which in turn have created problems like microclimatic change, flooding, etc. the state's encouragement of urbanisation has led to destruction of habitats, road congestion, air pollution and serious sewerage problems. All this has resulted in the gradual development of 'ecological anomie' in the mind of the citizen and state alike where they forget their interminable link with the land and thus act without regard for the consequences of their actions.

Urbanisation

As a result of state encouragement, the last 50 years have seen a rapid increase in urbanisation both in the state (J&K Development Report, 2003:10). Srinagar City has grown to about 800 sq km from 50 sq kms in the last 5 decades and Jammu City shows similar growth. (note on Environment and Development - J&K Perspective, 2001:1)

As the population of cities grows, so does the collective human impact on the environment, for example, the problem of waste management in cities has escalated to alarming proportions as

> There is practically no sewerage, sewage, garbage and bio-medical waste disposal facility in the state and most of the garbage, sewage, etc drains into water channels and rivers resulting in water pollution (*ibid:* 2)

Increased urban prosperity and spread of consumerism has led to an increase in vehicle ownership and combined with an indifferent attitude to the environment has meant that

> The condition of the roads and vehicles is not good, resulting in a high degree of air pollution. (*ibid:* 1)

But it is not just the increase in the ecological footprint of urban communities that is to blame. As modernisation's attendant philosophies of consumerism and individualism embedded their roots more deeply into the Kashmiri psyche, people grew out of the traditional mind-set that had been intimately attuned to the preservation of the environment. The consequence was a growing indifference towards the state of the environment, or ecological anomie. People began to look at individual components of the environment simply as commodities that could be exploited in the quest to extract material gains. An example of this is the increasing encroachment on the water of lakes in Kashmir.

People have filled in large tracts of lake water to construct houses and shops without considering that their acts endanger the very survival of lakes like the Dal. (the J&K State Development Report, 2003:221).

Land Use and Agriculture

Though Kashmir has laws dating back from monarchical times restricting land use[12], the state has in the past put forward various development policies that have altered the traditional land use pattern. The first of these was the land reforms that brought more land under cultivation: even steeper slopes covered by forests. The practice of changing the use of agricultural land was also started by the government. (note on Environment and Development - J&K Perspective, 2001:1)

The transformation of agriculture subsistence to commercial came about as the state encouraged the use of chemical fertilizers and pesticides. As their use increased over time, their impact on the environment became apparent.

> Most of these chemicals leach into the water bodies, lakes and wetlands resulting in eutrophication and shrinkage in surface water area. (note on Environment and Development - J&K Perspective, 2001:2)

With the land reforms, as the area of landholdings shrank, people did not have enough land left over to allot for fodder. (Aaradhana, 1998:6) As a result, there is continuous grazing on forest land with the result that perennial grasses have almost disappeared and given way to weeds. Soil erosion is also a problem. (*ibid*)

Forestry Policy

J&K was once one of the most heavily forested states in India, home to a variety of Himalayan tree species and valuable medicinal herbs (Singh, 1991:81). The forest supported valuable species like the Hangul and Snow Leopard, and contributed to soil and water conservation and flood mitigation (A. R. Wani, 2004:175). Traditional lifestyles did not interfere with the forest, though depending on them for fodder and fuel, since their capacity to impact was small. There was also a strong realisation that the forest needed to be preserved to ensure the continuance of the supply of natural resources that supported livelihoods: there is an old Kashmiri Sufi saying, "food will last as long as the forest will."

Since the 1940s, the State began exploiting its forests commercially on a large scale, taking charge of forest management, forestry policy and sales from forest land. However, its policies have been based on the commodification of forest and not on an appreciation of their ecological value. As urbanisation increased demand for food, the forest department started to fell trees at an ever increasing rate, taking the average to 116 lac trees felled per year. Not enough effort was put into regeneration of forests, resulting in the denudation of vast tracts of forest areas (note on Environment and Development - J&K Perspective, 2001:2)[13]

The State also initiated encroachment upon forest land through other developmental schemes like the "Grow More Food" Programme that was formulated in 1948 as part of the land reforms and aimed at conversion of forest area to agricultural use. Initially, 5000 acres were affected but now this area has been extended considerably: unofficial estimates place at 14000 hectare acres. (A R Wani, 2004:175)

Thus, due to cumulative effect of the State policy and the modernisation pressures, at present only 19 per cent of the land area is under forest as opposed to the 30 per cent requisite to ensure ecological stability (Dar, 2004:218): the forests are in a critical condition.

Industrialisation

Though the state is not as industrially developed as the rest of the country, the state government's industrialisation drive has meant that

There are a number of polluting industries like cement plants and leather tanneries in J&K province as well as brick kilns, stone crushers etc, that pollute both air and water. (note on Environment and Development - J&K Perspective, (note on Environment and Development - J&K Perspective, 2001:2)

This propagation of polluting industries is a result of the State Aid to Industries Act (1961) under which no industry need prove itself eco-friendly before state assistance is granted. The State Pollution

Control Board, the government body in charge of environment protection, is impotent as it has no say in the decisions of the Board of Industries. (Dar, 2004:236)

The people of the surrounding areas, who initially opposed pollution industries, ultimately had to surrender and accept jobs in the same establishment as compensation (MA Wani, 2004:87). In recent years, as pressure over environmental concerns has been mounted both by civil society and the central government's own environmental policy, the State government has been pushed to put forward plans to limit the effect of these industries. But these plans focus mainly on confining industries to hilly areas (*ibid*) which seems to forget the impact of the pollution produced on the forests and wildlife; forest being located mostly in the higher reaches (as agriculture and settlements take up almost the entire valley floor of Kashmir).

Treatment of industrial effluents is still considered a non-issue, but the dumping of hazardous wastes like Mercury into the rivers creating serious short and long term implications not only for the bio-physical but also the human environment, which may be possible to reverse.

Public Works Projects

The goal to build modern infrastructure led the state to pursue some bizarre public works projects without considering the value of ecosystems and traditional ways of maintaining them.

Traditional ways of life had worked within these ecosystems, but modernisations stress on applying technology to mould nature led to large scale, high cost projects that aimed at supplanting them. For example, road building, deemed essential to the furthering of development in the state, meant building on top of natural canals flowing through the summer capital Srinagar (J&K State Development Report, 2003:223). These canals had not only been the transport lifelines of the city, but also provided natural outlets to the water of lakes that form "*important repositories of unique biological diversity.*" (Zutshi, 2000:18) After they had been filled up, the lakes began stagnation, their self-cleansing mechanisms broken down. Urbanisation compounded the problem as increasing amounts of untreated sewage started being dumped into the lakes leading to reduction of water depth, eutrophication and a burst of excessive macro vegetation, threatening not only the survival of the lakes but also important native species like Snow trout and Chara.[14] (ibid 20)

The remaining canals are now just gutters into which solid waste and sewage is dumped both by the residents of the areas as well as the city Municipality. (Swami, 1998:25)

Other public works projects were equally insensitive to the environment, the most glaring example being the state's most ambitious public health institution- the Sher-e-Kashmir Institute of Medical Sciences, built on land created by filling in part of the Aanchar Lake. Over the years the daily disposal of nearly-untreated human and bio-medical waste has turned the once thriving habitat into no more than a cesspool.

Kashmir's Himalayan climate entails abundant rainfall both in summer and winter, which, combined with the topography and temperate climate, have created an extensive system of underground springs, streams and ponds. These have constituted not only an important habitat for various species but also a valuable natural resource for hundreds of years. Village communities evolved traditional regimes of cleaning and maintaining these water resources that not only constituted their drinking water supply but also supported irrigation. Every autumn the entire village would gather to clean and desilt all the village ponds, streams and irrigation canals. This tradition was known as 'Halsheeri'. Domestic and human waste was turned into compost for the fields and the villages had strict rules against polluting the local water source. But when the government started supplying piped drinking water to villages and providing tube wells for irrigation (J&K Development Report: 2003: 245), the direct dependence of the population on the water resource was broken. Over the next decade the tradition of Halsheeri was abandoned. The water sources have since fallen into neglect and in most villages domestic waste and sewage is being dumped into the streams and canals. Water pollution and siltation have become acute; the former leading to diseases like Gastroenteritis, Typhoid and Cholera and the latter contributing to worsening of flood situations in recent years. (Chadha, 1991: 68)

In the traditional Kashmiri system based on Sufi and Vedanta philosophy, there was a strong recognition of symbiotic connection between the biophysical ecosystem and human life. The concept that the ecosystem itself was sacred and needed to be preserved from violation as the governing principle for human behaviour, germinated from this. Protecting the ecosystem from outside or inside exploitation was a collective responsibility. (Ramakrishnan, Rao, Saxena and Maikhuri, 2004: 55)

But, with its various developmental interventions the state replaced the community as the primary determinant of the relationship between man and the environment. This became possible because of the natural resources and directly administered this ownership in a way that it hadn't been able to do in the feudal system.[15] It thus was able to operate at a level between communities and their surroundings, clouding the traditional recognition of their symbiotic relationship. The people were able to shrug off their responsibility to maintain the resources over which they no longer had ownership. (James, 2004: 78)

Looking at nature simply as a set of resources to harness through application of technology, the state came up with high-cost development projects for maximum and immediate impact. In the process the environment was pushed to the sidelines for decision-making. The result was myopic policies like establishing polluting industries in the ecological heart of the Himalayas.

And as individuals and communities became exposed to the 'modern' way of relating to the environment, ecological anomie grew as prevalent short termism made people seek immediate monetary gains from the environment without caring for long-term effects, giving rise to acts like filling up lakes to build houses or illegal logging of forests and timber smuggling.

Conclusion

The highly centralised Planned Economy model of development developed in Kashmir as initiated by *Naya Kashmir* has aimed for large scale changes in traditional social, economic and political structures. It has implemented policies to ameliorate anomalies in agriculture, develop industry, expand secondary and tertiary employment and develop modern infrastructure to increase economic growth. This answers my question in the affirmative: i.e. the state's developmental policies were based on the Modernisation model as they did aim at bringing about a transition from traditional to 'modern' in Kashmir's economy, society and polity.

And as to my second question, the data clearly demonstrates that the development policies of the state were based not just on Socialist/ Communist ideals but on the entire structuralist model and linear continuum of Modernisation theory- land reforms that strengthened individual property rights instead of establishing community ownership of land in the state, being the perfect example of this. In its uncritical imitation of the Modernisation model, the State did profound damage to the society and environment of Jammu and Kashmir.

So did these high costs of Modernisation outweigh its benefits? That question, of course, is vast enough to warrant a separate study.

Bibliography

- Aaradhana, PS (1998): Himalayan Ecology. New Delhi: Rajat Publications.
- Alam, SM (1988): 'Effect of land reforms on resource use efficiency in J&K' *Agricultural Situation in India 1988.*
- Balsubramanyam, V (1984): 'The Agricultural Sector' The Economy of India, London: Weidenfeld.
- Banerji, JK (2002): Agrarian Revolution and Industrialisation' in Bakshi, SR: *History of Economic Development in Kashmir.* Kashmir: Gulshan Publishers.
- Bardhan, PK (1984): *The Political Economy of Development in India.* New Delhi: Oxford University Press.
- Beg, MMA (2002): 'Social and Economic Orders of the Present Age and Our Decision' in Bakshi, SR: *History of Economic Development in Kashmir.* Kashmir: Gulshan Publishers.
- Berger, MT (2001): 'The nation-state and the challenge of global capitalism', *Third World Quarterly,* Vol. 22, No. 6.
- Bhagwati, J (1993): *India in transition.* Oxford: Clarendon Press.
- Bhandari, L and Debroy, B and Saran, R (2004): 'India's Best and Worst States', *India Today* 16 Aug.
- Bhat, MS (1991): 'Integrated Rural Development in J&K: some field experience', *Journal of Rural Development,* Vol. 10, No. 2.

- Bhat, MS and Alam, S (1987): 'Growth Performance of Jammu and Kashmir Agriculture', *Agricultural Situation in India (Nov).*
- Bhat, MS and Misri, ML (1994): *Poverty Planning and Economic Change in Jammu and Kashmir.* New Delhi: Vikas.
- Chadha, K (1991): 'Pollution and Ecological Balance in Jammu and Kashmir State' in Chadha, SK (ed): *Kashmir: Ecology and Environment.* New Delhi: Mittal Publications.
- Choudhary, S (1990): 'Does the Bill give power to people?' in Mathew, G (ed): In *Panchayati Raj in J&K.* New Delhi: South Asia Books.
- Coleman, V (2004): *Why the New EU is like the old USSR.* <http://www.vernoncoleman.com/tneuiltou.htm>(accessed 28th July 2004)
- Common, MS and Stern, DI (1996): 'Economic growth and Environmental Degradation: The Environmental Kuznets Curve and Sustainable Development' *World Development.* Vol. 24, No. 7, pp. 1151-1160.
- (1956): *Constitution of Jammu and Kashmir* <http://www.aryawat.com/kashmir/constitution.htm> (accessed 28th July 2004)
- Dar, MA (2004): 'Air Pollution: Legal Control Mechanics in Jammu & Kashmir' in Bhatt, S (ed): *Kashmir: Ecology and Environment: New Concerns and Strategies.* New Delhi: APH Publishing.
- Development Review Committee on Jammu and Kashmir (1975): *Report of the Development Review Committee on Jammu and Kashmir.*
- Foster-Carter, A (1985): *The Sociology of Development.* Ormskirk: Causway.
- Gaffney, J (ed) (c1988): *France and Modernisation.* Aldershot: Avebury.
- Gare, A (1993): *Nihilism Incorporated: European Civilisation and Environmental Destruction,* Bungendore, NSW: Eco-logical Press.
- Goldblatt, D(1996): *Social Theory and the Environment.* Boulder, CO: Westview Press.
- Gunder Frank, A (1983): Crisis and transformation of dependency in the world system, Norwich: University of East Anglia, Development studies discussion papers; No. 113.
- Hidenheimer, AJ and Johnston, M and LeVine, VT (eds) (1989): *Political Corruption: a handbook.* New Brunswick (NJ): Transaction Books.
- Huntington, Samuel (1984): 'Will More Countries Become Democracies?', *Political Science Quarttely,* Vol. 99, pp. 193-218.
- James, AJ (2004): 'Water Resources Management: Issues and Concerns' in Bhatt, S (ed): *Kashmir: Ecology and Environment: New Concerns And Strategies.* New Delhi: APH Publishing.
- Klaren, P (1986): 'Lost Promise: Explaining Latin American Underdevelopment' in Klaren, P and Bossert TJ (eds): *Promise of Development.* Boulder, CO: Westview Press.

- Krueger, AO (1974): 'Political Economy of Rent Seeking Society', *American Economic Review,* Vol. 64, No. 3.
- Lal, D (1988): *The Hindi Equilibrium,* Oxford:Clarendon Press.
- Latham (2000): *Modernisation as Ideology.* Chapel hill: University of North Carolina Press.
- Lipset, Seymour Martin (1981): *Political Man: The Social Bases of Politics,* Baltimore: Johns Hopkins University Press.
- Lipton, M (1991): 'Agriculture, Rural People, the state and surplus in Asian Countries' in Breman, J & Mundle, S (eds): *Rural Transformation in Asia.* Oxford: Oxford University Press.
- Mattoo, A (2002): 'An agenda for a new Kashmir', The Hindu, 28 Oct.
- Melosi, MV (c2001): *Effluent America: Cities, Industry, Energy and the Environment.* Pittsburgh: University of Pittsburgh Press.
- Mir, SA (2004): 'Legally you can't do it, practically you do' Letter in Greater Kashmir, 29 July.
- Mol (1995): *The Refinement of Production: Ecological Modernisation and the Chemical Industry.* Utrecht: Jan van Arkel/International Books.
- Murphy, J (2001): 'Ecological Modernisation: The Environment and the Transformation of Society', OCEES Research Paper No. 20, Mansfield College, Oxford.
- Norberg-Hodge, H (1992): *Ancient Futures: Learning from Ladakh.* Delhi; Oxford: Oxford University Press.
- Planning Commission, Government of India (1961): *Jammu and Kashmir Review of Progress,* Planning Commission, Government of India.
- Planning Commission, Government of India (2003): *State Development Report: Jammu and Kashmir,* Planning Commission, Government of India.
- Planning Department, State Government of Jammu & Kashmir (1960): *Jammu and Kashmir State Draft of Third Five Year Plan,* 1961-66 Planning Department, Jammu and Kashmir State Government.
- Planning Department, State Government of Jammu & Kashmir (2001): *Note on Environment and Development -Jammu and Kashmir Perspective.* Planning Department, Jammu and Kashmir State Government.
- Planning Department, State Government of Jammu & Kashmir (1991): *Jammu and Kashmir Digest of Statistics: 1960-1990,* Planning Department, Jammu and Kashmir State Government.
- Planning Department, State Government of Jammu & Kashmir (2003): *Jammu and Kashmir State Planning Department Report,* Planning Department, Jammu and Kashmir State Government.
- Prakash (2000): 'The Political Economy of Kashmir since 1947', *Contemporary South Asia.* Vol. 9, No. 3, pp. 315-337 (23).

- Punjabi, R (1995): 'Kashmir imbroglio: the socio-political roots', *Contemporary South Aisa.* Vol. 4, No. 1.
- Ramakrishnan, PS; and Rao, KS, Saxena, KG and Maikhuri, RK (2004): 'Managing Natural Resources for Sustainable Mountain Development' in Bhatt, S (ed): *Kashmir: Ecology and Environment: New Concerns and Strategies.* New Delhi: APH Publishing.
- Rostow, WW (1971): *The Stages of Economic Growth:* A Non- Communist Manifesto London: Cambridge University Press.
- Sadhu, AN (1989): 'Agricultural Transformation in Jammu and Kashmir', Paper Presented in the Seminar on: *Economy, Society and Polity in Jammu and Kashmir,* organised by Centre for Research in Rural and Industrial Development, Chandigarh, from 31st Oct – 2nd Nov 1989, in Srinagar.
- Schumacher (1973): *Small is Beautiful: A Study of Economics as if People Mattered.* London: Blond & Briggs.
- Sen, A (1999): *Development as Freedom.* Oxford: Oxford University Press.
- Singh, G (1991): 'Regeneration of Forests in Jammu & Kashmir State' in Chadha, SK (ed): *Kashmir: Ecology and Environment.* New Delhi: Mittal Publications.
- Smith, WC (1965): *Modernisation of a Traditional Society,* London: Asia Publishing House.
- Spybey, T (1992): *Social Change, Development and Dependency.* Cambridge: Polity Press.
- Swami, P (1998): 'To save a Lake', Frontline Vol. 15, No. 11, 23 May – 5 Jun.
- United Nations Development Program (2003): *Jammu and Kashmir Human Development Fact Sheet. <http://www.undp.org.in/Programme/undpini/factsheet/J&K.pdf>*(accessed on 28th July 2004)
- Varshney (1995): *Democracy, Development and the Countryside.* London: Cambridge University Press.
- Verma, PS (1992): *Jammu and Kashmir at the Political Crossroads.* New Delhi: Seema.
- Wani, MA (2004): 'Degeneration of Environment in Kashmir Valley: Need for Immediate Awakening' in Bhatt, S (ed): *Kashmir: Ecology and Environment: New Concerns and Strategies.* New Delhi: APH Publishing.
- Zapf, W. (2003): *Modernisation Theory and the Non- Western World.* Paper Presented to the conference: *Comparing Process of Modernisation,* University of Potsdam, 15-21 Dec.
- Zutshi, DP (2004): 'Dal Lake: Environmental Issues and Conservation Strategy' in Bhatt, S (ed): *Kashmir: Ecology and Environment: New Concerns and Strategies,* New Delhi: APH Publishing.

Notes

1. Mystic philosophies that developed out of mainstream Hindu and Muslim thought. They saw man as an organic part of the complex natural and spiritual world around him, the balance of which he had to continually strive not to disturb.
2. It was a document that electrified the State and transformed J&K's politics, economics and society. (Mattoo: 2002:1)
3. This was more for political than developmental reasons, as Rs 103.50 lakhs were allocated just for defence and during this period more backward states like Bihar had received only 70 per cent funding (Prakash: 2000:2).
4. About 8 per cent of the GDP, only agriculture and defence recorded higher spending (Prakash, 2000: 3).
5. 8.4 per cent of planned expenditure in the second plan (1956-60) was allocated to industry (Report of the Development Review Committee on J&K: 1975:11).
6. State expenditure can exceed internally-derived revenue because the majority of salary funding comes through grants given by the Indian central government.
7. For example, employment schemes like Training of Rural Youth for Self-Employment (TRYSEM) and Jawahar Rozgar Yojna and rural housing schemes like the Indira Awaas Yojna.
8. The single line system was based on the idea of a three tier system – the lowest being the traditional village governance committee or "Halqa Panchayat", then the Block development Council that comprised the heads of all Halqa Panchayats of the area as well as government officials and finally the District Planning and Development Board that included the local MLA or MLC along with the other government officials. Halqa refers to a village or such contiguous number of villages as may be determined by the government from time to time; based on the restriction that the population of the Halqa should not exceed 3000 in hilly areas and 4500 in the plains (J&K State Development Report, 2003: 241).
9. For example, villagers given Jersey cows sold milk from at depressed prices to the middleman, who sold it on at high prices, reaping profits as high as 66.6 per cent (Prakash, 2000: 7).
10. Though changing the use of agricultural land in this way is illegal under Section 133 of the Land Revenue Act of 1939, the past decade has seen this trend growing as the separatist conflict undermined the authority and effectiveness of the state.
11. The maldistribution of growth in favour of urban centres meant that the growth rate for urban population between 1981 and 2001 was a staggering 98.77 per cent (J&K State Development Report, 2003:210)

12. The land is classified for residential use ('Abadi Deh') irrigated prime agricultural land ('Abi Awwal'), secondary agricultural land ('Abi Duam'), orchard, wasteland and forest under the land revenue act of 1939.
13. In looking for other ways to maximise its profits, the forest department carried out ill throught out schemes like encroaching on the surface area of lakes like Wullar and bringing it under plantation. This obstructed the water flow and led to siltation of the lake bed and shrinkage in lake area, thus threatening the survival of the largest fresh water lake in Asia (A.R. Wani, 2004:139).
14. The number of Chara, an important native plant species, has fallen from 12 to only three in the period from 1953 to present (Zutshi, 2000:20).
15. As the State's representatives dictated policy even at the village level as opposed to the traditional village 'self- government' (Panchayati Raj) system that even the local landlord was answerable to.

21

That Ray of Hope

— Humra Quraishi

Kashmiris are emotional and warm people. Bonding takes off rather too spontaneously…In the 90s when the stray dogs menace hadn't quite reached alarming levels, I could walk around the streets of Srinagar city, see for myself stories unfolding in every single lane and by-lane. Later, for fear of getting bitten by strays, I was left with little option but to hop into auto rickshaws; hear the drivers offload the grim happenings, the complex build ups, the characters involved. Together with that see and sense and grasp some harsh realities…

This generation of the Kashmiris has grown up in the midst of curfews and crackdowns. They have survived in an atmosphere riddled with insecurity together with apprehensions of the aftermath. Coupled with this, stands out the fact that employment avenues are shrinking. Recreational facilities cum cultural events are rare…a rarity for the youth surviving the Valley. Even when hyped concerts are staged - such as the Zubin Mehta conducted concert which was staged at Srinagar's Shalimar Gardens - the young Kashmiri enthusiasts are kept far away. Those musical strains only for the who's who; leaving one to wonder rather aloud - Why host cultural shows in a locale when the locals are not allowed to come anywhere near the venue? Why put the city under another round of security strain?

Also, there are none of the symbolic 'Jantar Mantars' in Srinagar. Just about no platform from where the young can voice his or her anguish at the complex builds ups amidst changing sociological patterns.

Also there is an apparent disconnect between the young Kashmiris living in the Valley with the youth living in the other cities and towns of the country. Few interactive forums or platforms and fewer occasions where they could get to meet and talk and discuss.

Though, of course, a large number of Kashmiri students study in the universities and colleges dotted in and around the cities of this country, but they keep to themselves... On several occasions when I'd spoken to Kashmiri students studying in the Aligarh Muslim University and also at the New Delhi situated Jamia Millia Islamia and asked them the crucial 'why' they kept to themselves, confined to their own little groups and did not really mix around, they had detailed two basic reasons - 'the locals are not very comfortable with us getting friendly with them ...they know the police keeps a watch on us - where we eat or where we go or where we stay ... we are aware of this constant watch on us.' Their second reason was this, 'we, the Kashmiri students, can understand each other's problems... none of the non-Kashmiri students from here have ever visited the Valley, so they are unable to comprehend what we and our families go through...the realities we face.' And when I had asked these Kashmiri students if they had talked about these 'realities' to the Kashmiri politicians based in New Delhi or in Srinagar, they had given me those looks as though I should be aware of the political complexities of the day, along the strain that gone are those days when there existed that basic connect between the rulers and those ruled. Not just layers of security that come in way but also the political will to try and reach out to the hapless.

Never mind, if the political characters have developed a thick hide or are hiding under those security covers, the apolitical students from the SAARC countries have taken the bold decision to reach Srinagar to study along with the Kashmiri students...In fact, that's one of the positives I did get to see last Summer (July, 2015) when I was visiting the Valley...Amidst all the gloom in the Kashmir Valley, there'd stood out a ray of hope when I visited 'UNESCO Madanjeet-Singh Institute of Kashmir Studies' situated in the midst of the University of Kashmir. I had heard about this Institute drawing students from the SAARC countries, but had never got to see it function from close quarters. Well, till last summer when I happened to meet the director of this Institute, Professor Gull Wani, at a dinner hosted by the Valley's

CPI (M) leader, Mohammed Yousuf Tarigami. I asked Gull Wani if I could visit the Institute and interact with the students and faculty. And the next afternoon I was there…talking to the young research scholars, hailing from the various countries of this subcontinent. That afternoon it was an experience in itself to hear Afghanistan's Mona Hossaini, Bhutan's Kabita Kharka, Nepal's Bishnu Pokhral and Indu Dhungana, Bangladesh's Sharmin Tamanma, Subarna Dhar, Tanjina Ahmad, Mohammad Zakaria and several others. They offloaded their experiences of residing on the University campus, narrated their interactions with the Kashmiri fellow students and faculty members.

Stories of human connect and bonding emerged…one narration after another. In fact, as a student from Nepal had detailed that when she'd visited the Maqdoom Sahib dargah one of the caretakers asked her if her family was all safe and okay after the earthquake disaster that had hit Nepal. 'It was truly touching...he looked so concerned about that tragedy hitting my country.' Another student from Bangladesh spoke of the marriage function she'd attended that weekend in one of the rural locales of the Valley; detailing the warmth and hospitality. I still recall her words to the effect that the host Kashmiri family (of one of her fellow colleagues at this Institute) had made her feel absolutely at home and language constraints didn't really come in way.

Not a single negative feedback. Though as a journalist I couldn't control my probing prowess; but even after throwing endless queries about this or that, not one negative or lukewarm response. These students sitting amidst their Kashmiri colleagues looked relaxed discussing different aspects connected to their customs and cultures and those connected offshoots.

Of course, I'd had asked them about their parents' initial reactions when they decided to travel all the way from their home countries to this Srinagar based Institute. Much along the expected strain they told me that their parents' reactions ranged from absolute anger to shock riddled with apprehensions. But within weeks they seemed more or less at ease. As one student from Bangladesh said, 'My parents' first reaction was - Is this the only educational Institute in the world you could find to study! But after reaching here and writing to them that the atmosphere around was safe and serene, they felt reassured…'

It was one of those moving experiences to interact with these young men and women of this subcontinent. There seemed an intermingling of diverse cultures and opinions and views cum viewpoints. I could have spent many more hours in that interactive session with these young scholars. It was one of those afternoons where conversation just flowed…flowed on along spontaneously.

I do wish and hope these students write about their experiences so that the masses get to grasp the fabric is intact…still intact. In fact, one of the students had told me she was busy writing her debut novel. Hopefully it should be carrying inputs of her stay in the Valley; after all, a writer cannot be writing in a vacuum, there has to be background or foreground for that take off!

There's something special to this region…it beckons

In fact, that afternoon during my interactive session with these young students, I'd kept thinking about those bygones – centuries back when the Sufis had travelled to the Kashmir region, from far flung foreign lands. Not letting geographical hurdles come in way, these Sufis came from Central Asia, Iraq, and Iran etc. And after they had reached the Valley, they did not move any further; settling down in and around Srinagar. What seems absolutely surprising is that these Sufis never ever went back to their homelands, even when turmoil had settled down in their homelands. There could be several explanations for this but the most probable one is that the local population had been totally taken up by their selflessness and simplicity and not just accepted them but gave them the needed anchorage. None of those prefixes-foreigner or outsider and certainly not the 'other'- were hurled at them. Historian GMD Sufi writes in his volume 'Kashir'- "deeply imbued with Sufism of the age and country from which they emigrated these Sayyids and their followers seem to have stimulated the tendency to mysticism for which Vedantism and Buddhism had already paved the way." In his memoirs Mughal Emperor Jehangir has focused on the very simplicity that these Sufis not just believed in but actually practiced in everyday life – "though they have not religious knowledge or learning of any sort yet they possess simplicity and are without pretence. They abuse no one. They restrain the tongue of desire and foot of seeking. They eat no flesh, they have no wives and always plant fruit bearing trees in the fields so that men may benefit by them, themselves desiring no advantage ..." And Abu'l Fazl records his meeting with Wahid Sufi, "Here an enlightened anchorite has come to my view - for thirty years he has, in an unnoticed corner, been gathering happiness on an old mat."

And so influenced had been Mughal Prince Dara Shikoh with his spiritual teacher- Akhund Mulla Mohammad Shah, who had come all the way from Badakshan - that he had built in Srinagar, the unique school of Sufism, "Kas - I – Mah", at the instance of his spiritual teacher. This Sufi school was the first of its kind in the whole of Asia. Even today the dilapidated remains of which can be witnessed in Srinagar. Though in a run-down condition yet its grandeur stands out amidst the scenic beauty. There's the Dal Lake down below and the range of mountains standing tall and lofty, and somewhere in between stands out this structure, lying close to the Chashme Shahi springs. In fact, each time I am standing there, gazing at the grandeur of Kas- I - Mah, I am transported far beyond. Wondering and wandering how these Sufis had travelled towards the Kashmir valley, in search of refuge and became one with the people. No, they were not kept at bay and nor labeled 'refugees' and nor 'suspects'. Instead, accepted and made to feel comfortable. A contrast to today's so called modern and developed times when there lurks an air of suspicion and distrust. More so, as we spot a 'foreigner' around...maybe someone hapless seeking refuge. Also, isn't seeking refuge a state of the mind? So many times don't we close our eyes and mentally transport ourselves from a difficult situation to a peaceful one, as though finding ways and means to survive, to move our thoughts from a this to that...

Opening the eyes back to the present day. Getting back to that ray of hope – these young students from the SAARC countries traveling all the way to Srinagar have actually proved that the people of this subcontinent are one. Compatible in the midst of diversity of thoughts and beliefs, views and viewpoints, living conditions, changing sociological patterns and formats and much more.

And Kashmiris in keeping with their age old tradition of hospitality have welcomed these young student scholars with much warmth. Human bonding at its best!

Index

H

I

M

R

S